LOSING THE BATTLE, WINNING THE WAR

LOSING THE BATTLE, WINNING THE WAR

How We Can Defy the Odds We're Given

Ben Parkinson

With Jerome Starkey

SPHERE

First published in Great Britain in 2021 by Sphere

1 3 5 7 9 10 8 6 4 2

A CIP catalogue record for this book
is available from the British Library.

ISBN 978-0-7515-8027-3

Typeset in Goudy by M Rules
Printed and bound in Great Britain by
Clays Ltd, Elcograf S.p.A.

Papers used by Sphere are from well-managed forests
and other responsible sources.

Sphere
An imprint of
Little, Brown Book Group
Carmelite House
50 Victoria Embankment
London EC4Y 0DZ

An Hachette UK Company
www.hachette.co.uk

www.littlebrown.co.uk

For Mike, the Boss.
Always a little further.

In my opinion, I am confident that Bdr Parkinson will *not* achieve functional walking with prostheses. His physical amputee rehabilitation to date has been to facilitate his neurorehabilitation, but I do not believe that it should be continued further as he will not achieve functional walking. L Bdr Parkinson's rehabilitation should be aimed at wheelchair independence.

PROFESSOR RAJIV S. HANSPAL
Hillingdon Hospital, Uxbridge,
20 November 2008

Expert opinion requested
on behalf of Defence Medical
Rehabilitation Centre, Headley Court

Of all the factors, which make for success
in battle, the spirit of the warrior is the
most decisive. That spirit will be found
in full measure in the men who wear the
maroon beret.

'MONTY', FIELD MARSHAL THE
VISCOUNT MONTGOMERY OF ALAMEIN

Note on the Text

Jerome Starkey

The first time I met Ben, at his home in Doncaster, I asked him if he saw himself as lucky or unlucky. He had just finished a work-out and was sitting in his gym kit, in an armchair, with the stumps of his legs exposed. His back was sore from recent surgery and I was still getting used to his slur, which is a result of his brain damage.

'Lucky,' he said, without a second's hesitation.

It was the answer I was hoping for.

'Why?'

'Because I have got a twin brother. And he's ginger.'

Ben doesn't remember the explosion. He can't tell you what it feels like to fly out of a gun turret and land face-first in the stony dirt. He doesn't remember the sound of the blast or the taste of blood pooling in his throat. He doesn't remember the courage of his comrades as they saved his life.

From the injuries sustained in service to his country, he suffered serious, lasting brain damage which wiped long sections of his memory. It affects his movement, his speech, his concentration and every aspect of his life. But it hasn't dimmed his wit.

Ben was twenty-two years old when he was blown up in southern Afghanistan, in September 2006. I flew out to Kabul that year to cover the war as a journalist. I lived there for the next five years and I visited the places where Ben fought.

Ben was often described as the most seriously wounded soldier to survive the war in Afghanistan. I saw first hand the staggering advances in battlefield medicine which helped soldiers like Ben survive injuries that would have been fatal in earlier wars. But even by the standards of Afghanistan, Ben's injuries were off the scale. From the moment his friends sliced into his throat to help him breathe, on that bomb-scorched patch of desert, he was pushing the boundaries of what modern medicine can achieve. Throughout his recovery he has charted new territory. He has constantly surprised and inspired his doctors by setting and achieving goals far higher than they dared imagine. It is a testament to Ben's unshakable determination that he never let his doctors' bleak prognoses limit his soaring ambitions.

This is Ben's story, so it is only right that it is written in his voice. But it has been a collaboration. We have drawn on many sources to tell this story in the fullness it deserves.

For the things Ben can't remember, his friends, family, colleagues and carers have shared their memories. Medical notes, news reports, military records, legal papers and official investigations provided the rest. Some names have been changed to protect the innocent – and sadly, on occasion, to spare the incompetent.

In almost every instance, the scenes recorded in this book were recounted by one of the people who was present. In a few instances, where that was impossible, some scenes and some dialogue have been reimagined to convey the drama and the personalities involved.

This book is Ben and his loved ones' account of how he overcame horrific injuries to lead a full and fulfilling life. Ben will tell you that all of us face challenges in our lives and often they feel insurmountable, but together we can find the strength to overcome almost anything.

He is living proof that it is true.

Preface

The landmine that changed my life was probably a green metal drum about the size and shape of my sixth birthday cake: a Victoria sponge slathered in white icing, which was identical to my twin brother Dan's.

I was born in Doncaster, an old coal-mining town in South Yorkshire, on a sunny spring day in 1984. I arrived exactly fourteen minutes after Dan did (the original age before beauty!). There was never any chance of the nurse mixing us up. We were the opposite of identical. Dan was fair haired and fair skinned. As he grew up, he was wiry. I was dark haired and dark skinned, and always built like a house. By the time we turned six, Danny was the competitive one. If he hit you, it hurt – which was great, because he used to look out for me at school and most of the time he saved his fighting at home for our older brother, Philip. I couldn't be bothered to fight. I was always more laid back.

We celebrated our sixth birthdays at the newly opened Donny Dome, a concert venue and leisure centre, and the only place in Britain with a split-level ice rink. For a bunch of thirty children from Bessacarr First School it was a waterpark wonderworld, with interlinked pools and brightly coloured water slides, where the lifeguards told us off for running and we squealed with excitement until we collapsed with exhaustion. Mum and Dad were still together then and we lived up near the racecourse. It was a happy time in a happy childhood.

In the canteen at the Donny Dome, Mum set the identical cakes out on the same table and Danny raced me to blow out his candles before I did mine, and we dished out slices of cake to our friends.

Danny was given his first football that year. I was given a little box of soldier figurines because I was obsessed with the army.

That night, after the party and the presents and the birthday cakes, Mum gave us one more gift. It was a book called *Finn Family Moomintroll*, a story about trolls and goblins in a magical mountain land. Mum read to us until our eyes were heavy with sleep and then she kissed us both goodnight. It became my favourite book as a child, and my favourite character was Snork. He was a bulbous purple creature who turned green when he was frightened. He was obsessed with rules and details, which was nothing like me. I think I just liked the sound of the word Snork. But there is one scene in the book where Snork acts as a judge to settle a dispute. Mum said I was the peacemaker when Danny and Philip used to fight. Snork became my nickname.

By the time Mum turned the light out and said goodnight, the green birthday-cake-shaped landmine that would one day explode underneath me while I was on tour in Afghanistan had been laid. Every day that I went to school it was waiting for me to get there. The days that I skipped school, the days that I pestered the recruiting sergeants at the recruiting office in Donny, the days when I missed my exams, the days when I did my first parachute jumps and earned my maroon beret, the months that I was serving in Iraq and Kosovo, and all those carefree days I was chasing girls and scoffing Big Macs – that massive, silent metal anti-tank mine was waiting for me on a wadi's edge, 3500 miles away.

I was never one for rushing, so it would have to wait a while.

BATTLE I

Work Hard for What You Want

vs

Let the Dream Go

1

My mum tells a story about one of my first sports days, when Danny and I were at primary school near our home in Doncaster. It was only a small school, but it had great big playing fields out the back and I was in the final of the egg-and-spoon race, competing against my best friend. My friend really, really wanted to win.

When the PE teacher said go, I sprinted off the mark and I was in the lead immediately. I could hear all the parents cheering from the sideline but I didn't look at them. I was staring at the egg in front of me, concentrating on not dropping it. When I realised I was winning I stopped dead in my tracks.

I was nearly at the finish, so I turned round and waited for my friend to catch me up. I knew that he wanted to win, so I let him overtake me.

I was never very competitive. Some people are like ocean waves hitting the rocks every day. Other people are like rocks, letting the waves break over them. I was always more of a rock than a wave. I did my own thing as life crashed on around me.

I think that if I'd been blown up back then, I wouldn't have survived. Not because I was smaller and weaker, but because I hadn't found the will to win yet. I hadn't found the steel inside me that I needed to fight. You don't need to be born a fighter: you can learn it.

On the morning of my history GCSE, when I was sixteen, Mum got a phone call from my headmistress at Hall Cross School to say I hadn't turned up at the exam hall. It was the third exam I had missed that week.

I don't know why I didn't like school. I could tell you the teachers were bad or the classes were big or that nobody inspired me. But that wouldn't be true. It was a good school. My brothers went to the same school and they both did OK. I had loving and supporting parents. I had friends.

The problem was with me. I was lazy and unmotivated. Before I joined the army, I was happy to coast along. I let life wash over me without ever really trying to change it.

Mum left work and came home to look for me, but I wasn't at the house when she got there. I wasn't on the low wall at the bottom of the garden where I used to hang out with my best friend, Chris. So she drove around the neighbourhood, scouring my other haunts, getting angrier and more upset as every moment passed.

Eventually she found me sitting on a grassy bank underneath a railway bridge with a bag of six Big Macs. Chris, who lived across the road from us, was sitting next to me. He had one Big Mac, the other five were for me.

I was always the big kid in my year. Taller and stronger than the other lads – and always hungry. I was never bullied and I had plenty of friends. But I just didn't get excited by the things that excited other people. I never liked playing football and I didn't really support a team. Schoolwork I found incredibly boring.

I can't remember what Mum yelled, but she was at her wits' end with me.

'Chill out, Mum,' I said. 'I don't need GCSEs.'

'Do you want to be a failure for the rest of your life?' I was so laid back, I was horizontal. 'Of course you need GCSEs, Ben!'

'I don't need GCSEs,' I said. 'I'm going to join the army.'

As long as I can remember, I had always wanted to be a soldier.

My great-grandad on my mum's side was at Dunkirk. He was a military policeman tasked with marshalling the British retreat as German bombs rained down on the beach and the flotilla of small boats sailed across the Channel to the rescue.

'Not the best place to be directing traffic,' he used to joke.

My grandfather served in the merchant navy and he told me terrifying tales of convoys stalked by German U-boats in the icy

North Atlantic and how they tried to save the sailors whose ships were going down but sometimes couldn't make it in time.

Dad's dad was in the Royal Air Force. He enlisted at fourteen with dreams of being a sergeant pilot but he was too young to start flying so they trained him as a fitter. By the time the war broke out he was a qualified mechanic. They told him fitters were more valuable than flyers because they took longer to train and were less likely to die, so his dreams of getting airborne were put on hold until the war was over. But they did come true. In 1946 he flew all over America in a Lancaster bomber as part of a goodwill tour. Then from 1948 to 1949 he was in and out of Germany as part of the Berlin Airlift, the massive allied operation to relieve the Russian blockade designed to starve West Berlin.

I didn't want to go to sea. I didn't want to fly. I wanted to be a soldier, and not just any soldier. I wanted to be a Para.

The Parachute Regiment was formed in the midst of World War Two, on Winston Churchill's orders, to give the army a unit that could parachute into battle. They were designed to operate far ahead of the regular army, and often behind enemy lines, which meant they had to be fit, fierce and self-reliant. They had to be the best. The first parachutists were drawn from the commandos, who were then the best-trained troops we had. Paras were the first troops into mainland France in June 1944. The day before the D-Day landings, they used gliders to capture a bridge over the Caen Canal, three miles behind the beaches, to cut off the German supply lines.

I can't say where my dream of being a Para came from. Perhaps it was a schoolboy diet of war films. In my head it was simple. The British army was the best in the world. The airborne were the best of the army. That made them the best of the best. Since the age of fourteen, I had been going to the army recruiting office in Doncaster as often as I could, to feed my obsession. The office was on Hall Gate, sandwiched between a strip club and a church. I was too young to care about sex or salvation.

Phil, my older brother, was artistic. Dan, my redheaded twin, was the practical one. Both of them are over six feet tall and well built, but because Dan's the smallest of the three of us we nicknamed him the runt. Both of them were good at school. Dan got his A levels and joined our dad as a cabinet maker. Phil went to university and became a graphic designer.

I left school in the summer of 2000 without a single GCSE. But I wasn't worried. I was happy. I was one step closer to my dream.

2

The only problem with my plan to quit school and enlist in the army was that I needed my parents' consent. Mum and Dad got divorced when I was nine, but they were still on speaking terms, which meant I couldn't play them off against each other. My only option was to wear them down.

'They'll eat you alive,' Dad said.

He was right.

'What about Welbeck?' Mum asked.

She wanted me to join the army sixth form college and get some A levels, but that was never going to happen. I had given up on school.

The compromise was Harrogate, home of the Army Foundation College.

By the time Mum and Dad drove me to the recruiting office to swear my oath of allegiance, I had worn them down so far, for so long, they were glad to see me go.

For most of my life up until that point, the British army had only really been to war once, on Operation Desert Storm in the Gulf, when they joined with America to force Iraqi troops out of Kuwait in 1990–1. But things had started to pick up not long before I joined. A week before my fifteenth birthday, RAF Tornado jets began bombing Serb positions in Kosovo. Three months later, in June 1999, a crack squad of Paras led an airborne assault to seize the strategic Kaçanik Pass. The pass was the only road that led from Macedonia, where the rest of the British force was based, to the Kosovan capital Pristina. It wound through a natural fortress of steep forested hills and towering cliffs. The ribbon of road was the only flat ground, and unless we controlled the hills, troops on the road could be easily ambushed. The Paras' task was to secure the valley with a squad of Gurkhas, so that engineers could check the bridges for booby traps before the cavalry rolled in a few days later.

It was thrilling to see British troops in action on the evening news. It was the most exciting mission since the Falklands and General Sir Mike Jackson, the gruff commander with droopy eyelids, became a household name.

Three days before I swore my oath of allegiance, Chris and I decided it would be a good idea to bleach my hair with peroxide. My great brown mop went luminous orange. Mum was furious. I looked ridiculous. I was tall and gangly, my face was covered with acne, and after years of teasing Dan for having ginger hair I had turned myself into a carrot-top.

Mum made me cut it off before she drove me to the recruiting office to swear the oath of allegiance. Every serviceman, whether they are in the Royal Navy, the Royal Air Force or the Army, has to swear an oath of allegiance when they join. I had to swear the oath to take up my place at Harrogate. I stood in the careers office in a baggy shirt and a badly tied tie, brimming with excitement. Dad handed over the signed papers.

'Right, Ben,' the recruiting officer barked while my parents watched on. 'Repeat after me.'

He was an old-school sergeant major with a voice embroidered by Marlboro Reds.

'I, Benjamin Parkinson,' he said.

It felt like a marriage vow.

'I, Benjamin Parkinson,' I repeated. My voice was quivering. I couldn't believe it was happening. After so many years of waiting, I was actually joining the army.

'Swear by Almighty God,' I continued. I was sixteen years old and I thought I knew everything. I certainly knew the oath off by heart. I had read it a hundred times and I had to stop myself running ahead of him.

'That I will be faithful,' the sergeant major said.

I stared at the bristles of his moustache.

'That I will be faithful,' I continued, 'and bear true allegiance to Her Majesty Queen Elizabeth II, her heirs and successors and that I will, as in duty bound, honestly and faithfully defend Her Majesty, her heirs and successors in person, crown and dignity against all enemies and will observe and obey all orders of Her Majesty, her heirs and successors and of the generals and officers set over me.'

I was smiling so hard my cheeks ached.

'Congratulations, Parkinson,' the sergeant major said. It was the first time anyone had called me by my surname. 'This'll be the making of you, young man. That's for sure.'

We said our goodbyes and made to leave. 'One more thing,' the sergeant major said.

'Yes?' I asked.

'Stay off the peroxide.'

3

A few weeks later, as I packed a kit bag with my favourite clothes and a toothbrush, news came in of a rescue mission in Sierra Leone, in west Africa. The Paras and the SAS had launched a deadly jungle raid to rescue five British soldiers who had been taken prisoner by a drug- and drink-soaked rebel militia. The rebels were called the West Side Boys, and they treated their prisoners appallingly. Troops from 1 Para launched a diversionary attack while a squad of SAS stormed the headquarters, rescued the prisoners, killed a dozen West Side Boys and captured their leader, effectively destroying the group as a viable force. But they also lost one of their own. He was a twenty-eight-year-old gunner, who had joined the SAS and never got the chance to meet his unborn child.

I thought about that mission as Mum drove me north along the A1, to the Army Foundation College in Harrogate. I thought a bit about the soldier who had died, but mostly about the thrill of a successful mission. I was proud that the British army had rescued their mates in the jungle. It was a message to our enemies that said, 'Don't mess with us.' In my mind, being a soldier was all about ops. It was all about swooping in and winning. The reality came as a shock.

My daydreams screeched to a halt when we pulled up to the guard hut on the edge of camp. It was the first time in my life that I had been on an army base and it felt like entering a different world.

It was bewilderingly big, for a start. There were four or five vast square buildings that remined me of prison blocks, and something that looked like an aircraft hangar. In between there were neat rectangular lawns, mowed in perfectly straight lines like the tennis courts at Wimbledon.

Before I knew it, a soldier led me to a dormitory where I was given a set of bright red tracksuit bottoms and a navy blue T-shirt. I felt the first pang of homesickness.

My first few weeks were awful. Forced marches, square bashing, early starts and classes, classes, classes. It was basic stuff – mostly English, maths and map reading – but I had to do the work.

The army had different rules. If you weren't five minutes early you were late. If you were late you got press-ups or a run. You always had to rush. Then you had to rush some more. They spoke a different language. Food was scoff, teas were brews, the dining room was the cookhouse and my bed space was my grot, which had to be kept gleaming. New recruits were crows and everything we did was gash. Gash went in a gash bag.

Exercise was phys or PT, which stood for physical training, and the men I came to dread the most were known as PTIs – physical training instructors. Their job was to beast us until we were threaders. Marching with a rucksack was a tactical advance to battle, otherwise known as a TAB. If something was good it was hoofing or gleaming, and if it looked cool it was ally. Gossip was gen, stories were dits, and if you managed to pick up something extra it was buckshee. We slept out in doss bags and washed clothes in the dhobie.

There was so much to learn, but the biggest shock was being unpopular.

Up to that point I had taken it for granted that people liked me. I never had to think about it. I always had friends. Even when I was bunking off at Hall Cross in Donny, the teachers had liked me.

I thought I was friendly and funny and easy to get on with. It all counted for nothing at Harrogate. If you couldn't keep up on the runs, if you couldn't keep time, if you couldn't keep tidy you were less than nothing to the directing staff. I was plodding down a corridor in one of those prison-like classroom blocks one day, not really looking where I was going, when I barged into a sergeant by mistake.

'Hands out of your pockets!' he bellowed at me. 'And look where you are going! Do you need glasses, Parkinson?'

'No, sir,' I mumbled.

'Don't call me sir, Parkinson! I work for a living!'

'Sorry, staff,' I corrected myself.

He pulled out a black permanent marker from his pocket and drew a pair of glasses on my face.

'Maybe these will help you see,' he said.

There were days when I wondered if Mum and Dad had been right. Maybe I had made a terrible mistake. I was properly unhappy for the first time in my life. I hated the discipline. I couldn't keep up on the runs, I couldn't march straight and I couldn't even blend in because I was head and shoulders taller than the other recruits.

I imagined going home to Doncaster and telling Mum, my stepdad Andy, Dad and my stepmum Sue, Phil and Danny and my younger stepsister Emma that I had given up. They were right: I couldn't hack it. The shame made me angry and sick. Then I imagined sticking it out through the winter. More PT, more drill, more beastings from the DS. More discipline. It made me feel ill with dread.

For the first four weeks at Harrogate, no one was allowed to leave. They had confiscated our mobile phones and we could only call home from a phone box. In our bright red tracksuit bottoms and standard-issue navy T-shirts, it felt like being in prison.

'Parkinson,' the DS sneered. 'Do you like it here?'

It was the end of the fourth week and every recruit had a one-on-one interview.

'No, sir. Not really, sir.'

'Don't call me sir, Parkinson,' he barked. 'I work for a living.'

'Sorry, staff,' I said for the hundredth time.

'Pack it in then,' he taunted me. 'Now's your chance.'

He was the same sinewy little man who had welcomed me on my first day. I remembered how friendly he was then, how he had reassured the anxious mums that their boys would be looked after. Now he was a monster.

'Pack it in,' he repeated. 'Half your class has already gone.'

'No, staff,' I mumbled.

'No?' he asked, feigning surprise. 'You want to stay?'

'Yes, staff. I want to stay.'

'Speak up, lad, I can't hear you.'

'I want to stay,' I said loudly. 'I am going to make it.'

And once I had made that decision, life felt a lot easier. A few guys had quit, but it wasn't anything like half the class. That was normal. A few more dropped out over the next few months. That was normal too. But the rest of us grew closer because we all had one thing in common. We had decided not to quit. Failure is a state of mind, and unhappiness can be too.

Not that anything got easier, of course. The phys got harder. The runs got longer, the hills got steeper and the weather was terrible that winter. One of the PTIs had a boxer dog called Tyson who he brought on all our forced marches. Tyson set the pace and every time the PTI whistled the dog ran slightly faster. I love dogs. I always have. But when my lungs were screaming, my legs burning and my back was raw from hauling a rain-soaked rucksack, there were times that love of dogs was tested.

It all paid off. Harrogate transformed me. By the time I turned seventeen, in March 2001, I was over halfway through the course and I was loving it. I had started to make friends and I had learned an important lesson. Your friends made all the bad times – the speed marches and square bashing – much easier to bear.

I met Pagey, a dour lad from Hull who ended up in the same airborne regiment as me, and he became a lifelong mate. He was there the day I survived. He knelt by my head in the desert, wiped the blood out of my eyes and told me I would make it.

I discovered that I loved the outdoor life. I loved clambering over walls and flying along zip lines. I loved leaping into cargo nets and leopard crawling in the freezing mud. I loved the night-time dorm raids between rival platoons. I loved the teamwork with my mates. I loved the firing range. And I loved the banter between the lads. I loved being a soldier.

It had taken guts and determination and a lot of hard work, but for the first time in my life I had found something I was good at.

4

In the cookhouse at Lille Barracks, where my regiment was based, there were two types of soldiers. There were those who held their heads up high as members of the airborne brotherhood. Then there were the rest of us, the crap-hat Toms like me.

I had joined 7 Parachute Regiment Royal Horse Artillery. They are the airborne gunners who leap out of planes with Howitzers to support the airborne infantry.

Toms are new recruits. Hats is what the Paras call any soldier who isn't airborne, because they haven't earned the right to wear the maroon beret. You earn the right to wear the beret by passing the Paras selection course. It is a brutal week-long physical test known as P Company. Until you passed you were a hat. You were no one.

The division between hats and airborne affected every aspect of camp life, but it was most obvious at mealtimes. In the queue for the cookhouse the airborne lads could jump ahead and the hats had to let them pass. When we finally got to the canteen there was a choice of water, orange or blackcurrant juice from three dispensers. Hats were allowed to have water or orange juice, but on absolutely no account could they drink the blackcurrant, because that was 'maroon juice' and it was for airborne trained men who had earned their maroon berets. Hats weren't allowed to eat with the other men. We had to sit behind a screen, in a place that everyone called hat corner.

Hats got all the worst jobs. Until you passed P Company, you were stagging on the gate on sentry duty, sweeping out the gun park and making all the brews. It was almost impossible to get promoted.

P Company is a gruelling mix of runs, with and without ruck-
sacks, a log carry, a stretcher race, a boxing match and an assault
course sixty feet off the ground. It is a ticket to a place in the airborne brotherhood.

Unless and until I passed P Company, I was not a full member
of the regiment. I was a hat, and hats were second-class soldiers.

Before I even got to 7 Para, I had failed P Company twice already.
In August 2001, when I passed out, proud as punch, from the Army
Foundation College, I moved up to Catterick and joined an intake
of the Parachute Regiment.

Catterick is the main infantry training base for the whole of
the British army. All the infantry were there, from the Guards
to the Gurkhas and a hundred hat regiments no one had heard
of. The Paras' sense of being special started from day one. We
were kept separate, in a part of the base called the depot, and
the message from the training staff was clear. The Paras were the
toughest, meanest, strongest regiment in the British army and the
only way we were going to get in was if we could prove that we
deserved a place.

Some of the stuff at Catterick I was used to. I knew how to
polish my boots and make my bed the way sergeants liked it. But
the phys went up a level and I struggled with the runs. The other
recruits called me 'Cut Glass' because no one in my family was
serving time in prison.

My first shot at P Company came at week twenty-one of the
thirty-week combined infantry course. I got injured. I couldn't
run, so I was back-squadded and had to start basic training all over
again. The second time, I wasn't fast enough. I came in too slow
on the speed runs, so they offered me a choice: I could either back-
squad again, or I could transfer into a hat regiment. I thought a
transfer meant giving up my dreams of being a Para. There was no
way I would give up.

Then someone told me that I could transfer to one of the Paras'
attached arms. That was news to me. The attached arms were units
like 9 Parachute Squadron Royal Engineers, or 216 (Parachute)

Signal Squadron. They were airborne units that provided specialist military skills to support the Paras in battle. Crucially, for me, they were all airborne trained. Unlike the Para Reg, which only lets you join after you have passed P Company, the attached arms let you join first and take P Company later on. It meant I could move forward with my career and still have a chance to earn my wings. Deep down in my soul I was determined to wear the maroon beret; I was determined join the airborne. So I chose 7 Para Royal Horse Artillery.

It was the best decision of my life.

A few weeks after I moved to Catterick, the planes flew into the World Trade Center in New York and it felt like a lightning bolt struck the camp. By the time I left, we were at war in Afghanistan where the green metal drum in the desert was waiting for me.

But I had two different wars to fight before then.

5

From Catterick I moved to Larkhill gunnery school, on the edge of Salisbury Plain, and from there I moved to Aldershot, where 7 Para were based.

I was cashed up and carefree. I was eighteen years old and had discovered drink and girls. I was brilliant at drinking, but not so good with women. Scoring with a girl was known as bagging off and I was known as bagless. I was far more likely to go to bed with a kebab than any of Aldershot's finest.

Nights out in the town, on champagne and vodka Red Bull, always started at the Traf or North Camp Bar, where we played pool, then on to the Peggy Bar. We always ended up in Cheeks, a sweaty club with a sticky dance floor in an old cinema where the drinks were £1 a bottle.

I shared a room with a lad called Martin Cartwright, who is still one of my best mates, and two other lads. We partitioned off our beds with curtains, but if one of them bagged off they would bring the girl back and crack on.

'Mind if I join in?' someone would ask.

'Fuck off! Do one!' was the standard reply.

I was usually passed out by then, or else I had stopped in Belly Busters, the kebab shop outside camp, for a midnight feast. In later years we used to break into the cookhouse to steal food.

One night I'd been out with a bunch of guys – Brownie, Martin, Mozza, Phil Armitage and Pagey, my mate from Harrogate. We stopped at the cookhouse, on the way back to the block, and 'liberated' a whole tray of Cornish pasties. We went back to Mozza's room to eat them. Mozza had a freezer, so we stacked the ones we couldn't manage in there and left.

The next morning, the battery sergeant major was hammering on Mozza's door. Mozza was still drunk from the night before.

'There was a break-in at the cookhouse last night, Morris,' Sergeant Major Shorrocks said. 'And there is a trail of crumbs all the way from the cookhouse, all the way across camp, and it leads directly to your door.'

Mozza had been so drunk he couldn't even remember what had happened. He looked guiltily at his freezer and a pile of crumbs on the floor in front of it.

Before he had time to concoct a reply, Shorrocks swung open the freezer door like a TV detective revealing the key piece of incriminating evidence. Inside was not what he expected. It was jam-packed with Mozza's uniform. There were shirts, shoes, camouflage fatigues and army boots – all frozen.

'I don't know what you're talking about, Sergeant Major,' Mozza said.

Shorrocks glared at him.

Mozza had passed out while we were still in his room. I was still hungry, so I kept on eating the pasties until they were all gone. Then I decided it would be funny to freeze all of his kit. Which was just as well. With no evidence of stolen pasties, Mozza was off the hook.

Lots of things that happen in barrack blocks should probably stay in barrack blocks. I can't tell the bad stories here because my mum is going to read them. Suffice to say we had a lot of fun. We played awful drinking games and there were girls with names like One-Armed Mandy, who knew her way round camp better than the junior ranks.

I was terrible with money. The weekend after payday I lived like a millionaire. I would be skint by the end of the week. I got used to having nothing in the bank account, but a few months after I got to Aldershot I realised something had gone wrong. I wasn't getting paid at all. I asked one of the lance corporals what he thought I should do, and he said stay in bed.

'I wouldn't go to work if I wasn't getting paid,' he said.

I've always been easily led, so I did as I was told. We were supposed to parade every morning at 0730 hours, in the gun park. My protest lasted until 0733 when Rudy Fuller burst into my room and found me lying in bed watching telly. Rudy was a senior corporal in those days, just about to make sergeant. He was a short, wiry man with a fiery tongue – always annoyingly fit and making me run faster on phys. He was famous for colourful insults that were usually delivered with a healthy spray of spittle, at full volume, a few inches from the recipient's face. And they were forgotten as soon as the bollocking was done.

'Parky, what the hell are you doing?' he asked. He was totally confused.

'I ain't been paid. I'm not coming to work,' I told him.

'Listen, lizard lips, I don't really give two shits!' Rudy said. 'You're in the army, you daft shit. You can't go on strike.'

'I haven't been paid,' I repeated. But as I said it, I knew I hadn't thought this through.

'Stop acting like a screaming hat!' he said. 'The battery sergeant major wants you on parade ten minutes ago. Get the fuck out of your stinking piss-stained bed and get your limp dick on parade. We'll sort your pay out later.'

When I got to the gun park, the rest of the lads were doing press-ups as punishment for me not being there.

That afternoon Rudy took me to see the pay gadgies. Someone in the paperclips corps, as payroll and admin were affectionately known, had ticked the wrong box. I was paid by the end of the week.

6

Before they sent you up to Catterick to take P Company, 7 Para ran a three-week training course called Pre-Para to make sure you were ready. It was scored on points like P Company was, and at the end of the course we would all line up on the tarmac to hear the directing staff's verdict.

I was on every Pre-Para course for two years. And every time it ended the same way.

'Parky!' the DS would bark.

'Yes, staff.'

'Fail!'

Everyone would laugh and I would smile it off. In a way it didn't bother me, because nothing really bothered me. But a fail meant sweat and tears for nothing. I couldn't help looking left and right and thinking, I worked harder than him, and him. How has he got through and I haven't?

There were times I failed because I was injured. That was fair enough. There were times I failed because I just wasn't fit enough. That was fair enough. There were even times when I knew that I just hadn't dug deep enough. That was fair enough as well. But the hardest times to pick yourself up again were when I thought, I have done all right this time, and the DS still barked 'Fail!'

It is gutting to watch the guys you've bonded with on Pre-Para heading up to Catterick without you. It's even tougher when they come back, jumping the queue at the cookhouse, filling their cups with maroon juice and never on the rota for stag duty.

You start to question yourself. You think, What more can I give when there's nothing left in the tank? What's the point? I have given everything. If I come back again, what will be different next time?

I guess that is where grit and determination come in. The first thing I learned was not to let it get me down. Some guys sailed through P Company first time. They were always the little wiry fellas who were built for running. Good for them. They made great soldiers, but I was learning a valuable lesson every time I failed. It was like life was preparing me for a much tougher, longer battle to come.

Each time I failed, I picked myself up again. And the first thing I did once I had dusted myself off was head out with the other lads for the end-of-course party in Tiffany's, Aldershot's finest strip club, where I would drink myself to oblivion. (The nights on the smash in Tiffany's were optional; picking yourself up after failure is not.)

The next thing I would do was look for ways of improving myself. Passing P Company started and ended with me. I knew I had to get fitter, so I joined the F Battery boxing team and got the proverbial kicked out of me three times a week. I wasn't a good boxer, but I kept on going back for the fitness.

On my sixth attempt at P Company, I was fitter than I had ever been. I knew the routine. I knew all the tests. I was convinced that, this time, I would make it. I made it through all the tests. I didn't get injured. When I lined up for the last parade, I was sure that I had made it.

'Parkinson!'

'Yes, staff.'

'Fail.'

Giving up then was a viable option. There were plenty of people at 7 who were convinced I would never make it. People had written me off – and that wouldn't be the last time in my life that happened. I could have stayed a hat and sat in hat corner for the rest of my life. But that wasn't who I was. I wasn't ready to give up. I didn't know it then, but I was learning an important lesson, a lesson that would save my life. No matter how impossible, no matter what the doubters think, you have to keep on trying.

A year later I went back for the seventh time. P Company starts with hell week and culminates with test week, which is eight tests over five days. You are always exhausted before you start. On the first morning of test week, all the candidates were lined up on the depot parade ground at Catterick. The officer in command gave the same speech I had heard so many times before.

'If you have come this far, you have got what it takes to succeed,' he said.

I had an extra reason to dig deep this time. Rudy – the corporal who'd got me out of bed when I went on strike for not receiving my pay – had been posted up to Catterick. He was on the directing staff. If I failed this time it would be a double defeat.

'Just dig out blind on every bit, Parky,' Rudy said. 'Dig out blind and you'll make it.'

It is fair to say that after so many fails, I knew what expect – but to be honest, that only made it worse. Day one starts with a ten-miler, running with 35lb in your bergen, plus water and weapon. It's designed to simulate the move from a drop zone to an assembly area and it has to be completed in one hour, fifty minutes. From that we went straight into the trinasium, an assault course built of scaffolding sixty feet off the ground.

All of us on the course had been assigned a number which the directing staff used instead of our names. During the trinasium you could be jumping between scaffolding boards, wriggling over the shuffle bars or leaping onto the cargo net. They would call out your number and issue a command. Hesitate for a second and you failed. Second day was always brutal because it started with a two-mile speed run that you have to finish in eighteen minutes. Running fast was my worst event.

After so many years, after so many P Companies – and because of my brain injury – they all blur into one another. The only thing I really remember about my seventh attempt was the milling. Milling is sixty seconds of pure-aggression boxing and it is unique to P Company. Once we had finished the two-miler we changed into PT kit and marched over to the gym. The DS paired us off by size and we stood nose to nose with our opponents, psyching ourselves up until the whistle went. When your sixty seconds start you are not allowed to defend yourself. You are not supposed to drop your head or form a guard. It is sixty seconds of aggression, trying to fill the other man in.

Rudy paired me off with a giant officer for the boxing. Officers live in a different world to enlisted men like me. They are the army's commanders. Most of them have got uni degrees and they are all trained at Sandhurst before they join their regiments.

If a soldier ever punched an officer it would be an act of gross insubordination. You would probably do time in the army's Glasshouse prison, and then you would get kicked out with a dishonourable discharge.

'Bash the living daylights out him,' Rudy said. 'It's the only time you are ever gonna be allowed to twat an officer and not get in the shit.'

We went hell for leather in that minute. Punching, reeling, punching, reeling. We had about fifteen seconds to go when he clocked me square on the jaw and I staggered backwards. If I left the fight I failed. It was only a split second, but my instinct took over; I channelled every ounce of aggression I had through my fists. I stormed back at the officer and pummelled him with a dozen blows until I heard the whistle.

The last event was the stretcher race. On the morning of the final day we were broken into teams. The stretcher weighed 175lb and we had to carry it four and a half miles, to simulate a battlefield casualty extraction. The worst part of the stretcher race was the long, steep, muddy slope known as Stretcher Hill. Everyone was digging blind by then, pushing through the pain, but from the top of Stretcher Hill you know you're almost home.

Then came the moment of truth. Back at Helles Barracks we changed into clean uniforms and lined up in three ranks for the final beret parade. We all knew that finishing was not the same as passing. Everything depended on our scores.

The company commander strode onto the parade ground. Rudy was behind him, holding a tray of maroon berets.

The company commander said a few words to all of us. It was something about the airborne brotherhood, the history of P

Company and the glorious history of the all-arms airborne regiments like 7 Para. Then he walked along the lines, man by man.

It was like a medal parade. The commanding officer would call out each man's number and that man would come to attention. Then he would say pass or fail. If it was fail, he moved straight on to the next man. If it was pass, he would say a few words.

I was seventh in line. All the men on my right had passed. I held my breath and braced as the OC stepped in front of me and called out my number.

'Pass,' he said at last. 'Congratulations, Bom Parkinson.' I fought to stop myself crying. 'I gather it's not your first attempt.'

'No sir,' I said, grinning. 'I enjoyed it so much I did it seven times.'

'Seven times? That's got to be a record.'

He took my beret from the tray and handed it to me.

'Welcome to the airborne.'

7

Almost as soon as I passed P Company we deployed to Kosovo to hunt suspected war criminals. Kosovo was a party. We spent most of the time in civvies, driving round in civvy cars on covert surveillance missions. We kicked down a few doors.

It was the winter of 2005. It was freezing, and apparently the only time I came close to using violence was when I threatened to kill a man who kept his dog outside in the snow.

For Christmas that year a couple of Page 3 girls flew out on one of those morale-boosting trips for the troops. Someone had the bright idea of playing *Blind Date* in fancy dress.

I was 'voluntold' that I was one of the contestants. I dressed up as Captain Caveman and ended up winning the date with a gorgeous girl called Peta. The only place I could take her was for a pizza in the Naafi. It wasn't exactly romantic, with all my mates at the other tables.

On the date she gave me a signed picture of herself. She had written, 'To Ben, you were the best.'

'Thanks,' I grinned. Then with a shrug – and loud enough for the lads to hear – I said, 'I've had better.'

When we got back in February 2006 the regiment had moved to new barracks in Colchester, with the rest of the Parachute Regiment. I did my jumps course, earned my wings. That's when I was 'voluntold' to make up strength in I Battery.

It was the best news I could have ever asked for. I Battery were going to Afghanistan and I was going with them.

BATTLE 2

Enjoy the Ride

vs

Dwell on
the Negatives

8

The desert in Helmand looked flat, at first glance, but nothing was quite as it seemed. The terrain was a gently undulating plain, criss-crossed by a web of ancient river beds, called wadis, that cut into the ground like the creases in a giant's palm. Some were so fine you barely noticed them. Others were deep furrows. They were canyons cut by centuries of floods that surged through the desert then left it parched again.

There were only three of us in the WMIK, an open-topped Land Rover with two mounted machine guns. Phil was at the wheel, H was in the passenger seat and I was in the gun turret, called the cupola, on top cover. We had hardly been driving for five minutes when we reached the wadi where it happened. It is impossible to count the millions of decisions that had brought me to that precise place at that precise time. From joining the army six years earlier to winning rock, paper, scissors, which meant I'd chosen for us to ride right flank on this patrol. And there were still more decisions to come, while the mine sat waiting for me in the ground.

The wadi was what we called dead ground. The lie of the land, the dip in the ground, meant we couldn't see it from where we were camped, so in theory an enemy could use it to sneak up on us unnoticed.

From the lip of the plain, where we stopped, to the bottom of the wadi floor was probably a drop of four or five metres. Then from the bottom, the empty river bed was probably only ten metres across. It was bigger than a crease, but it certainly wasn't a canyon. It was somewhere in between. We could find a way to cross.

I glanced left at the main column. They were about fifty metres away. The slopes of the wadi were much gentler there. It was an easier place to cross. The cavalry had recce'd the route and led them to a place where we could get the lorries over. Half the main column had already crossed. Ahead, in the distance, I could just make out the lead Scimitars, light tanks with 30mm turret guns that fire bullets the size of milk bottles. They were half a mile beyond us. They looked like little black Dinky cars, sending up huge plumes of dust in their wake.

H stopped the WMIK at the edge of the slope. The way in looked quite gentle, but the far side was craggy and steep.

'This'll be fun,' he said. 'Whaddya reckon, Parky?'

I lifted up my goggles to get a clearer look. I had a better view from the gun turret. The wadi floor was strewn with stones like rugby balls but it was nothing the WMIK couldn't handle. The far side looked more problematic. There were parts that were almost like little cliffs. It looked as though there was a narrow path, possibly a goat track, in between the steepest rocks.

'Aim for the goat track,' I said.

There was always something about wadis that made me hold my breath. It was instinctive. We are trained to use terrain to our advantage in the army. I knew that wadi crossings made us vulnerable. Our ingress and egress routes were limited. We were being channelled by the landscape, which meant we were sacrificing some of our initiative.

We made it to the bottom and bumped over the rugby balls. Some of these wadis flooded every spring, when snow in the lower mountains melted, but most of them drained the seasonal rains that brought the Kuchi nomads with their low, brown woollen tents and goats that grazed the sudden flush of pasture.

I looked right along the wadi floor, scanning the rocks and crevices for anything unusual, for splashes of colour or unnatural straight lines. Anything that indicated people may have been there.

My knuckles turned white as I held on to the gun. I tried to brace myself with my legs against the ammunition boxes so I could stop my hips getting slammed from side to side as we bounced over the boulders.

We crossed the bottom without incident and I looked up at the goat track. It was slightly wider than I had realised.

'Reckon we'll make it?' H asked.

'You're good,' I said.

He put the WMIK into first gear and pressed the accelerator. The WMIK lurched forwards and I felt my body armour bang the back of the gun turret. I wondered if we had enough momentum to carry us up the slope. The wheels started to slip, then they caught, then they slipped. H was wrestling with the steering wheel to keep us on the track, which led through the crags at an angle. Suddenly the wheels gripped again and we lurched over the lip onto flat ground.

'Nice one,' I said to H.

We were just beginning to pull away when something underneath us went *click*. There was a deafening boom and the world went white. The WMIK flew into the air.

But I'm getting ahead of myself. First we should talk about Iraq.

9

The roar of a fighter jet shook me awake in my shell scrape, a shallow man-sized trench which each of us had dug to protect us if we were shelled. The radios on the gun net crackled into life.

'FIRE MISSION BATTERY!' a detachment commander yelled. I was sleeping fully dressed and I grabbed my gas mask and my helmet. The guns were only yards away. We were in Kuwait, five kilometres south of the Iraqi border. Our biggest fear in those days was that Saddam Hussein would attack us with chemical weapons.

'Six guns!' Rudy bellowed. Rudy was now a sergeant and he was my gun commander. His voice was calm and clear that night in Kuwait.

'H-E!' he called out. 'L-1-0-6. Charge: Super!'

I could see his breath in the beam of his head torch as he read the orders off his notepad.

'Bearing 1-2-3-4 mils,' Rudy continued.

I stood ready at the breech with a ramrod.

'Elevation 5-6-8-9 mils!'

As soon as the shell went in I pushed it up as far as it went. The Number 2 slammed the breech closed. The Number 3 was at the controls. He punched in the numbers and the barrel dipped and swivelled.

'Ready!' he called back to Rudy.

The moon was so bright we cast shadows on the sand.

'At my command,' Rudy bellowed. 'Five rounds fire for effect!'

The barrel recoiled with a deafening boom. Somewhere in the darkness a distant pillbox had been turned to rubble. Saddam's wretched conscripts never stood a chance. It was 19 March 2003.

I was eighteen years old. I didn't realise it at the time, but 7 Para had just fired the first shots of the ground war. The coalition of the willing had declared war on Iraq.

None of us slept that night. As dawn broke and the guns went silent Rudy came over with an empty cartridge case. 'There you go, Parky,' he said. 'Youngest man on the gun. You get to keep the case from the first shot of the war.'

I was part of F Battery and we had been loaned to the US Marines Expeditionary Force that was spearheading the invasion. We captured the Rumaila oil field, which Saddam's men had set ablaze as they retreated. Thick plumes of stinking black smoke towered like toxic feathers out of the desolate plain.

On the second or third day we came under attack from a barrage of Iraqi artillery. Saddam had a battery of Russian D30 Howitzers that were well dug in around the highway to Baghdad. It was terrifying.

The first thing we knew was when the radar siren went off. We had a new piece of kit called a MAMBA in the gunline. It was a lorry with a massive sensor that could pick up almost anything fired our way from up to forty clicks away. It was a Gucci bit of kit that we had bought from the Norwegians. When the Iraqis tried to mortar us, the MAMBA told us immediately where the bomb was going to land, how long it would take to get there and, most importantly for us, where it came from.

The Iraqis' guns were bigger than ours. They were spread out and well hidden. We were the opposite. We were totally exposed in the desert.

'Like a pair of dog's bollocks,' Rudy said.

But we were faster, and our fire was more accurate. The only way to win an artillery duel is to send your shells the other way.

We moved position constantly to keep up with the Marines' advance. Whenever we stopped we dug shell scrapes and built defensive berms in case we came under attack. One day, when we had just crossed a bridge to the north of Rumaila, Rudy put me on stag duty. It was my job to keep watch in case anyone tried to sneak up and attack us from behind.

'Grab the jimpy, Parky. Watch our six,' he said.

I was exhausted.

I stared into the filthy haze. The sky and the dust and the desert were the same shade of grey.

Next thing I knew, there was a deafening crack on the top of my helmet. My heart was in my mouth. I thought we were under attack. I blinked at the desert, confused and disorientated. What the hell had just happened?

'Parkinson!' Rudy screamed. 'You ever fucking fall asleep on stag again, you won't have to worry about the Iraqis. I'll fucking bury you in the desert and leave you there for Saddam and his men to bum you.' Lesson learned: I never fell asleep on stag duty again.

I turned nineteen near Nasiriyah, with my gas mask clipped to my hip and my chemical warfare suit close by. I was always hungry, always tired. Hours of nothing were followed by explosions of adrenalin. Then from nowhere came a deluge. It rained so hard the ground became a quagmire. Our shell scrapes filled with water and we were slipping in the mud as we tried to move 70lb boxes of shells.

The days rolled into each other. The battery had a moustache-growing competition – I made an excellent Mexican bandito – and the gun teams challenged each other to see who could eat the entire contents of a 24 ration pack the fastest. It was four thousand calories of muesli, chicken curry, sausages in spaghetti, Yorkie bars, peanuts, bully beef, chicken pâté and biscuit browns. I won it every time, and even then I was still hungry.

War was mostly waiting and no sleep. Then just when you thought you were getting some rest someone would scream 'Gas!' We'd fumble for our masks in the suffocating heat, but it was always a false alarm. Tony Blair had misled us. There were no weapons of mass destruction in Iraq.

But we made the best of it. Some time in the middle of April, about two weeks after my birthday, we got our first bags of mail sent up to the front by the British Forces Post Office (BFPO). Rudy was up at the command post when the battery sergeant major said there was post for our gun.

'Get some men up here to collect it,' the sergeant major said. He waved at eight grey post bags stacked up next to a wagon.

'Which ones for B Sub?' Rudy asked.

'All of them.'

Most of it was for me. I got nineteen parcels in one day. Mum had got everyone she knew to send out birthday cards and care packages. They were full of magazines and food. Glorious food! Most of the guys were sent Haribo sweets which had melted in the heat into giant bag-sized globules. My family had sent tins of custard and ginger cakes, beans and sausages and noodles. It was better than gold.

In one box there was a homemade cake. Fred, my stepdad Andy's dad, was a confectioner and he had baked me my favourite kind of fruit cake. On the top, in icing, he had written 'Happy 19th Birthday Ben' and he had wrapped it in a maroon ribbon, the colour of our berets. There was a 2kg weight limit for parcels sent in the BFPO and Fred had weighed it out precisely so that the cake, the silver cardboard plate, the icing and the ribbon, the box and the wrapping came to exactly 2kg. It was 2kg of pure morale. I dished it out to everyone and the cake was gone in a matter of minutes, but it buoyed us up for weeks, knowing people at home were thinking of us – and remembering just how good it had tasted.

Two weeks later, on 1 May, President George W. Bush stood on the flight deck of an aircraft carrier and declared an end to major combat operations in Iraq. We moved into peacekeeping mode. We set the guns up inside a camp near Basra, but rarely fired them any more. We spent most of our time out on foot patrols. Me and my mate Brownie adopted a stray dog. He was a scrawny sand-coloured thing with a white-tipped tail and we named him Dangerous Dave because he used to follow us out no matter how sketchy it was. The locals didn't want us there – we were foreigners with guns walking uninvited through their towns. Kids would throw stones at us and the adults gave us death stares.

'Why the fuck are we patrolling through this town where everyone hates us?' Phil Armitage asked once. Dangerous Dave was scampering along at our feet.

I always carried the GMPG on patrols. It was a belt-fed machine gun known as a jimpy that weighed 14kg. On top of all the ammo, water, body armour, med kits and radios we had to carry, it was heavy. But that was the price of being 6′ 4″.

'If owt happens, Parky,' Phil said. 'We'll duck and you just do a circle with the jimpy. Just do a fucking circle.'

I never had to do a circle. The rest of the tour was quiet.

10

Three years later, in March 2006, the British army deployed in strength to Helmand for the first time in over a hundred years, and I went with them. We were part of a NATO-led International Security Assistance Force (ISAF). In broad terms, our mandate was to support the Afghan government, which meant helping them fight the Taliban. British troops had been in Afghanistan since the US-led invasion in 2001, but this was my first deployment there.

In 2001 the mission had been strictly limited to toppling the Taliban and catching Osama bin Laden. The special forces hunted al-Qaeda in the Tora Bora mountains near the border with Pakistan. A handful of regular troops set up a Kabul garrison.

They called the British base Camp Souter. It was named after Thomas Souter, one of the last survivors of the last stand at Gandamack, when the band of battle-weary and bedraggled British soldiers were massacred in the retreat from Kabul in 1842. You can always rely on people in the army to have a sense of humour.

With time, the mission shifted into nation building. NATO created ISAF with a UN mandate. Regular British troops were put under ISAF command. Afghanistan was a deeply conservative, tribal country that had been traumatised by more than thirty years of violence. The last time Afghanistan was peaceful was in 1973, just before King Zahir Shah was deposed by his cousin Daoud. Five years later, Daoud was killed in a coup, which triggered a civil war. In 1979 the USSR invaded and the Americans saw a chance to bloody their nose by backing the anti-Russian mujahideen.

It was a bloody war: by the time the Russian army limped out of Afghanistan in 1989, they'd lost fifteen thousand soldiers, and more than a million civilians had been killed in the crossfire. They left behind as many as seven million unexploded landmines, and conditions ripe for another civil war. The factions that had beaten them turned their guns on each other. Afghan government ministers shelled each other for control of Kabul. Prisoners were tortured, raped, beheaded and in at least one instance, squashed beneath a warlord's tank. A country fragile at the best of times was shattered into fiefdoms loosely controlled by rival militias whose members were often no better than thugs. Their commanders levied taxes from checkpoints on the roads and kidnapped and killed on a whim.

All I knew about the Taliban when I arrived in 2006 was that they were our enemy. They were a bunch of hardline Islamic crazies who banned girls' education, made women wear burqas and held public executions in football stadiums. The truth is slightly more nuanced. They were actually born in the 1990s as a sort of vigilante movement in response to the chaos of Afghanistan's civil war.

According to the legend, which has no doubt been embellished, the movement started in response to a particularly heinous crime committed by a militia commander in the southern province of Kandahar. Mullah Omar, the Taliban's one-eyed leader, had been a local village mullah when a teenage girl was abducted at gunpoint and taken to a nearby base, where she was repeatedly raped by a commander and his men.

I was ten years old in 1994, when Mullah Omar led a band of about thirty Talibs, or students, who surrounded the commander's compound in the fruit orchards near Zangabad. They rescued the girl and, in an act of poetic justice applauded across Afghanistan, they hanged the commander from the barrel of his own tank. By the time they captured Kabul two years later – promising peace and rule of law – people were so weary of bloodshed that students from Kabul University welcomed them with flowers.

The Taliban's rule was brutal. When they captured Kabul in 1996, they stormed a UN compound where a former president, Dr Najibullah, was sheltering with his brother. Najibullah, the last of the Russian puppet presidents, was castrated and his body dragged around the city lashed to the back of a pick-up truck. Then they hanged his corpse from a lamp post and stuffed his pockets with money to show that he had sold his loyalty to Moscow.

Under the Taliban regime, every aspect of people's lives was curbed and controlled. Women were banned from leaving the house without a male escort. Men had to grow their beard at least a fist's length below their chin or risk being beaten in the street by the vice and virtue police. The economy ground to a halt. Then, in March 2001, they used tank shells and dynamite to commit one of the most spectacular crimes against antiquity ever seen. Mullah Omar, who was now the self-styled leader of the Muslim world, ordered his men to destroy the ancient Buddhas of Bamiyan, as idols of other gods. These two magnificent statues – one fifty metres high, the other thirty-five metres high – had been carved into a cliff and had stood unmolested for fifteen hundred years, but they couldn't survive the Taliban.

In 2001 and 2002, after the US invaded, there was a palpable sense of euphoria. Amid the devastation there was hope that a new era had dawned. And apart from the odd rocket hurtling in from the nearby mountains where disgruntled Taliban were hiding out, Kabul was largely peaceful.

In 2004, ISAF expanded to the north and Britain sent a garrison to Mazar-e Sharif, an ancient Silk Road town near the border with Uzbekistan that is best known for its magnificent fifteenth-century Blue Mosque. I was twenty years old in 2004. I wasn't paying attention to what was happening in Afghanistan. I had just got back from the war in Iraq and I was struggling to get fit to pass P Company. But 2004 was an important year for Afghanistan. It was the year that it held its first democratic elections. It was the year Britain suffered its first casualty, when Private Jonathan Kitulagoda was killed by a car bomb in Kabul.

By the time we arrived in 2006, things had got much worse. Afghanistan was facing a full-blown insurgency. The odd rocket attack and occasional suicide bomb had snowballed into a guerrilla campaign. The Taliban had regrouped in the lawless mountains of Pakistan, and they wanted the foreigners out.

11

By September, I was coming to the end of my tour. We had already lost fifteen soldiers including two very popular officers from 7 Para, Captain Alex Eida and Captain Jim Philippson, who had been killed in separate Taliban ambushes. Then on 2 September the death toll doubled overnight when an RAF spy plane crashed, killing all fourteen on board. Four days later, on 6 September 2006, the taskforce suffered what came to be known as the Day of Days. It was when our friend and comrade Mark Wright was killed in Kajaki.

Mark was a mortar fire controller in 3 Para who was killed by a landmine as he tried to help his mates who were stranded in an unmarked Russian minefield. The events that led to Mark's death started when a three-man sniper team left their hilltop lookout at the Kajaki dam to try to reach a nearby ridgeline. They wanted to get a better view of, and perhaps a clearer shot at, an illegal Taliban roadblock in a village in the valley below.

Kajaki wasn't like the other platoon houses. The base was built on the edge of a massive hydroelectric dam that the Americans had built in the 1950s. It consisted of a small turbine hall next to the dam wall and a couple of stone houses that had originally been built to house the construction workers. The Russians used it as a base in the 1980s and according to the local lore, they were left behind, skinned alive and thrown into the turbines when the rest of their comrades withdrew in 1989. We had also heard stories of some French special forces who met a very unpleasant death a few years before we arrived.

But for us, Kajaki was different. It was the oasis in the mountains.

Compared to the hell-hole towns of Sangin and Musa Qala, where our troops were holed up in platoon houses surrounded by hostile Talibs, Kajaki was a holiday camp. It was the rest and relaxation post with a massive natural swimming pool.

Mark had been flown up there to give him a break after a rough few months in Sangin. Chill out, swim in the dam, take it easy, they said. If only.

Mark wasn't part of the sniper patrol, but he was part of the quick reaction force (QRF) that scrambled to go and help them when the first mine went off.

The patrol had followed an old goat track down a barren brown hill on the southern side of their lookout. At the bottom they followed a wadi until they reached a crossing point. Lance Corporal Stuart Hale, the sniper, leapt over the wadi and heard something go *bang*. The explosion blew his foot off.

The other two lads applied a tourniquet to his bloody stump. When the QRF arrived, they cleared a 'safe-lane' to a patch of flat ground where a helicopter could land. The most senior soldier in the QRF was Sergeant Stuart Pearson. He was walking back along the safe lane when he stepped on a second mine, which blew off the bottom of his leg.

With two men down a few yards from each other they realised they were in a minefield. It seems crazy now, but they didn't have metal detectors. They just hadn't been issued that widely in 2006. In the years that followed, every single British foot patrol in Helmand would be led by a 'Vallon man', who swept the ground in front of his feet with a metal detector looking for mines. On our tour, all we had were our eyes, our fingertips and metal rods like meat thermometers to poke through the sand.

The lads told headquarters that it was far too dangerous for a chopper to land. They needed a winch rescue, like the coastguard do all the time. But the British Task Force Helmand only had six Chinooks and none of them had a winch.

There are lots of reasons why we didn't have the kit we needed. Soldiers and their commanders always want more of something. More men, more guns, more armour, more helicopters. That's the nature of war. But a couple of things stand out in Afghanistan. Firstly, I think the politicians and the generals underestimated the threat. Secondly, and this is even more shocking, the army was prohibited from buying the kit it needed until after the government announced that we were going to Helmand. I only learned this years later from the Board of Inquiry that the army held to investigate the circumstances surrounding my injuries. All the planning and preparation for Herrick 4, which was our tour, was halted for two months because of the government's decision not to announce the deployment until January 2006. During that delay, the MoD and the Treasury refused to pay for special kit, known as Urgent Operational Requirements, which our commanders knew we needed.

'As a result,' the inquiry said, 'many key items of equipment arrived in theatre late and some even failed to meet the Op Herrick 4 deployment at all.'

When a massive twin-rotor Chinook helicopter arrived, without a winch, a problem with the radios meant the soldiers couldn't communicate directly with the crew. The lads on the ground tried to use arm signals to tell the pilots not to land, but the pilots didn't understand. They lowered their 12-tonne chopper into the unmarked minefield.

As they did, the downdraught sent rocks scuttling along the ground. Exactly what happened is still disputed. It could have been the downdraught from the rotors. It could have been a stone sent hurtling in the blizzard of rocks. It could have been a mine flipped over in the wind. Something triggered a third explosion, which tore into Mark's torso. He wasn't killed outright, but his arm was hanging off and his face and throat were burnt.

Then another young soldier tripped a fourth device – and he also lost a leg. To start with Mark was conscious, cracking jokes, but it took so long to get a helicopter with a winch team he died on his way to the military hospital.

It was amazing how the guys had all run in to help each other, even when they knew the risks. But it was terrifying how many of them had got hurt and how long it had taken to get them out.

When we heard about what happened, one of the officers came round to remind everyone about the right drills for a mine strike.

'You can't just charge in to help your mates or you'll be brown bread too,' he said.

'If we've got to deal with one casualty, we don't want to deal with two. Remember your drills. Check the ground. If you need to clear it, clear a path with the mine kit.'

'But what if your mate's bleeding out? What if there isn't time?'

What would I do, I wondered. Would I wait? Or would I run in?

Three men had lost legs that day, three others were seriously injured, and Mark lost his life. This was the tour the government had hoped would pass without a single shot.

Well they got that wrong. We fired a million bullets. We were attacked with rifles, rockets, mortars, mines and improvised explosive devices. And we fought back with everything we had, from fast attack jets and Apache gunships to brute force and bayonets.

The level of violence came as a shock, especially to the politicians. But violence was what we trained for. It was what we were good at. But there is no way to train for losing your friends and the deaths of our comrades hit all of us hard.

Unless you were there when it happened, the first sign that someone had been killed or badly injured was something called Op Minimise. All calls home would be banned for twenty-four hours to make sure details of the death didn't trickle back to the family before the army had a chance to tell them officially.

There was always a hush that would fall over the guys as they learned who it was and what had happened. You might take a few minutes out. Sometimes we'd come together for an evening prayer or a few of us would get into a huddle. But there really wasn't time to stop and grieve. We were all at war, with a job to do. We just had to crack on.

But whenever there was Op Minimise it always made me think of home. My mind would go to my family and my girlfriend, Holly. She was small and dark and absolutely gorgeous. We had met about six months before I deployed. A lot of my mates worried that relationships would struggle when we spent six months abroad.

Things with Holly had been a bit tempestuous, but overall I felt really lucky. When I saw her on my RnR, the one-week holiday in the middle of the tour, she had the most amazing news. She told me she was pregnant. She told me that when I finished my tour, when I came back to England in September, I was going to be a dad.

12

Helmand is one of the Taliban heartlands. It is a long, thin desert province, about two and half times the size of Wales, that stretches from the foothills of the Hindu Kush mountains in the north to the baking-hot Desert of Death three hundred miles to the south. Running the length of the province is the mighty Helmand River. And it has been fought over for thousands of years.

The terrain in Helmand fell into three categories. There were the towns, like Sangin and Musa Qala. These were mostly made of mud-walled compounds and narrow alleys, built around bazaars of one-room shops. Outside the towns there was a ribbon of lush farmland that flanked the banks of the river. This was known as the Green Zone. The farms were fed by canals from the river. Farmers grew pomegranates and apricots in low-walled orchards, and grapes which hung off earthen berms. A handful of fields were given over to maize, but most of the farmers grew opium poppies, which were used to make heroin.

The canals made getting around the Green Zone difficult and dangerous. There were only certain places where vehicles could cross the channels, while the walls of the orchards and hamlets provided perfect cover for Taliban ambushes.

The third part of the province was by far the largest. It was the desert. A vast moonscape of stony ground that changed colour through the day. At dawn it started a pinkish purple. There was always half an hour, most mornings, when the ground glowed orange in the low sunlight, but as the sun climbed higher it sapped the colour from the stones until everything was khaki-grey.

Before we deployed that summer, a small team of soldiers,

diplomats and development experts had produced a detailed plan for what they thought we could achieve with the battle group – about three thousand soldiers – at our disposal. According to their plan, the taskforce would focus its efforts on securing Lashkar Gah, the administrative capital, and Gereshk, the commercial capital about fifteen miles to its north. But almost as soon as we arrived that plan was thrown out of the window.

Instead of concentrating our effort on a so-called Afghan Development Zone, small bands of troops were strung out up and down the province. We found ourselves defending towns like Sangin, Now Zad, and Kajaki – dusty, tribal towns that would soon become household names.

Without fully realising what was happening, British troops were sucked into a complex turf war between rival groups of warlords, tribes and opium smugglers. One group happened to be in government, and they used the British army to fight their enemies.

Our mission was to help the government. So when a desperate provincial governor, appointed by the Afghan government in Kabul, said the district centres were about to be overrun we sent garrisons to defend them. The garrisons were bands of thirty to a hundred men in fortified mud-walled compounds, the infamous platoon houses.

They were perfect Taliban magnets. The troops inside were regularly outnumbered and outgunned. They were hard to resupply by road and it wasn't much better by helicopter. We had no choice but to weigh in with our 105mm artillery guns and helicopter gunships, at rag-tag men in flip-flops. Our strategy in Helmand in 2006 was like kicking a hornet's nest again and again and again – and killing the hornets when they swarmed at us.

It was bonkers, but we loved it. As long as no one on our side was getting hurt or killed, war was fun. We longed to get into firefights because that was what we had trained for. The adrenalin, the noise, the training kicking into action. It was brilliant.

The most dangerous place to be was in a platoon house. They were under almost constant attack. After that it was the Green Zone, because there was a constant risk of ambush. The safest place was in the desert. Out in the desert no one could attack because they couldn't get near.

I spent time in all three zones because I was part of a mobile patrol called the Movement Operations Group, or MOG. Our job was to drive around Helmand looking for trouble and to help the guys pinned down in the platoon houses.

If things were quiet and we were in the desert, we had to find ways to kill time. Sometimes we played cricket, with jerry cans for a wicket. Sometimes we played touch rugby. Once we held a desert Olympics, which included a pistol-shooting competition and fireman's lift.

All of us were fit. We'd had six months off the booze with nothing but Op Massive – getting massive in makeshift gyms – for entertainment. Looking back now at the pictures of before I got hit, I had a six-month-summer tan, a six pack and a beard. I was only twenty-two. In Para speak, I looked pretty ally.

13

A couple of days before I was hurt, we camped in the dun brown deserts outside Musa Qala, the most dangerous place in the world for British soldiers. Musa Qala was a low-rise town of ancient mud-walled compounds and modern concrete homes built with the proceeds of the only local industry, opium production. It was more than fifty miles from the main British base at Camp Bastion. Musa Qala was the northernmost major town in Helmand, and it was deep in Taliban country.

The lads in the platoon had been fighting for their lives. They were constantly running low on food and ammunition because choppers that tried to land always risked being shot down. A Danish armoured column had refused to resupply by road because they said it was too dangerous.

The MOG had tried to break through a month earlier but it ended in disaster. That was when we lost Alex Eida, a 7 Para captain, and two Household Cavalry soldiers when their wagon was hit by a roadside bomb. It was a well-planned Taliban ambush. The war had clicked up a gear. In the first two weeks of September, four of our guys were killed in the Musa Qala platoon house and six more were seriously wounded.

I didn't realise at the time, but the situation was so desperate that British spies had cut a deal with Musa Qala's elders to let the garrison leave. Tuesday 12 September 2006, the day I survived, was the first day of the ceasefire.

The MOG was a massive armoured column. Bits of it could break off if we had specific tasks like a reconnaissance mission but on that Tuesday morning we were all parked together on the plain in what we called a desert leaguer. We weren't trying to hide. We were a deliberate show of force. We were there as back-up and our guns were aimed at suspected Taliban firing points in case the deal went south.

The day started much like any other.

'Fuckin' hell, Parky,' H said as he kicked me in my sleeping bag. 'You're snoring so loud the Taliban can hear you in Kandahar.'

'Urgh,' I groaned, wiping a few hours' sleep out of dusty eyes. Everything was covered in fine brown dust like talcum powder. The dust got everywhere. It clogged your eyes, filled your nose. It made the hair on your head feel stiff.

'Snoring is a show of force,' I said.

I had been in the army five years by this point. This was my third operational tour and we had been in Afghanistan for nearly six months. I felt like I had been doing it all my life.

Phil was sleeping on a thin foam roll-mat next to me. He twisted a pair of grubby earplugs out of his dusty ears, inspected them for signs of wax, and held them up to H.

'Borrow these if you like, mate. I've only used them once.'

I pulled on a pair of shorts that were stiff with three days' sweat and grabbed a shovel from the wagon and walked into the desert where I dug a shallow hole to take a shit.

The ground stretched flat and barren as far as I could see. The only things that lived out here were tumbleweed and flies. We had been camped for a couple of days now and the flies were getting bad.

'Take your time,' shouted Phil at my back. 'I'll get the brews on, shall I?'

The desert was a strange place. It didn't feel that dangerous. We had parked our wagons in a circle. About a dozen light reconnaissance tanks, which belonged to the Household Cavalry, formed the outer perimeter. Our three guns, 105mm Howitzers, were in the middle. Next to them were the six-wheeled Pinzgauers, full of rations and ammunition. Three of the Pinzes belonged to 7 Para. We used them to tow the guns. One belonged to the Engineers, who did mine clearance and demolition; one belonged to the LEWT, the light electronic warfare team; and one belonged to the drone team led by a hot female lieutenant. She was the only woman on the MOG. Overall, there must have been around ninety guys on thirty wagons. We even had our own armoured ambulance, a tow truck in case one of the tanks broke down and a handful of Ford Rangers for the Afghan National Army.

We had gun sights, night sights, thermal imaging scopes, man-portable radars and a hand-launched Desert Hawk drone. We were out of range of the enemies' mortars. We could see for miles in every direction. There was no threat from the air. There was only one place that we couldn't see. We couldn't see underground.

The orders to move came at the hottest part of the day: a pleasant 52 degrees Celsius – the gun officer had logged it. We were moving camp, mainly for health reasons. We never stayed in one place for more than a couple of nights. Firstly, it's bad drills to set patterns. Sit too long in one location and the enemy has time to find ways to attack you. Secondly, for hygiene. With ninety blokes eating, shitting and pissing in the desert, disease could be more deadly than the Taliban. An outbreak of D&V – diarrhoea and vomiting – could knock a company off the battlefield almost overnight.

The gun crews folded up the Howitzers and hitched them to the Pinzgauer lorries. I pulled on my Osprey body armour and climbed into the WMIK's turret. A WMIK, pronounced 'wimik', is an open-topped Land Rover with a pair of belt-fed machine guns mounted on the chassis. One gun is fixed to a swing arm next to the front passenger seat. The other is mounted on a gun turret in the back.

WMIKs are good desert vehicles. They are fast and light, built for shoot-and-scoots. They were modelled on the legendary jeeps the SAS used in the Second World War to strike behind enemy lines in Libya. The only disadvantage is that they are almost totally unprotected. What you gain in speed and manoeuvrability you lose in inches of steel armour.

I can't remember, and no one has told me for certain, what I was wearing on my lower half. Some people said I still had shorts and flip-flops on. The rules and regs were clear: I should have worn my desert boots and full-length trousers. But it was hot, it was the end of the tour, and we thought wearing shorts was ally. It could have made a difference, but I will never know.

The black metal of the turret gun almost burnt my hands to touch. I checked the ammo boxes at my feet and fed a belt of bullets into the machine gun. The brass glistened like gold in the fierce overhead sun. I yanked back the cocking lever and thumbed the safety catch as the lever flew forward and the first round entered the chamber. Sweat stung my eyes as I pulled on my radio headset.

'Two clicks east, towards Musa Qala,' I heard somebody say on the gun net. We were heading to a new campsite, about two kilometres closer to Musa Qala town. We were travelling in the hottest part of the day because the Taliban rarely attacked when it was this hot, which meant we were unlikely to have to stop and set the guns up to smash them.

A squad of four cavalry recce tanks rumbled out on point. They always led the column because their Scimitars and Spartans, armed with 30mm canons, had the most armour and the biggest guns. To all intents and purposes, they looked like little tanks.

We all knew the order of march. We had done these moves a thousand times. The tanks went first, the wheeled vehicles went in the middle. Then there were more cavalry tanks at the back. Dust and diesel filled the air and the desert's eerie calm was suddenly replaced with the clank and growls of heavy armour on the move. I wrapped a rag around my face to stop me choking on the dust and I looked across at the rest of the convoy. We looked like a scene from a *Mad Max* film.

The other WMIK pulled up next to us.

'Left or right?' their driver shouted.

Our task was to protect the convoy's flanks. We would ride off to the side as an extra layer of defence.

I raised my fist for a game of rock, paper, scissors. Left or right didn't make much difference. We were both along for the ride, whatever happened. Rock, paper, scissors was how we decided everything.

I went rock. He went rock.

I went paper. He went paper.

I went scissors. He went scissors.

I went rock. He went scissors.

'Ha!' I laughed triumphantly. Then I shouted, 'We'll go right!'

He nodded and the driver spun the wheel to peel off into position.

We moved off to the right side. We drove parallel to the main column, about sixty metres to its south. We were the outriders, moving up and down the column to protect the main body from a side-on attack.

'Opal two zero, this is Opal four. Radio check.' It was H's voice on the gun net.

'Opal four. You are Lima Charlie,' came the reply.

'All good, Parky?' Phil asked.

'Roger,' I said. 'Hot.'

'I'm sweating so much it feels like I'm pissing myself,' Phil said.

'Hot?' H said, surprised. 'You should have said, lads. I'll turn the air-con on.'

With that, we started to accelerate. I pulled my goggles down and felt grateful for the breeze.

BATTLE 3

Fight for Your Life

vs

Give Up and Let Go

14

Captain Kirby stepped out of the car and adjusted his peaked cap. He could see the flickering lights of a TV inside and he felt his throat tighten as he walked up to the house and knocked on the front door. It was a bright blue door with nine panes of clear glass above the letterbox. I knew that door well. It was the door to the house I grew up in.

Mum and Andy had just settled down to watch the six o'clock news. There was yet another story about Afghanistan.

'I'll get it,' Mum said. Might be the window cleaner, she thought. She still owed him some money.

At 5' 11", Mum is a tall woman. She has short, wavy brown hair and spectacles, and she is made from a potent combination of love and steel. She is the sort of mum that my friends loved to visit, but they knew never to cross her.

Archie, her beloved Scottish terrier, was sitting on her lap when she heard the knock. He leapt off in a flash and Rory, his fellow Scottie, raced him yapping to the door.

When Mum stepped into the hall the dogs were in full voice. She saw Kirby through the glass. Khaki suit and sash, polished shoes, the peaked cap. The uniform for formal duties.

'Andy!' Mum yelled over the dogs. She grabbed the wall for support. 'Andy!'

She was frozen to the spot and she refused to answer the door. It was as if that blue half-glass door could hold back the tsunami of pain that she knew was coming her way.

Andy came out of the sitting room. He is like my second dad. He is a lean, energetic man with barely a hair left on his head and a face well creased with smile lines. Andy is an electrician, a problem-solving, practical man who supports Sheffield Wednesday and his beloved Doncaster Rovers. Like every self-respecting Yorkshireman, he tells it like it is.

He looked at Mum, then he looked at Kirby through the glass. He opened the door.

'Mrs Dernie?' the soldier asked, speaking past Andy to my mum.

'Yes,' she said.

'Your son has been very seriously injured in a landmine explosion in Afghanistan.'

The dogs didn't understand. They were scrambling around Mum's feet.

'No!' Mum gasped. 'He hasn't! It's impossible.'

'All I can tell you is that Ben has been very seriously hurt,' Captain Kirby replied. There aren't many worse jobs in the army than informing next of kin.

'But Ben's in Bastion,' Mum protested. In her mind I was nearly home. I was among the sprawling mass of sand-coloured tents and the rolled-dirt airstrip, almost on the aircraft in fact – a creaky RAF TriStar that belonged in a museum – that would carry me safely home. 'He's waiting for his transport out.'

I had called home the day before. There were only six days to go on my six-month tour and I was excited about coming home.

'Right, that's it. I'm done!' I'd said. 'I'm mongin' it now. Just cleaning guns and that, to hand over to Marines.'

'That's brilliant,' Mum had said. I could hear the joy in her voice.

'Yeah,' I lied. 'It's boring.'

I wasn't in Camp Bastion, of course. I was on that final op – Operation Lewanay – in the desert west of Musa Qala. Lewanay is a Pashtu word that means crazy, but I didn't know that at the time. It was just one last mission to me, and then I could fly home.

'He's not going to die, is he?' Mum asked.

'He might do,' Kirby replied.

Some of the seven million mines that the Russians had left behind in 1989 were bright plastic butterfly mines that were scattered out of helicopters and mistaken for toys by local children. Some were anti-personnel mines, primed with just enough explosive to take off a man's foot, but not kill him. The one I hit was an anti-tank mine. Probably a TM-62 or similar. It looks like a metal birthday cake, about twelve inches across and packed with 15lb of high explosive TNT. It had been waiting for me for most of my life.

I don't regret what happened. If it hadn't been me who got blown up that day it would have been one of my mates, and they might not have made it. For that alone, my injuries were a small price to pay.

I think God wanted me to survive. I wasn't religious before this happened, but getting blown up will change a person. I am convinced there is someone upstairs who wanted me to make it and he was looking out for me.

15

In the first few thousandths of a second, when a mine explodes beneath a car, the floor jolts up so suddenly it can shatter a man's ankles before he hears the blast. A fraction of a second later, before the pain reaches the brain, tiny bits of shrapnel start tearing through the chassis. The third stage is the shockwave. A superheated pulse of air builds up beneath the vehicle and punches it into the sky.

The mine exploded underneath the right rear wheel of our open-topped Land Rover. Some people said the wagon was thrown as high as a telegraph pole before crashing back down to the stony ground. It landed upside down, on its bonnet.

All of the following account is based on what my friends have told me, and the army's formal investigation.

'Stop! Stop! Stop!' someone yelled across the net.

'Contact minestrike. Wait out.'

It was 1431 hours in Afghanistan. That was 11:01 a.m. in England. I was twenty-two and a half years old. The convoy came to a halt. Then lots of things happened at once.

The gun officer, Lieutenant Sam Bayley, was in a WMIK in the main column about two hundred metres ahead of us. Sergeant Major Leigh Dawes – the most senior non-commissioned officer and the most experienced gunner in the convoy – was driving.

'That's one of ours, boss,' Dawes said.

Before he finished speaking, he had spun the vehicle out its tracks and floored the accelerator as he raced towards our wreckage.

The scene that greeted them was carnage. The WMIK was upside down beneath a thick pall of smoke and desert dust that lingered above the wreckage. In the silence after the blast there came a sound like hail. Bits of metal and debris were falling out of the sky. Occasionally a larger lump would thud into the ground.

'Someone stop that fucking WMIK!' a clipped cavalry voice called over the net. 'It could be a fucking minefield.'

Sergeant Major Dawes slammed on the brakes and stopped about fifty metres short. He and Lieutenant Bayley jumped out. They grabbed their SA80 assault rifles.

'Right, boss,' Dawes said to Bayley. 'You run in my footsteps for the first half. I'll run in yours for the second. OK?'

'OK,' Lieutenant Bayley agreed.

Phil had been trapped inside by the steering wheel. I think he was knocked unconscious. When he came round, he was upside down and disorientated. He could smell smoke and taste diesel that was running over his face and stinging his eyes from a ruptured fuel line. *Ammunition*, he thought, and fought to get out as fast as he could before our ammo boxes caught fire.

The next voice on the net was Rudy's. 'That's Parky's WMIK,' he said.

Rudy was in the front passenger seat of one of the Pinzgauer lorries. He scanned the ground outside the cab for any signs of mines, then leapt down and ran towards us. Phil had managed to wriggle free and was sitting in the dirt about five metres away from H, who had been thrown clear by the explosion. They were covered in white dust and looked a bit like ghosts.

'My eyes!' Phil screamed when Rudy reached him. 'I can't fucking see!'

'Man down. Man down. Multiple casualties,' Rudy said on the net as he ran towards the carnage. He gave Phil a quick once-over. If a casualty is shouting it is normally a good sign. He ran to H, who was lying on his side, shaking uncontrollably. It looked like he was fitting. More people arrived. Someone knelt down next to H.

'Where's Parky?' Rudy asked Sergeant Major Dawes.

They looked around but they couldn't see me. Then they looked at the upside-down WMIK. Then looked back at one another with the same awful thought that I had been crushed underneath it.

'Oh fuck,' Rudy mumbled. He paced around the wreckage, peering inside, but there was no sign of me. He looked up and scanned the ground.

'Shit!' Rudy said as he recognised a crumpled lump about fifteen metres away. 'That's him.'

Lieutenant Bayley and Sergeant Major Dawes had both run past the lump without realising it was me. They were so focused on the WMIK and the dazed human shapes in front of it they didn't notice the crumpled heap lying motionless in the dirt.

When Rudy got to me, he said it looked as if my feet had been dipped into a meat grinder. Both my heel bones were exposed. I was lying on my front, half conscious and making a faint gurgling sound.

Rudy and Sergeant Major Dawes reached me almost at the same time as Corporal Matty Oliver, who everyone knew as Olly. Olly was a specialist trauma medic from the Royal Army Medical Corps who had been attached to 7 Para for a couple of years. His wagon was near the back of the convoy. They were crossing the wadi when the bomb went off. He grabbed his med bag and sprinted forward on foot.

'Severe trauma to the feet and shins,' he said calmly and methodically as he knelt at my side assessing my wounds. 'No breath. Weak pulse. We're gonna need a MERT.'

MERT was the medical emergency response team, a flying trauma ward that usually came on a Chinook.

'Tell 'em we've got one cat alpha, Parky is P1.'

It was the military jargon for the most serious battlefield casualty. It meant that I needed urgent surgical intervention.

There was always a MERT on standby at Camp Bastion, but Bastion was at least a twenty-minute helicopter flight away.

'I've got to get him breathing,' Olly said.

He only had minutes to save my life.

When Olly rolled me over, my face was such a state he didn't recognise me. I was bleeding from my eyes, my nose and my mouth. I had a deep gash across the top of my head.

Olly tried a chin lift. It is a simple procedure, exactly as it sounds, to open up my airway, but my jawbone was a mush. I had broken it in four places.

Next, he opened my mouth, pulled out blood and bits of teeth with his fingers and inserted a J-shaped plastic tube to try to open my windpipe. He was going through a standard procedure to secure a patient's airway, but that didn't work either. He could see blood was pooling in my throat. It was drowning me.

By this point other people had started to arrive. My good mate Bernie and Captain Armstrong, the forward air controller, had run in on the tyre tracks of Sergeant Major Dawes's WMIK.

'You're all right, Parky,' Bernie said as he knelt at my head. 'You're gonna be all right, mate.'

Olly was working methodically and fast. He directed Rudy and Captain Armstrong to focus on my legs. They said my shattered shins felt like socks full of snooker balls as they tried to wrap bandages around the wounds.

At the same time, Olly pulled out a long, soft plastic pipe from a sterile packet in his med kit. It was a nasopharyngeal airway – a nose hose – which he pushed up my broken nose, through the nasal cavity and down the back of my throat. As soon as the tube was in blood gushed out of it.

'Shit,' Olly cursed. He was running out of options. 'How we doing on the MERT?'

Rudy shook his head.

The nose hose had made a small improvement. I managed to squeeze Rudy's hand, but I still wasn't breathing properly.

Olly told Bernie to get the oxygen bottle and hold the respirator over the nose hose.

The other gun commanders, Paul Challoner and Lewis Johnson, were establishing a cordon when the cavalry's armoured ambulance pushed up from the rear.

It stopped about fifty metres short and Corporal Paul Hamnett, the cavalry's medic, climbed over the bonnet to get as close as he could. He scanned the ground for mines then eased himself onto the dirt. It was only later, when I was long gone and they were extracting from the site, that they found a dark metal disc half buried in the dirt in the ambulance's tracks. They had driven over another mine, but by some miracle it hadn't gone off.

'What have we got?' Paul said as he knelt down opposite Olly.

'I think we've got to do an emergency crike,' Olly said.

'Shit.'

'Something's blocking his airway. I've tried everything else.'

Crike is slang for surgical cricothyroidotomy. It means cutting through the skin of the throat to open up the airway, like a tracheotomy, and inserting a breathing tube. It was right at the limit of their training.

'You ever done one before?' Olly asked Corporal Hamnett.

'Only on a pig. You?'

'On the dummies, in training,' Olly said. 'And the dummies always died.'

16

Corporal Hamnett leant close to my face to listen to my gurgling. The effort to breathe was encouraging. It showed I was still fighting. Olly tore open the crike kit and handed Hamnett the scalpel.

'Hold him still, lads,' Olly said.

The crike kits weren't included in their standard-issue med kits, but both of them had acquired a few before we hit the ground.

Bernie held my head. Rudy, Sergeant Major Dawes and Captain Armstrong had my body. Olly held my neck with both hands and pulled the skin over my larynx tight. Corporal Hamnett cleaned the skin with a disinfectant wipe, then he took the scalpel and pressed it into my throat.

He made a small, simple incision in my windpipe.

As soon as the knife went in they heard a whistle as my lungs expanded and sucked air past the scalpel. Paul took a pair of tongs from the crike kit and prised the small incision open. The whistle changed pitch. Olly inserted the plastic tube and secured it with an inflatable cuff. At last, I was breathing again.

'Fuckin' 'ell, Parky, you had us worried there for a second,' Rudy said.

Bernie moved the oxygen mask from my nose to my throat. He was doing two seconds on, two seconds off.

'How we doing with the MERT?' Olly asked as he taped the crike in place.

No one answered.

I know that I was semi-conscious because in his account to the Board of Inquiry, Corporal Hamnett said he tried to get a drip in my left arm but I fought him off. Olly tried the other side. I had lost a chunk of flesh around my left elbow, the bones were broken and the arm was limp.

'That's it, Parky, nice and still,' Olly said. 'Thank God you've got veins like fucking drainpipes.'

Rudy and Captain Armstrong had untwisted my shattered legs and packed the wounds with twelve first field dressings.

The good news was there were no obvious signs of external bleeding. The bad news was my blood pressure was dropping. Olly could feel my pulse getting weaker. He scanned the rest of me for injuries.

'Lucky you've got such a tiny knob, mate. Bomb's clean missed it.'

My low blood pressure told them I must be bleeding internally. When they pulled open my eyelids, one pupil was normal, the other one was totally blown. It was a sign of a brain injury.

'Where's that fucking MERT?' Olly cursed.

'Nine-liners's gone to Bastion,' Sergeant Major Dawes said. The nine-liner was the 999 call for a medevac. It told them who we were, where we were and what to expect when they got here. 'No ETA just yet.'

The lads from the electronic ordnance disposal team, the bomb squad, had moved up on foot and cleared a safe lane to the bomb site along the tracks of the ambulance. It was slow work. They were using metal detectors which beeped at every shard of metal from the wreckage of the WMIK. They marked the safe ground with white spray paint and anything suspicious they marked red and moved around it.

Once they reached the spot where I was lying they pushed on, further east, clearing a path about 150 metres long to an emergency helicopter landing site, where the MERT was due to touch down.

'Right, lads,' Sergeant Major Dawes said. 'Let's get him on the stretcher. He's a big fucking unit. On my count: one, two, lift!'

They heaved me on to the stretcher. Then they carried me along the safe lane to the helicopter landing site. Phil and H were already there. They were dazed but walking wounded.

'Where's the fucking MERT?' someone said.

'It's on its way.'

'You sure?'

'Fuck,' someone said more quietly. 'It's still not wheels up.'

'What the fuck is going on?' Dawes demanded.

Trauma medics often talk about a golden hour. If a patient gets to surgery within the first sixty minutes of being injured their chances of survival are massively increased. The helicopter's records show the mine exploded at 1431. Fourteen minutes later, at 1445, they received the nine-liner warning them of three casualties five miles west of Musa Qala. For some unknown reason, it took almost half an hour for them take off. At 1514, the Chinook left Camp Bastion.

Olly tried to splint my legs while he was waiting for the Chinook. The Sager splint in his med kit was a long piece of metal with Velcro straps. The metal went between the patient's thighs. It worked by strapping the damaged leg to the good leg with the metal in the middle. Olly gave it a go, but as he told the inquiry, it took his brain a little while to realise that my legs were beyond splinting.

'Leave it, mate,' Corporal Hamnett said.

'I wish the fucking MERT would hurry up,' Olly said.

It was a twenty-four-minute flight from Camp Bastion.

At 1538, an hour and seven minutes after the explosion, the Chinook thundered into view. Two Apache gunships flew either side as escorts. Someone popped a smoke flare into the helicopter landing site and a blue plume billowed upwards to signal our position.

'Parky, you dodgy bastard,' Rudy said. 'Can't believe you're short touring.'

17

Bernie and Sergeant Major Dawes covered me in a poncho to protect me from the blast of dust and pebbles when the Chinook touched down.

The first man off the ramp was Pagey, my best and oldest army mate from Harrogate. He's a solid lad with a square set jaw. He had been attached to the MERT as part of their force protection detail. He was basically a bodyguard for the doctors and the helicopter whenever it went on missions.

Lieutenant Bayley warned him that it was me under the poncho. Pagey ran over and knelt at my head.

'Eh up, Parky,' he said, doing his dour best to sound cheerful. 'You're gonna be all right, lad. Hear me?' He had to shout to be heard over the roar of the engines. 'It's Pagey. I'm here, mate. I'm here on the MERT. You're gonna be OK.'

He pulled out a first field dressing from his webbing and mopped the blood from my eyes.

My friends have told me there were some angry exchanges between the MERT and the MOG. Olly told the inquiry that somewhere along the line messages had got mixed up. The MERT was expecting only two casualties. As soon as Phil and H were on, the pilots wanted to take off.

A doctor ran off the back with a med bag and knelt in the dirt next to my stretcher. His uniform was clean and pressed. My mates were covered in dust and dark spots of blood.

Olly shouted out my vitals to the doc as a handover briefing. 'Faint, irregular pulse. Possible internal bleeding. Suspected brain injury. Five litres of fluid, no morphine. Let's get him on the chopper.'

'What's this?' the doctor shouted.

'What?'

'Who did the crike?' the doc asked. Olly told the inquiry the doc seemed surprised at the extent of my injuries.

'I did,' Olly said.

'We did it together,' Corporal Hamnett weighed in.

'Why?'

'He wasn't breathing,' one of them yelled back.

The doc was a pro. He had worked on the London Air Ambulance in peacetime and he was one of the guys who wrote the manual for training combat medics. But I had some of the worst injuries he had ever seen. At least that's what he told the inquiry. He said the crike had saved me, but he also said it was a procedure that 'not even a highly experienced emergency doctor or anaesthetist would undertake lightly'.

My mates were impatient. They thought he was dawdling.

'Who's this fucking thunder-cunt?' Rudy muttered to Sergeant Major Dawes.

We were thirty metres from the Chinook's tail ramp. The pilots were waving at us. They wanted to take off.

'Let's get him on the helicopter,' Sergeant Major Dawes addressed the doctor. 'Now, sir!'

The pitch of the engines increased.

The doctor was a colonel.

He measured my pulse and the oxygen levels in my blood. I was hypovolaemic. There wasn't enough blood pumping through my veins, which meant there wasn't enough oxygen reaching my brain. Even though I was breathing oxygen from the bottle, the lack of blood meant that there weren't enough red blood cells to carry the oxygen from my lungs to my brain. My heart was working overtime to try to compensate. My pulse was like a sprinting man, but my blood pressure was so low they couldn't get a reading.

The engines changed their pitch again. The pilots wanted to leave.

'What the fuck's going on?' Dawes said on the net.

'They're not happy on the ground. The pilots want to take off and circle until the doc's done whatever he's doing.'

'No way!'

'They say they'll come back.'

'No fucking way. They're not leaving without Parky.'

Apparently, someone from 7 Para ran on to the chopper and had a 'frank exchange of views' with the pilots. They knew that if the chopper took off there was a chance it would never come back. That was always the thing with helicopters.

The doc measured my responsiveness on the Glasgow Coma Scale. It runs from 3 to 15. Anything less than 9 is a coma and indicates a severe head injury. He gave me a 7.

Then he gave me ketamine and a couple of other sedatives to inhibit my gag reflex. He was effectively putting me in a medically induced coma so that he could put me on a mechanical ventilator. It took a bit of time, but he told the inquiry this was in order to optimise my ventilation and transport me more safely. About fifteen minutes after landing, Pagey, Rudy, Sergeant Major Dawes and Bernie carried me on to the helicopter.

I needed an urgent blood transfusion to treat the hypovolaemia. But the MERTs didn't carry blood in those days because they didn't have fridges on board and blood would go off in the heat. After I was injured, they got round that problem by carrying blood products in iceboxes. It has saved countless soldiers' lives.

By the time we reached Camp Bastion, my vital signs were desperate. My Glasgow Coma Scale score had plunged to 4, which is only one point above brain dead. My injury severity score (ISS) – another scale that doctors use to grade their trauma patients – was written on the handover notes. It runs from 1 to 75. At the top of the page, someone had written 'ISS – 75' in black felt tip and ringed it three times.

By rights, I should have been dead.

Rudy's crew unhitched their gun and aimed the barrel directly at my WMIK. They fired high-explosive shells into the wreckage until it caught fire.

The cavalry used their 30mm cannons to obliterate the radio sets and sensitive jamming devices that had been scattered in the desert.

In the army, we call this denying. We were destroying our own kit to make sure there was nothing of any use that could fall into enemy hands. And for those few minutes, as my mates unleashed the might of their guns at the scene of my injuries, there was a brief moment of catharsis.

Afterwards they retraced their route back to the camp where we had spent the previous night. For the next two days, whenever they looked east they saw a haunting plume of smoke from the burning wreckage of my WMIK.

18

The Chinook landed on a patch of gravel about two hundred metres from the tented hospital. An ambulance was there to meet me. It was 1616 hours, an hour and forty-five minutes since I was injured.

When the MERT crew signed me over to the Emergency Department, the first thing the medics did was to start a blood transfusion. Later that afternoon, a call went out across Camp Bastion for blood donors because stocks in the hospital fridge started to run low. Over six and a half hours they gave me thirty units – more than ten litres – of blood and blood products. A man my size and build might have about seven litres of blood in his body, which means they must have flushed me through completely.

As those first drops of haemoglobin dripped into my veins, the trauma team whisked me into an X-ray room and they scanned my torso with a mobile ultrasound.

The operating theatre was a DRASH tent – a deployable rapid assembly shelter – set up with two surgical bays, each equipped with a simple operating table, some trolleys and a light. At that point the surgeons' priority was to stop the internal bleeding the ultrasound had revealed was in my torso. It explained why my pulse had got so faint. The bleeding would kill me if it wasn't staunched. I also had a severe brain injury that needed urgent treatment.

Unfortunately, the British field hospital in Helmand didn't have a CT scanner, so the surgeons couldn't assess my brain injury in enough detail to intervene. The closest CT scanner, and the closest allied military neurosurgeon, was a forty-minute flight away at a Canadian military hospital in Kandahar.

The surgeons at Camp Bastion had one overriding priority. They wanted to get me as stable as possible as quickly as possible so that I could survive the flight to Kandahar.

Initially the plan was to perform a laparotomy – to open up my abdomen – to identify and staunch the internal haemorrhage. Then they planned to set my legs with external fixators and send me on my way. But as every soldier knows, no plans survive first contact with the enemy. Things always change in the heat of battle. By the time I came out of surgery, they'd amputated both of my legs.

19

A squad of Royal Air Force firemen carried my stretcher up the tail ramp of an empty C-130 Hercules. The air was hot and smelt of dust and jet fuel inside the barren fuselage. The nurse and an anaesthetist strapped my stretcher to the floor and clipped the drips and pumps and monitors to a strap stretched taut between the ceiling and the floor.

The aircraft's yellow-tipped propellers spun up one by one into a faintly luminous blur, while the medics buckled into canvas seats with their backs to the aircraft wall. We hurtled down the rolled-earth runway and climbed steeply out of range of enemy guns and missiles.

Kandahar Air Field was a massive Canadian and American military base, complete with coffee shops and restaurants and shops the size of small supermarkets. Unlike Camp Bastion, which had only been built a few months earlier, KAF was attached to an old civilian airport and the base had been there since the invasion, in 2001. When we arrived, more problems arose.

First of all, it took three hours to get a CT scan. I don't know why, but that's what is recorded on my medical notes. The Hercules was grounded and the RAF medics forced to stay with me because there was no one from the Canadian hospital available to take over my care. They must have been swamped with other casualties.

The second problem was much more serious. When I was finally admitted, the Canadian medics revealed that the consultant radiologist needed to interpret CT scans had finished her tour of duty and flown home. No one had replaced her.

The third problem was the worst. There was no neurosurgeon at Kandahar.

So I couldn't have the operation that might have saved my brain.

20

As soon as Captain Kirby left, Mum picked up the telephone and dialled my brother Philip's number. Then she called Danny. Then she drove round to Dad's house with Andy. Dad and his wife Sue lived near the racecourse. Everyone had questions, but Mum didn't have any answers. They all came round to Mum's house to await Captain Kirby's return. He had promised to come back when he had some more information. He said he was waiting for 'a signal' from Afghanistan.

It was after 10 p.m. when the doorbell finally rang. Kirby had come with another officer, and both of them looked grave.

'There is no easy way to tell you this,' Captain Kirby told the family. 'But we have had to amputate both of Ben's legs.'

The words cut Dan like a bone saw. He is not a man who cries easily, but something flipped inside him and he started sobbing inconsolably. Mum was on the sofa. She had Philip on her left and Andy on her right, both of them holding her hands.

'We can cope with that,' Mum whispered, trying desperately to be strong.

'And I am afraid Ben has suffered significant chest injuries,' Captain Kirby went on.

'We can cope with that,' Mum said again.

'And a very serious head injury.'

There was a silence for a moment as the words sunk in.

'Is he blind?' Mum asked, her voice breaking. 'Please don't let him be blind. He's got beautiful eyes.'

'I don't know,' Captain Kirby replied.

When the soldiers left, Andy showed them to the door.

'What are we looking at here?' Andy asked as they stepped outside onto the drive. 'Everyone wants to know but no one dares ask the question.'

Captain Kirby said nothing.

'Is Ben going to make it back alive?' Andy asked.

Captain Kirby took a deep lungful of air and considered his reply.

'Ben has a very serious head injury,' he said. 'We don't expect him to survive.'

The next morning 7 Para sent a soldier to tell Holly, who was seven months pregnant by this point. She was staying with her parents in Bury St Edmunds.

It should have been an officer for a jack job like that, but for some reason, that day it fell to a lance bombardier. Someone the same rank as me. It was the second-lowest rank in the army. We can only guess what the chain of command had told him. When he reached Holly on the Wednesday, he kept on calling me 'the body'.

'The body will be repatriated,' he said.

He called me the body three times.

'Bloody strong boy!' said Major Jim McGubbins. He was the officer who had accompanied Captain Kirby the night before. When he turned up at Mum's house alone the next day, he could scarcely conceal his surprise. 'He's still alive!'

McGubbins said the plan had changed. They were flying me straight to Birmingham. He didn't say why. He may not have been told. But my family got the impression they were bringing me home as fast as possible so they could say goodbye.

21

The inside of a C-17 is almost thirty metres long and wide enough to carry a Challenger II battle tank. The one I flew back on, with a Critical Care Air Support Team looking after me, had been fitted out like an intensive care ward. It wasn't so much a flying ambulance as a flying hospital.

We took off under cover of darkness and flew to the massive allied air force base at Al Udeid, in Qatar, to refuel. Then on to Birmingham airport, where I was handed into the care of a civilian West Midlands ambulance that took me to Selly Oak hospital.

Now, I don't say this lightly, but Selly Oak was a dump. It was a crumbling Victorian dump. The place was built as a poorhouse in the late nineteenth century and had been falling down ever since. By the time I got there, two days after my survival day, it had already been condemned. Everyone was waiting for a new 'super hospital' to open up next door, but it wouldn't be ready for another four years.

You might have thought wounded soldiers coming back from a war where they risked life and limb for their country would be treated in specialist military hospitals by dedicated military doctors and nurses who were experts in trauma caused by bombs and bullets. You might have thought that convalescing patients would be surrounded by their wounded comrades who would boost each other's morale with the banter and gallows humour that doesn't go down very well on a civilian ward.

That is not what happens.

God bless our politicians. They closed all the military hospitals in the late 1990s, just before they declared two major wars, in Afghanistan (2001) and Iraq (2003).

Selly Oak was already an overstretched NHS hospital when, in April 2001, it was designated the Royal Centre for Defence Medicine. The idea, a cost-saving exercise, was that Selly Oak would be a centre for excellence for military medicine. A place where military medics would stay sharp in peacetime by working in the NHS.

The reality, in 2006, was that the system wasn't working. The Army's Board of Inquiry into how I was injured and treated would find that civvy medics and their military counterparts had fallen out and didn't trust one another. Meanwhile, rival branches within the military system were fighting amongst themselves.

The doctors and nurses who worked there were trapped on a sinking ship, doing their best to treat their patients in a system built to thwart them. Of course, the people who suffered through all of this were the ones who needed help the most: wounded servicemen and women. It was all over the papers at the time. One lad was left in agony because the hospital didn't give him his meds for fourteen hours. Another guy dived under his bed whenever someone slammed a metal bin lid. One man had to wallow in his faeces for a night, because his colostomy bag wasn't emptied. The staff just weren't ready for the number of military casualties, with multiple complex injuries, coming back from Iraq and Afghanistan. They weren't ready for people surviving with what used to be unsurvivable wounds.

In 2006, from Afghanistan alone, there were eighty-five men and women airlifted off the battlefield. Of those, thirty-one were deemed serious enough that their families had to be informed with the dreaded knock on the door.

Compared to other wars, the number of dead and wounded wasn't huge. But the nature of our injuries was new. Advances in battlefield medicine and the fact that we all wore body armour meant people who would have died on the battlefield in the past were surviving with multiple, complex wounds.

*

Selly Oak's intensive care was a long, cavernous, paint-peeling ward on the second floor of the hospital, with about forty beds arranged along a central aisle.

They put me in a corner bed next to Sergeant David 'Paddy' Caldwell, from 3 Para's mortar platoon. Paddy had been shot through the neck in Sangin when he was calling in mortar fire. Opposite us was a Fijian lad who had been badly hurt in Iraq.

The room was filled with the sound of life support. Pumps and hoses sucked and gurgled blood and piss and the drugs that kept us all alive.

Bub! Bub! Bub!

Computers pulsed. Monitors hummed. Patients moaned.

I was totally comatose, but my parents remember that ward with horror. They remember how it looked that evening. And they remember how I looked. Beyond awful.

Visitors were only allowed in two at a time and they had to dress up in gowns with gloves and masks to limit the spread of infection. The room was pitch black apart from the pools of light over each man's bed.

Mum and Dad came in together. The first thing they noticed was my head. It was obscenely swollen. My face was as round as a football and the skin was deep purple, almost black, with bruising. My jaw was wired and there was a hammock under my nose collecting clear fluid that was leaking out of my brain. A clear, pinkish fluid was leaking from behind my head.

My abdomen was still wide open from the laparotomy in Bastion. The doctors had packed it with bandages and left it open to manage any infections. There were drips going into my arms and drains coming out of my chest. My left arm looked like it was hanging off at the elbow.

My legs were gone. My stumps were packed with wadding. There was a cage on top of them and a blanket over the cage to keep them warm.

'Ben, oh Ben,' Mum said. 'What have you done?'

She sat down next to the bed and rested her hands on the skin of my right forearm. It was the only bit that she could actually touch.

It was the only bit of me without pipes and wires and bandages. She leant forward and kissed my arm.

She saw that someone had pinned a rosary on my pillow. I am not a Catholic, but a nurse told my mum that I had been given the last rites.

'You're not going to need that,' Mum said. 'Come on, Ben. You can do it.'

It was Sue, Dad's wife, who noticed that my hospital wristband said I was twenty-nine, when I was only twenty-two. She mentioned it to Mum. Mum mentioned it to the doctors, but no one was really worried. Wearing the wrong wristband was the least of my problems. They thought I was going to die. But there was no way I was going without a proper fight.

22

Before they left the hospital that evening, my parents met a consultant orthopaedic surgeon, Mr Edward Davis, who became their main point of contact at the hospital. He was a fresh-faced, engaging man and a great example of someone doing their best to do a good job in spite of everything around them. Mr Davis led them to a side room to update them on my injuries.

'I'll start at the bottom and work my way up,' he said calmly. He started with my legs. He moved on to my abdomen and talked them through the operation to remove my spleen in Afghanistan. Then he moved on to my back. They had done more scans at Selly Oak, which showed I had broken my back. He said one of the vertebrae in the middle of my lower back had fractured and flipped forward.

'Don't worry,' Mr Davis said, 'his spinal cord is still intact. Everything is in line. We can pin it up. It's a straightforward operation.'

Then he talked about my head injuries. He said these were the most serious. I had what he called subdural and extradural haematomas. That meant something had ruptured inside my head and I had life-threatening bleeding inside my skull, which was putting pressure on my brain.

It was probably caused when I landed head-first in the dirt, rupturing the blood vessels between my brain and my skull. Blood had spurted out under pressure, like water from a burst pipe, and coagulated into thick, dark, livery clots, called haematomas. It was these semi-solid lumps of blood that were squeezing my brain out of shape, like a pressed balloon.

Bleeding on the brain is routinely treated with surgery. Mr Davis said a specialist team of brain surgeons would have to assess me and decide what course of action to take.

'Ben is very, very seriously injured and it is too early to know if or how he will recover,' Mr Davis said. 'If Ben had been hit by a car on the road outside the hospital and turned up here with even half of these injuries we wouldn't have expected him to survive, so how he's come back from Afghanistan we can't begin to know.'

He was trying to sound upbeat while managing my family's expectations, but my prospects didn't sound great. Perhaps understandably, some of my friends and relatives thought I might be better off dead.

'The thing you must focus on,' Mr Davis insisted, 'is that now he is here we are going to do everything we can for him.'

Mum came back into the ward. She kissed my arm again and said goodbye. She is the strongest person I know, but at this point even she thought I was going to die.

23

On Friday morning, at 8 a.m., they took me back into theatre at Selly Oak. The surgeons closed up my abdomen and the wounds on my legs, but they did not relieve the haematomas on my brain. They did not drill a burr hole to let the blood drain out, nor did they remove a piece of my skull and peel away the haematoma, which are the most common surgical treatments in such cases. But I wasn't a normal case. Instead, they inserted a bolt into my head to measure how much pressure the haematomas were exerting.

The surgeons at Camp Bastion had concluded that I needed urgent brain surgery, but they didn't have a CT scanner. They sawed off my legs so I would survive the trip to Kandahar, where they thought I could have brain surgery. At Kandahar they had a scanner but they didn't have a surgeon, so I was flown back to Britain. Now I was at Selly Oak and it turned out they didn't have a brain surgeon either. The brain and spinal specialists were based at the Queen Elizabeth (QE) hospital next door.

Mr Davis said that the hospital had taken fresh CT scans of my head, and the specialist team at QE had decided it was better to monitor the bleed than to treat it. If the pressure went over 25 they would re-evaluate.

In spite of the odds the doctors had given me, both in Afghanistan and back home in the UK, I clung on. Mum came every day. From the moment she realised that I wasn't going to die, she had one overriding objective and she pursued it relentlessly, for years, with every ounce of her formidable strength. Mum was determined to make sure I received the very best care available, the care she thought I deserved, the care she thought every wounded soldier deserved.

Jane Viggers, whose husband, Lieutenant General Freddie Viggers, was the adjutant-general, one of the most senior men in the army at the time, met my mum at Selly Oak. Years later, Jane told me that if it hadn't been for my mum fighting my corner every step of the way, she doesn't think I would be alive today. I have no doubt that she is right.

Mum would never say this herself. But I can tell you. Ever since that first night at Selly Oak, she's been at my side, fighting tooth and nail. Fighting against the systems that didn't know how to deal with someone like me. Mum gave up everything. She gave up her job, she gave up her life.

For years, she and Andy had been dreaming of retiring to a little cottage by a loch in Scotland. They had bought the cottage with their savings and had been doing it up, little by little, over the past few years. But all that disappeared the instant I was hurt. Mum gave it up to help me. She and Andy help me every single day. They are my greatest allies.

Most of the families of wounded servicemen were housed in an old nursing block called the Alexandra Wing, but that was already full by the time I was injured. Major McGubbins instead arranged for Mum and Andy to stay in a B&B. Each morning, Mum would get up too early for breakfast and drive to the Alexandra Wing where she could park the car. Then she walked over to the ICU. She would spend the next sixteen hours at my bedside. She read me stories. She talked to me. She kept looking at the pipes and drains, and the lines that twitched across the screen.

One of the numbers on the monitor showed the pressure from my brain bolt. It started creeping upwards almost as soon as I came out of surgery on that first Friday morning. As soon as it hit 25 Mum ran out to find a nurse. The nurse called a doctor. Mum came back to the ward and told me what was happening – even though I was unresponsive. She talked to me as if I could hear.

Nothing happened.

She went to find the nurse again. The nurse promised things were in hand.

The pressure hit 33.

'Look! Can you not see?' Mum screamed. 'My son has got a brain injury. He needs surgery. Why are you not helping?'

She begged the nurse to do something.

A doctor arrived.

'We are not going to intervene,' he explained to Mum. 'We think the pressure is spiking. It is not continually over 25. It is fluctuating up and down.'

The next day, in my medical notes, it states the doctors thought I was coning. Coning is when the pressure inside the skull is so great that the brain stem is forced out through a small opening at the base of the skull, where it meets the spinal cord. Coning leads to brain-stem death, which is fatal. If I was coning I would have died.

They sent me for another CT scan of my head, which showed a 'bright area' of bleeding, which could have been a new bleed or an old one getting worse.

'We think Ben has had a stroke,' the doctor said.

A few days later they removed the bolt.

They did not operate.

24

The Tuesday after I was injured, I was scheduled to have an operation on my back, to pin up the fractured vertebra. This was the operation Mr Davis had said was necessary but straightforward.

A specialist spinal neurosurgeon, Mr Andre Jackowski, had written in my notes that I needed a pedicle screw – a sort of metal scaffolding that supports your spine – around the T10 to T12 veterbrae, which sit at the bottom of the rib cage. 'It will aid rehabilitation,' he wrote.

He warned that if my spine wasn't fixed it would get worse when I regained consciousness and started moving around.

'These fractures deform into increasing deformity,' he wrote. 'If [Ben] needs to go to theatre again, then would be a good time to fix the T11 fracture.'

Unfortunately, on the day I was due to have surgery there was a major traffic accident in Birmingham. The surgeons were called away and my operation was postponed.

Mr Davis told us not to worry. My operation was urgent, so the hospital would find a slot soon. A few days later they wheeled me into theatre for the third time since I got back to England. They set my broken jaw and performed a skin graft on my stumps. But by then the doctors had changed their opinion about fixing my spine.

My notes that day record that the risk of my abdomen bursting open when they rolled me onto my front was considered too high to make the operation viable.

Two days after that, my temperature was through the roof, my face was hot and clammy, I had blisters break out on my skin. I had contracted an Acinetobacter infection.

If you're healthy, then Acinetobacter might be the same as a bad dose of flu. But my immune system was shot. I had thirty-seven serious injuries, I had lost my legs, had a massive blood transfusion and my spleen had been removed. Your spleen is really important when it comes to fighting infections because it filters bacteria out of your blood.

Acinetobacter is a tough, drug-resistant bug. Whereas normal bacteria get blitzed by sunlight, Acinetobacter thrives in sun-baked soil – such as in Iraq – in temperatures over 40 degrees. It had been doing the rounds in the US field hospitals. It was so common out there the Yanks had nicknamed it Iraqibacter. There were cases in Afghanistan as well. By 2006, with all the casualties coming back, it had started to lurk in British hospitals. I probably caught it in Selly Oak, and it was yet another thing that probably should have killed me, but didn't.

Mum spent the next ten days mopping my face with cold flannels, and she started reading to me. She read me *Stig of the Dump*, *Swallows and Amazons* and my old favourite, *Finn Family Moomintroll*.

Somehow, I managed to fight off the infection, but by the time I was back to 'normal' the window to fix my back had gone. The deformity Mr Jackowski warned us about had started.

Amazing, selfless people did amazing, selfless things to keep me in this world. I owe my life to medical science and the courage of my friends who risked their lives to keep me alive. For that I will always, always be grateful. Some will disagree, but I also believe that things could have been done differently and, if they had, maybe the outcome would have been different.

A few days after Mr Davis had explained the decision not to operate, Mum came into the ward and saw me sitting bolt upright in bed.

A new set of nurses on the night shift had lifted the back of my bed to make me sit up, which meant I was putting my weight through my broken vertebra. My lungs were filling with fluid because of too much time on my back. The nurses sat me up to stop me drowning, but that could have snapped my spine and paralysed me. These were the sorts of impossible decisions that the medics caring for me faced every day.

At the beginning of October a nurse took Mum aside and said, 'We are starting to notice a very marked curvature in Ben's spine.' It meant my injuries were getting worse not better. The nurse called Mr Davis and he sent me for an X-ray, which confirmed that my spine was warping out of shape.

'His own weight is forcing his vertebrae apart,' Mr Davis told Mum.

As Mr Davis explained what was happening, he stacked his fists on top of each other and gently rolled them apart to demonstrate the movement of my vertebrae. It was called a kyphosis. It was exactly the kind of spinal injury that not being able to have the earlier spinal operation left me vulnerable to.

'They will operate now,' Mr Davis said. 'I'm sure.'

On 8 October he wrote in my medical notes, 'Kyphosis to be managed surgically soon.'

Three of my vertebrae had moved so far apart that they had broken through the skin of my back and left me with an open sore the size of a saucer. It was always red and leaking.

The nurses laid me on an inflatable doughnut to try to keep the sore off the sheets, but invariably every time a new team came in to change the sheets the doughnut would get swept up by mistake and sent off to the laundry. I would be left with my weight on the wound again, until someone, usually Mum, realised what had happened and took action. I never thought I would be so grateful for having a mum so good at nagging.

I was still in a coma, so I had no idea no idea what was going on, but looking back now, the secondary injury to my spine was probably the worst thing that happened to me – and that's saying something, considering what I'd already been through. Thank God I had someone with me who could fight my corner while I couldn't.

We can all be heroes, but mostly you're a hero to someone else.

To survive bad odds, find yourself someone to help who's brave, who won't give up and who'll think of others before themselves. We all have to lean on people in our lifetimes, and you don't want someone who'll blow down when you do.

Not long after the X-rays had revealed my new kyphosis, Mr Davis asked to see Mum. The relatives' rooms were full, so he led her upstairs to the paediatric burns unit. The ward was shut at the time and there was no one else there. They sat in a play area, on soft, brightly coloured children's chairs.

'Diane, I am afraid I have some disappointing news,' he said. Then he knelt in front of her and clasped her hands. 'I am so, so sorry. They are not going to operate on Ben's back.'

The spinal specialists advised that the risk was too high. Dealing with full-blown kyphosis was a much more serious operation than the preventative surgery.

'The risk of infection with screw fixation, set against kyphosis, is too high. Therefore, recommend not to proceed at this stage,' they wrote.

Of all the injuries I suffered, the wounds that have made my life the most difficult today are the damage to my brain and my spine.

We will never know if my brain damage would have been less severe if they had been able to operate to relieve the pressure or if my abdomen would have ruptured if I'd had the spinal operation. What I do know, beyond doubt, is that the curve in my spine grew irreparably worse. It left me hunched and crooked.

25

There are a fragments of hope in every situation.

After I had spent two weeks in Selly Oak, Mr Davis decided to wean me off the sedatives that had kept me in a coma since I was stretchered onto the Chinook.

'We hope he wakes up,' he told Mum. 'We're not sure if he will, but it could take several days, so don't give up on the idea straight away.'

Mum started reading me books by Jeremy Clarkson. She knew that I loved Clarko, and his style of ranting, irreverent humour cheered her up as well. It amazes me that she kept the faith. The doctors had been honest and made it clear I would be unlikely ever to walk again. Even if I survived, they warned that I would probably be a vegetable, confined to a bed in a nursing home for the rest of my natural life.

Maybe it was because Paddy Caldwell was still in the bed next to me. In the weeks that I had been stuck in a coma, Mum had watched Paddy make incredible progress. It was really inspiring. He was sitting up and talking. He was eating and drinking as well, although he still couldn't use his arms or legs. Day after day, Mum sat with me and talked to me and told me not to let go.

At first, when the drugs were withdrawn, the only change Mum noticed was that the number of twitching lines on the monitor by my bed decreased from about 12 to 8. That was just because the doctors were doing less measuring. Then one day, about five days after the drugs had been withdrawn, Mum thought she noticed something serious on the screen.

The two most important lines showed my breathing and my

heartbeat. My heart was beating on its own. It had never stopped, and the heart rate line had a regular, rhythmic, reassuring signature. But the breathing line was much less good. It was regular, but it was red. Red meant I was not breathing by myself. I was on a ventilator.

Something had made Mum look up at the screen and she noticed part of the line had turned green. She stared at it, transfixed but unsure what it meant, as it drifted left to right and disappeared. And then it was gone and the line was entirely red again.

It was almost another hour before she saw green again. Exactly the same thing happened. A blip on the machine made her look at the screen and there it was, a bit of green – surely a bit of good news – sailing across the display. This time Mum called in a nurse to ask her what it meant.

'Green means Ben is breathing by himself,' the nurse said.

Mum's eyes flushed with tears as she felt a surge of hope.

'It's a positive sign.'

'He's waking up?' Mum asked, scanning the nurse's face for a glimmer of reassurance.

By now the line was red again.

'Hopefully. But you can never tell what is going to happen with a brain injury.'

And then it happened again, while the nurse was standing at the side of my bed. The line flashed green. I had taken a breath and someone had witnessed it. My brain – albeit the subconscious, autonomous part – was beginning to wake up.

Mum squeezed my hand while the nurse made a note on the clipboard at the bottom of my bed.

'We'll keep an eye on him as the drugs continue to wear off,' she said.

Mum leant over and kissed my forehead. My skin felt burning hot.

'Come on Ben!' she whispered. 'I know you can do it.'

Over the course of the afternoon I took more and more breaths by myself. By the end of that day I was breathing on my own roughly once every fifteen or twenty minutes. Sometimes I would take two breaths together and then nothing for an hour. Very slowly, over the next week, my autonomous breathing increased until I was taking one in every ten breaths on my own. Then it was one in five. Then, at the end of two weeks, every single breath was green.

I was breathing for myself!

I was alive and I was breathing. I might be a bed-bound vegetable, but at least I could breathe for myself. This was the first bit of really good news – the only sign of progress – since I had been injured.

It meant I wasn't brain dead.

Breathing is controlled by the brain stem, in the reptilian part of the human brain. In evolutionary terms it is the oldest, most primitive part of our grey matter. It controls our most basic functions, including our heartbeat and our breathing. It you think of the brain like an onion, with the newest and most advanced functions like speech, reason and emotions in the outer layers, the brain stem is buried at the bottom of the onion, where the bulb connects to its roots. It connects to our spinal cord.

If the brain stem dies it means your brain can no longer send or receive messages to the body and there is no chance of recovery. Machines can keep you alive, but you are legally dead.

Breathing on my own meant I was legally alive. Who can ask for more than that?!

This was the first time we knew for certain that my brain stem was still working. But before there was time to celebrate, I went and ruined it by overheating.

At first the nurses thought my temperature was linked to the Acinetobacter infection, but Mr Davis diagnosed it as something much more serious. It was a sign that my hypothalamus wasn't working. The hypothalamus sits on top of the brain stem and controls a whole range of bodily functions including thirst, hunger, sleep, mood and, crucially, body temperature.

My brain stem was working but my hypothalamus was either dormant or misfiring. My temperature control was haywire and I was cooking from the inside.

'We've weaned Ben off the sedatives. That's a bit like taking a car off a tow truck,' one of the doctors told Mum. 'We were hoping it would run on its own, but it hasn't started properly. We're going to give him some drugs to try and jump start it.'

My heart rate surged when they gave me the drugs, like someone was revving an engine hard, but eventually it settled and my temperature began to fall. Whatever they gave me, it worked. Now both my brain stem and my hypothalamus were working. There would be no letting go. I was fighting back.

BATTLE 4

Define Your Own Limits

vs

Let Others Tell You What
You Can and Can't Do

26

The lads from F Battery, which had been my unit before I was voluntold for Helmand, were still in Colchester. Initially, the commanding officer told them not to visit for a few weeks, to give my family some peace, but they ignored him.

Phil Armitage, Dean Wright, Mozza, Brownie and Stapes – a bunch of lovable reprobates – all piled into a beaten-up old car and drove up straight away. Selly Oak gave them a room in the Alexandra Wing to stay the night. There was only one rule at the Alexandra Wing: you had to be in by midnight.

After they had been to see me the lads went out on the smash in Brum. They hit it hard, very hard, because no one much likes seeing a legless mate in a coma. By the time they stumbled back to the hospital the Alexandra Wing, where they were billeted, was all locked up. The puddles in the potholes in the hospital car park were starting to freeze over. They tried to break in to the wing, but only half-heartedly. They couldn't get in without causing real damage. So the only option was the car. Five hairy-arsed blokes squeezed into a three-door hatchback and slept like sardines in the car park.

I am very lucky to have friends like them.

I was very lucky to have visitors. Other lads' regiments were stationed in Germany so didn't have mates who could pop by for a visit. It wasn't just my mates who came to see me. One day Prince Charles stopped in to say hello. He's Colonel-in-Chief of the Parachute Regiment. He came on his own and Mum said he was very friendly, telling her, 'I may be Ben's Colonel-in-Chief, but I'm not worthy of men like this.'

*

About four weeks after I reached Selly Oak they moved me off intensive care.

'We no longer believe that we will lose Ben to a catastrophic event,' one of the consultants told my mum. 'He is not going to die from a heart attack or a stroke.'

The doctors said their hope was that one day I would sit upright, and I might even leave hospital for short periods of time. That was a fair prognosis, based on what they saw in front of them, but Mum never set her sights that low. Even though, I was then, to all intents and purposes, a vegetable (we've got to face the facts here: I was immobile and unresponsive), something in Mum's heart told her the doctors were wrong. She believed in me.

'You don't know who you're dealing with,' she told them.

They moved me upstairs to the burns unit. Burns was the one major injury I hadn't suffered, but the ICU was being redecorated and they were clearing everyone out.

'Come on, Ben,' Mum would whisper to me. 'Just do something. Just let me know you're there.'

I like to think I could hear her. The truth is I don't know. But one day, when Mum was holding my hand, she felt a tiny spasm.

'Oh my God!' she yelped.

Then it happened again.

'He's moving his hand!' she shouted to no one in particular.

She ran to get a nurse. She needed someone else to see, to prove that it was real. Sure enough, the nurse confirmed I was moving my hand. They were small involuntary movements.

Each day I twitched more. Then I started to clench my fist. Mum would put her hand in mine so that she could feel me squeeze it. After a while I started squeezing so hard that Mum bought a pair of children's socks to put over my fingers, to stop my fingernails from cutting the skin of my palms.

Unfortunately, it wasn't the good news she had been praying for. It was a condition called tone, a symptom of my brain damage. My tendons were shortening.

'He should really be in splints otherwise his arms will totally curl up,' a doctor warned. So the nurses strapped my arms in splints. But Mum kept on believing.

About three weeks later, my cousin Caroline was visiting when the whole thing happened again. But it wasn't my hands this time, it was my face.

Caroline was a year older than me and we always used to stay at our grandmother's house together when we were kids. Mum was in my room, as usual, when Caroline arrived. They chatted for a bit, then Mum left to get a cup of tea and give Caroline some time alone with me. Mum was sitting at a corner table in the hospital canteen. She was staring at her tea when suddenly Caroline burst in.

'He's waking up,' she panted. 'Diane! He's waking up!'

They ran up to my room together and saw me pulling a face. I was clenching everything up. My eyes, my mouth, my cheeks were all bunched. I looked like I was taking a dump.

The nurses came in and sent for a doctor.

'Ben is not waking up,' he said. 'He's in pain. These facial expressions are an involuntary reaction to the pain that is caused by a build-up of calcium in his body.'

The doctor picked up my catheter bag, which was hanging from a hook at the side of my bed. He shook it slightly, then pointed to little white balls that floated in the urine like blobs of cotton wool. 'That's calcium,' he said. 'Because of Ben's injuries his body has gone into overdrive to try to repair itself. It's laying down excess calcium, which is building up in his kidneys. He's passing it in his urine and it's excruciatingly painful.'

I wasn't waking up, but it was still good news. Pain meant progress. The fact that I was feeling pain meant another part of my brain was working as it should. I was responding to a stimulus. The doctors increased my coma score from 3 to 6. These were tiny, tiny steps. But they were all steps in the right direction.

27

Sometimes, when you are climbing a large mountain, there are places where you slip and fall. Crevasses halt your progress and you have to build a bridge or find another way. Sometimes the ground gives way beneath your feet. My recovery has been like that. I have suffered setbacks on my journey, like everybody does. Life would be boring if it was too easy.

A few days after the doctors diagnosed my kidney stones, I suffered one of those setbacks. The nurses fed me a milky brown mush, which they pumped through a hose that went through my nose and into my stomach. It's lucky I couldn't taste it, because it definitely didn't look as if it was made from puréed Big Macs. It looked like it had been eaten once before.

One of the nurses was replacing my feeding tube when he made a mistake. Instead of slipping it down my gullet to my stomach, he pushed the plastic hose into my windpipe and the brown mush splurged into my lungs rather than my stomach. They tried to suck it out immediately, but the damage was done. I contracted pneumonia and my coma score plunged back to 3. To avoid it happening again the doctors inserted a new type of feeding tube called a RIG directly into my stomach, through the wall of my abdomen.

It was a tricky operation. The doctors took three attempts on three separate days because all the scars from my surgery in Helmand were in the way. Those were three days that I couldn't eat. But eventually they found a way to fit the valve and they could feed me again, and I was back on my way to the summit.

28

It was Bonfire Night when they moved me out of the burns unit and onto the military ward. A nurse said they needed the bed space because they always expected burns patients on Bonfire Night.

The military ward was called S4 and there's no point sugar-coating the fact that it was awful.

They put me in my own room at the far end of the ward, opposite the bay for female geriatrics. It was old ladies with dementia who always seemed to need the toilet but never managed to find it in time. They lived with the constant stench of stale urine and disinfectant. I know it wasn't their fault. The problem was there weren't enough nurses to help them. Mum volunteered to help the old girls. At least, she thought, she could show them to a toilet, but the nurses told her not to. They were worried that if Mum helped the old ladies, she might pick up an infection and transfer it to me.

There was a sink in my room that was permanently blocked and a toilet next door that used to flood two or three times a week. The water would run under the door into my room. Fortunately, I was still in a state of very limited consciousness, so I didn't realise how bad things were.

The good news was that I had a TV, something I hadn't had before. A week after I moved in, Andy was sitting with me watching the football highlights when he looked round at me and gaped. I was lying in bed. I was totally immobile, but I looked completely different. I had opened both my eyes.

It was the evening of Saturday 11 November, the day before

Remembrance Sunday, and someone had pinned a poppy to the corner of my pillow.

'All right, Ben?' Andy asked. 'You waking up?'

I blinked. It was eight weeks after the explosion. This was the first time I had opened my eyes.

'You all right?' he asked again.

Andy had no idea if I had heard him. The blink could have been a coincidence. I was staring blankly at the television in the corner of the room. My eyes gave my face a deranged expression because one of my pupils was still blown out like a saucer and the other was pinprick small. Andy looked at me, then back at the television. My eyes weren't moving and there was no discernible expression on my face. Andy had a sense that I was watching the ticker at the bottom of the screen.

'Sheffield Wednesday beat Leicester,' Andy said to me. 'That's two good things have happened today.'

The next day, S4 ward fell silent, or at least as silent as it was able, for the two minutes' silence. Dad, Phil and Danny had all driven down and they were sitting in my room when one of the army liaison officers came and opened the door to try and make the four of us feel more connected to the other lads on the ward. The phones in the ward reception were turned down, as were the beeps on all the monitors. The only sound they couldn't stop was the pump and squelch of the drips and drains coming out of our wounds.

It was exactly two months since my survival day. Almost sixty soldiers had died that year – twenty-two in Iraq and thirty-five in Afghanistan – making it the bloodiest year since the Falklands War for our forces.

I was still totally out of it. I couldn't think, let alone remember. But Remembrance Sunday had new meaning for everyone on that ward. We could have been one of those fifty-seven. But no one was getting rid of us that easily.

29

One day I blinked when Mum asked me to. At least that's what she thought. She tried to communicate with me by blinking. She would ask a question and say one blink for yes and one blink for no. The problem was I was so slow to answer that sometimes she wasn't sure if I was answering, or just blinking out of reflex.

Then I moved my right index finger. No more than a centimetre at first. Mum almost didn't believe it. She wondered if it was tone all over again. She stared at my hand for hours and it was perfectly still. Then I did it again. It was definitely a movement. A small, controlled, conscious movement. More than a twitch, it was a tap. It was hope.

Andy had been right about my eyes. I was seeing things again. I started following people in the room. Then I started to move my head. They were tiny movements, almost imperceptible at first, but if someone came into the room and they shouted a big hello, I would try to move my head to look at them.

My hands and my arms were still in splints, but by early December I could move my right thumb up and down. If my hand was flat by my side I could lift it almost vertical to say yes and horizontal for no.

The first time I did it, Mum burst into tears, she was so happy. She had always believed I was going to wake up. She had always believed that I would get better, but this was the first sign that she wasn't mad.

Then I started to nod.

Little by little, and then suddenly very quickly, I regained movement in my arms. One of my favourite nurses was called Roxy.

Every time she left my room she would raise her fist in a rock 'n' roll salute – thumb and pinkie outstretched – and she would shout, 'Rock on, Ben!'

I would try to lift my hand to respond. My movements were small, slow and clumsy and my fingers were immobilised by the splints, but none of that really mattered. What mattered was that I was trying. Every time Roxy came in or out of my room, I tried to wave at her. And every time, the neurons fired – forging new pathways in the damaged tissues of my brain. Every time, the muscles grew a little stronger.

One evening Roxy was looking through the window into my room and she saw me lifting my arms up to my face. It was by far the biggest movement anyone had seen me make, and it solved a little mystery.

The nurses had started to notice that my splints kept coming undone. It was strange because they were held in place with secure Velcro straps. Roxy realised I was trying to undo the splints with my teeth. I was ripping the Velcro open because the splints were agony.

In those days, I didn't qualify for any kind of proper rehabilitation therapy. It was a problem I would battle many, many times in the future. I was deemed too ill to have physio. My chances of improvement were considered too slim to warrant the scarce resources.

But I was lucky. Instead of formal sessions I relied on human kindness. I relied on nurses like Roxy and ward sisters like Shirley and her colleague Angie.

One day Angie came in with a present for me. She had a disabled son who had limited use of his hands, like I did. He used special crayons, which had great big thick grips to make it easier to hold them. When my splints were off I could practise holding the crayons. Drawing was exhausting. My body was still so battered that even just lifting my arms up would wipe me out. But I loved it. I longed for my splints to come off so I could try to draw more.

The sum of all these tiny improvements was a change in my diagnosis. I was officially reclassified. Instead of being in a coma, I was now in very low awareness.

For the first week or two they just let me enjoy it, but now that the doctors knew I could listen and understand there was something they had to tell me. It was something pretty awful.

Mr Davis volunteered to break the news. He came into my room and stood beside my bed.

'Hello Ben, can you understand me?' he asked, speaking deliberately slowly.

I moved my thumb up to signal yes.

'We have to tell you something, Ben.' There was concern in his voice.

'You were very seriously injured in Afghanistan. Because of the injuries you suffered, the doctors at Camp Bastion had to amputate both of your legs.'

There was silence. I made no response. Mum's eyes were ready to burst. Mr Davis leaned a bit closer.

'Do you understand?' he asked.

I moved my thumb upwards and I held it in the yes position for as long as I could manage. I could see the relief on his face.

'You've known all along, haven't you?'

I moved my thumb up again and the tears ran down Mum's cheeks. It was more than two months since I was injured. I was still in a state of very low awareness, but I didn't show any distress at having lost my legs. Even now, it is not something that upsets me. It is something that happened that can't be undone and there is nothing to be gained by wondering what if, or beating myself up about it.

Mr Davis was a good man. It doesn't matter how bad a system is. The world is full of good people doing what they can. Selly Oak was a dump, but there were amazing selfless people, like Mr Davis, like Angie and Shirley and Roxy, who were always going above and beyond.

My survival has been an extraordinary fight, but I could never have done it without people like them. Being injured has reinforced an important lesson I learnt early on in the army. You fight with the people on your left and right. They are your brothers and sisters in arms. Look after them and they'll look after you. It is important to have a good team.

30

By now, all the lads on my Helmand tour were home. Some of them came to visit me straight off the plane when they landed at Brize Norton. Some of them came on their post-tour leave, and some of them came a couple of weeks later, when they were back at work. They just kept on coming. Almost every day I had a visitor. It was another way that I was lucky.

The 7 Para lads were driving a three-hundred-mile round trip from Melville Barracks in Colchester. They didn't take too kindly when the nurses tried to lecture them about visiting hours. For a start, they thought all the medics were crap hats. Secondly, when you have just survived six months in Helmand and driven 150 miles to see a mate who is very nearly dead, rules about visiting times seem very petty.

One day Matty Norman turned up to see me. Matty was almost seven feet tall. 'You're disrupting the ward,' a squeaky little military nurse said. 'It is not visiting hours.'

Matty towered over this fella.

'I take orders from Ben's mum,' he said. 'Not some screaming hat who couldn't make it in the proper army. If she says I can see my mate, then I am going to see my mate.'

New Year's Eve 2006 came 110 days after my survival day. Sergeant Rudy Fuller came to see me with his wife, Emma.

Mum and Andy had been sitting with me all morning. They had no special plans to celebrate New Year's Eve because they were stuck in the B&B in Birmingham, away from all their friends and family, but Mum wouldn't have it any other way.

They said hello when Rudy arrived. He looked older than Mum remembered. The Afghan tour had etched its toll in the lines around his eyes. Mum and Andy went downstairs for a cuppa, leaving Rudy and Emma to catch up with me alone.

'What's this, mate?' Rudy asked in his chirpy Manchester accent. He was rummaging through the pile of teddy bears that all my visitors had brought.

'A pink fucking poodle, Parky? You having a laugh?'

He picked up an otter as well. He had one toy in each hand.

'Right, Ben. What's going to happen, mate, is this,' Rudy said. 'Mrs Poodle's feeling lonely.

'Are you lonely, Mrs Poodle?' Rudy asked her.

'*Ah ya! I am lonely, Rudy,*' Mrs Poodle replied.

'What about you, Mr Otter?'

'*Ya! Ya! So lonely.*'

'Mate, I think they like each other,' Rudy said to me, surprised by his own matchmaking. 'Otter's gonna bag off.'

'*Mmm! Mmm! Otter fancy sexy poodle,*' Mr Otter said.

'*Oooh! I vant you Mr Otter. I vant you so bad,*' Mrs Poodle replied.

'*Mmm. Ya!*'

This was X-rated teddy action.

'*Ah, ah, aaah!*'

Rudy was on his feet. He was really getting into it. Mrs Poodle was bent over the bars at the side of the bed and Mr Otter was going like a drunken gunner.

'*Ya! Ya! Flicken ma hoopen,*' Mrs Poodle said.

Emma was in hysterics. And – I had started laughing. I was laughing so hard my shoulders were shaking. It just encouraged Rudy even more.

'*Ya! Mr Otter, harder!*'

Suddenly the door opened and my mum walked in. Rudy froze. Mum looked at Rudy then she looked at me. She looked distraught. She left without saying a word.

Emma pulled herself together and scolded Rudy: 'Now look what you've done! Ben's mum probably gave him those teddies. Go and apologise. Now!'

'Sorry, mate,' he said to me sheepishly.

Rudy put the teddies on the end of my bed and went outside to find Mum. She was halfway down the ward.

'Diane!' he called out. 'Diane, I am so sorry.'

He ran to catch up with her.

'What were you doing?' Mum asked. Her cheeks were wet with tears.

'It, er . . .' Rudy stammered. 'It wasn't what it looked like.'

'What were you doing, Rudy? I need to know,' Mum insisted.

Fuck it, he thought. There's no lying to Ben's mum.

'Well, I was just taking the piss out of Ben for having a pink poodle, you know? I decided . . . I decided Mr Otter fancied Mrs Poodle and, well, it kinda just went from there.'

Rudy said it felt like ages that Mum just looked at him and said nothing. Then she smiled. She wrapped her arms around him and gave him a massive hug as she started sobbing.

'I've not seen Ben smile in three months and you just made him laugh,' she said. 'Thank you, Rudy. That's given me hope that he's still alive, you know, still alive inside.'

'Well,' Rudy said. 'At least we know he's still a sick, twisted bastard who likes his teddy porn.'

Rudy's pornographic puppet show had flipped a little switch in my mind. I had remembered how to laugh again.

31

In January the doctors decided to give me Botox. Not to make me more beautiful – they didn't have enough for that – but to relax my arms.

Botox is a poison. It is one of the most powerful toxins known to science and doctors use it to cause muscle paralysis. People put it in their faces to stop their wrinkles moving and they end up with a frozen face. It's great if you're trying to impersonate a blow-up doll.

It's also pretty useful if, like me, your brain damage means your arms are curling up like claws because of involuntary muscle tone. My tone problem had been getting progressively worse. About five months after I was blown up, despite the splints I had to wear, my arms were almost totally locked.

Botox was a miracle. The doctors gave me sixteen injections, eight in each arm, and the effect was instant. The muscles relaxed. Suddenly, I had my arms back.

No one could quite believe how successful it had been. It was amazing. From having no movement, suddenly I could wave my arms around in clumsy uncoordinated swoops. I was like an excited baby bird flapping his wings, when suddenly I caught the feeding tube that went through the skin of my abdomen into my stomach. I ripped it straight out.

It had only been held in place by an inflatable cuff because, up to that point, I was so immobile there was very little risk of it getting disturbed.

The ward nurse tried to reassure Mum that it wasn't a serious problem. She said it was easily fixed. All I needed was a specialist nutrition nurse to come and reinsert it. There was plenty of time.

She said there was a two-hour window for that to happen before the hole would start healing up. Two hours came and went.

The nurse explained that there was no one on duty that day who was qualified to do it.

That meant I needed another operation to reinsert the tube surgically. Then they told me there was no room in theatre. The surgeons were all busy. So I starved. For four long days I had nothing pass through my stomach because there was no one in the hospital who could reinsert a feeding tube.

If it wasn't for Shirley speaking up for me, it probably would have been even longer. One of the few advantages of S4 was that the civilians like Shirley, the wonderful ward sister, had no fear of military rank. It was on the third day of waiting for the operation that a colonel came to my room, and in the usual meaningless way he asked my mum if there was anything that I needed.

'Yes, there is something he needs,' Shirley jumped in. 'He needs this operation doing and they say there's no room in theatre. He hasn't eaten for three days. That's what he really needs.'

On the fifth day they found a slot and wheeled me into theatre. I had to have a general anaesthetic because the surgeon had decided to stitch the feeding tube to my stomach to stop me ripping it out again.

Twenty-four hours later the doctors started getting worried. I hadn't come round from the general anaesthetic. They said it was not unusual for people with brain injuries to take a bit longer to wake up again. On the second day I was still completely out of it, but now I was sweaty and feverish as well.

When a nurse came in to check the wound, she peeled back the dressing on my abdomen and placed her fingers either side of the new feeding tube that went into my stomach. The skin was red and swollen. She was gently kneading it when suddenly a fountain of hot pus burst out so fast it spattered the ceiling above my bed.

The nurse's face turned pale and she yanked the red emergency cord. Suddenly the room was full of men and women barking orders. I was in serious trouble again.

When the surgeons refitted the RIG they cut through an old scar in my abdomen and the wound had become infected. It wasn't just any infection. It was MRSA, the deadly drug-resistant superbug that was ripping through Britain's hospitals.

MRSA, or meticillin-resistant Staphylococcus aureus, is a bacterium that lives on people's skin and in their noses. A lot of people carry it without ever showing symptoms, but if it gets into the body through a break in the skin it can kill within twenty-four hours.

One of the reasons it is so deadly is that it doesn't respond to normal antibiotics. The doctors pumped me full of vancomycin, the drug of last resort. Vancomycin is modern medicine's last line of defence and its side effects are brutal. Once the drug went into my blood it was metabolised, like everything else, and it found its way out in my faeces. I had no control of my bowels in those days, which meant I often had to wallow in my own mess until someone could clean me. The vancomycin dissolved the skin on my arse. It was like sitting in cleaning fluid and the pain was excruciating. But it did its job: it brought the infection down.

When I stop and think about it, that was yet another occasion where I could have died, but I didn't. If MRSA had infected the weeping sore in the middle of my spine from where my vertebrae had parted, it almost certainly would have killed me. So, take it from me, even when things are desperate, even when things are so shit the shit *literally* burns, you can find a positive within it.

It was a terrifying time for my family, but once again, I survived.

32

One morning at Selly Oak, a soldier stopped my mum on S4 and asked her to make sure my room was tidy for a VIP visit.

'Oh yeah, who now?' Mum asked.

We'd had everyone from footballers to TV chefs, princes to politicians.

'It's the big one,' he said.

'Blair?'

He shrugged. But the plain-clothes policemen were a giveaway.

'Right! He's here,' one of the officers announced. 'Everyone to your beds.'

We loved the visits. It was always good to know you hadn't been forgotten.

My room was right at the end of the ward and the PM was working his way towards me. A few minutes before he was due, one of the RAF liaison officers knocked on the door and came in.

She had never had much to do with me before, but she started making small talk with Mum. She looked round the room, picking up pictures and saying, 'Oh, when was that taken?' Or 'Who's this?' or 'Where was that?'

At first, Mum just thought she was being nice. She thought it might have been part of the protocol, an advance party before the PM stepped in, but after a few minutes the questions wore thin.

There was a small window in the door to my room and Mum looked through it to see how Blair was getting on. She saw two plain-clothes policemen with their backs to her outside the door, like sentries.

'What's going on?' she demanded. 'Are they are keeping us inside?'

The liaison officer looked uncomfortable. At first she said nothing.

'What's going on?' Mum demanded again.

'We don't think it's appropriate for the prime minister to visit Ben because Ben can't interact properly with him.'

Mum was mortified.

I think I was the only patient on the S4 ward who the prime minister failed to visit that day.

People can make up their own minds about Tony Blair. I was never much into politics, but I am no fan of his, to say the least. He should have had the decency to visit me in hospital. I couldn't speak, so I don't know what he or his team were scared of.

I think he led us to war without enough evidence. He misled us about Saddam's weapons of mass destruction in Iraq. His government had no idea what they were sending us to in Afghanistan. It was his government that sent us to Helmand unprepared and under-resourced, with Snatch Land Rovers, not enough helicopters and without a proper field hospital.

They made the decision to deploy to Helmand months before they announced it to Parliament. That meant the MoD was not allowed to buy the extra kit it needed for the war until it was too late. By holding off on the announcement Blair was playing politics with our lives. We didn't have the right vehicles. We didn't have the right blast-proof cladding. We didn't have the right mine detectors. All of that would have saved lives.

Soldiers do not mind fighting. Going to war is what we are trained to do. It's our job. It is what soldiers want to do and we do it well. But no one wants to fight a war where decisions are governed by how much things cost, not whether or not it is right.

If you can't afford the right vehicles, enough helicopters, the right body armour or a proper field hospital then you probably shouldn't be fighting in a war of choice. It wasn't like we were invaded.

I was too ill to say any of that to Tony Blair, and his team were too cowardly to let him meet me.

33

From the moment I arrived at Selly Oak – and especially once I made it to S4 – there was one consistent message from all of the military medics, family liaisons and welfare officers.

'It might look bleak at the moment, but don't worry. There is light at the end of the tunnel. It is a bright shining light and it is called Headley Court.'

Headley Court was the military rehabilitation centre in the Surrey downs. In MoD speak, there was a 'patient pathway'. It was the route that patients had to follow on their journey to recovery. Everyone knew the pathway. There were posters all over S4 reminding us. As soon as you were well enough to leave Selly Oak you were given two weeks RnR at home, and then you went down to Headley.

'It looks terrible now, but you just wait,' the welfare officers told my mum. 'When he gets to Headley Court it's a miracle what they'll do for him.'

I was already inundated with miracles. Little by little, defying all expectations, I kept on improving. Small movements in my hands and head became bigger movements and I had more and more use of my eyes.

In the weeks that followed the MRSA I made two significant steps forward. The first step was the alphabet board. For the first time since I was injured, we found a way of communicating more than yes and no.

It was a painstakingly slow and frustrating process. The board was the size of an A3 piece of paper with large letters printed in alphabetical order. Mum would hold up the board at the side of my bed and point at each letter in turn. When she got to a letter I wanted I would give her a sign. It was usually a nod or a little thumbs-up.

The first word I spelled was h-u-n-g-r-y.

She laughed.

My sentences were simple. I asked about my brothers.

'D-a-n, P-h-i-l-i-p.'

I only had to spell a bit of a word and Mum would guess the rest.

There were hours when I was semi-lucid and strong enough to communicate. There were times when I was vacant and times when I was asleep. The times when I was vacant, I was mouth agape, head lolling and dribbling. I looked like the vegetable the doctors had predicted I would be. But my fleeting moments of lucidity proved the doctors could be wrong. I wasn't a vegetable. At least not all the time. My mind was not totally gone. And if the docs were wrong about my mind, perhaps they were wrong about my body too. Ever since my legs were amputated the docs had said I would never be able to walk. They said I would be lucky to get out of bed. But I had found a way to communicate. I would find a way to walk as well.

One thing Mum noticed about those first exchanges was they were either about right now, like feeling hungry, or about way back. I asked about people and places from my childhood.

One of the first names I spelled was C-h-r-i-s. He was my best friend from home. The one I was hanging out with under the bridge when I should have been taking my history GCSE. I had remembered that he was my friend, but I had forgotten we drifted apart when I left home at sixteen to join the army.

The second step forward was that the doctors thought I was well enough to sit up in a wheelchair. As the months had passed since my arrival, the sores on my back had started to heal and, despite the worsening kyphosis, the doctors said it was safe to sit up and move without snapping my spinal cord. Day by day they had increased the pitch of my bed.

I was still hooked up to the ventilator because while I was breathing mostly on my own there were still times when I forgot to breathe and the machine would have to kick in. Which meant sitting in the wheelchair was a massive operation. It took place in a physio room, which was on the floor above S4. Three medics would have to wheel me there on my hospital bed, towing my ventilator and the monitors in my wake.

When we got to the physio room the nurses would shuffle me to the edge of the bed and transfer me into a sling. The slings are basically canvas sacks that you sit in, underneath a crane. But I needed a special hoist for a double amputee because otherwise I would fall out. The medical world was not set up to cope with people with my injuries. The hospital didn't have a sling for a double amputee, so I had to wait an extra two weeks while they ordered one before I could start. Luckily I had practice in sitting around waiting from our days in Helmand. Soldiering is all about 'hurry up and wait'.

In one sense, this was amazing. It was amazing because the same doctors who thought I wouldn't survive were now saying that I was well enough to try to sit in a wheelchair. But in many ways, it was awful.

It was only when I sat upright that the horror of my back became apparent, and that everyone realised the scale of the damage. I had this egg-like lump sticking out of my back and it dug into the back of the chair when I tried to sit straight. I looked like the Hunchback of Notre Dame.

Worse than what I looked like was how I felt. Sitting up was agony. After five months lying on my back, simply sitting up was the most painful thing I had ever done.

The eerie thing was that I had forgotten how to scream. I was completely non-verbal. I hadn't made a single conscious sound through my mouth since they carried me onto the helicopter. In my head I was screaming but no noises came out.

The only thing I could do was flail my arms in wild, clumsy and pathetically weak punches at the medics trying to help me. I wanted it to stop.

The second time they took me to the physio room they dosed me up on morphine first. It wasn't quite as painful, but I still came to dread those sessions. The skin on my arse was still red raw from the MRSA – I looked like I had a spanking fetish – and there were no drugs on earth that could blank out the pain in my back and my hips. But I persevered.

I persevered because I had to be able to sit in a chair if I was going to get out of Selly Oak. I wanted to get to Headley Court. That was my short-term, achievable goal.

It was believed that if I could demonstrate that I could follow basic instructions like touch my left knee, then my right knee – which proved I'd be able to answer commands from the therapists – that would be enough for me to go to Headley Court.

'We will take you when you are ready,' they said.

And so, three times a week, the Selly Oak medics wheeled me upstairs and craned me into the wheelchair. And then we played children's games.

There was a massive set of Connect 4, about four feet square, in the physio room. The red and yellow pieces were the size of dinner plates. By picking up the pieces and choosing where to put them I was learning how to think again. I was relearning my coordination. I was following commands. I wanted to prove I was well enough to graduate to Headley Court.

Towards the end of January, after what must have been the four longest months of my mum's life, let alone mine, Selly Oak decided that I was well enough to be discharged. They no longer thought I needed to be in hospital. I had done almost a dozen physio sessions in the Connect 4 room, I was breathing by myself and, best of all, I had even started to eat the first few mouthfuls of real food through my mouth, instead of through a tube.

Food! It had never tasted so good, and that's saying something coming from me. I could only eat tiny amounts of soft, wet mush but after so long living on brown pulp pumped straight into my stomach, those first soggy mouthfuls of Mum's egg mayo sandwiches and chopped-up ham and cream cheese were mind blowing. Real food was the surest proof that I was back in the fight and not giving up.

For years afterwards I would carry on being told what I couldn't do, what I wouldn't achieve – but I would never have to listen to those people, because I had already proven them wrong. When I arrived at Selly Oak doctors thought I'd be in a coma or immobile for the rest of my life. I'd already smashed through those limits. Maybe it was because I'd had to fight so hard to pass P Company, or maybe it was during that fight for my life, but as soon as you've defied someone's expectations of you once, you'll know for ever that you can do it again.

BATTLE 5

Maximise the Opportunity

vs

Miss Out on a Chance

34

Leaving Selly Oak was not the same as being healed. I still needed a lot of help. The doctors said I was past the acute stage, which meant my injuries weren't going to kill me. What I needed now was intensive rehab, which an NHS hospital is not best placed to provide.

At first, we thought this meant I was off to Headley Court. Everyone on S4 longed for Headley Court because it meant catching up with the other lads from Herrick 4 and having access to the promised land where soldiers learnt to walk again.

Alan Mistlin, an RAF doctor, came to assess me. We thought it was just a formality, because my doctors knew how much I had improved. We went upstairs to the Connect 4 room. The nurses hauled me upright and hoisted me into the wheelchair. I touched my knees, I moved my head. I played Connect 4.

I craned my neck to look at him.

'Ben, I am not going to admit you,' Colonel Mistlin said. 'You are too hunched over in your chair. You have to be able to self-transfer, to get yourself in and out of your chair. And I'm afraid your consciousness isn't improving fast enough.'

I wasn't alert enough to feel much, but Mum was devastated for me. For weeks and weeks I had been sucking up the pain, playing Connect 4, and then it felt like the goalposts had moved.

It didn't make sense. The promised land of rehab had refused to accept me, because I needed too much rehab. Selly Oak said I was well enough to leave. More than that, they were discharging me. But Headley Court wouldn't take me. So, on top everything else, I was homeless.

The system wasn't set up for soldiers with my injuries.

'Where's Ben going to go?' Mum asked.

35

Etched into the stone of the hospital in Putney were three words that turned my blood cold. They were three words no patient ever wants to see or hear. Three words I would have to fight with every ounce of strength in mind and body to make sure they never, ever described me.

'HOSPITAL FOR INCURABLES'.

The Royal Hospital for Neuro-disability was a place for the unluckiest people on earth. From the outside, it looked like a mighty stately home, somewhere between Buckingham Palace and Wellington Barracks, set in a rump of landscaped gardens in south-west London. Inside, it was hell.

One of the wings was human storage. There was no other way to describe it. Patients trapped in persistent vegetative states or with worsening degenerative conditions. Sunken cheeks, bared teeth, wide eyes and lolling tongues.

Putney was a place of last resort. Its name had been changed for the sake of political correctness, but the old one was accurate. Most of the patients here would never leave. Most of them were incurables. There was a bench in the garden with a plaque that proved it. It said: 'In gratitude for sixty-three years' residence.'

I desperately wanted to be in a military hospital. I needed to be egged on and inspired by my fellow wounded comrades – not trapped in an asylum. But Headley Court couldn't yet take me and Selly Oak said I had to leave. In February 2007, nearly six months after I was injured, Mum reluctantly agreed that I would go to Putney for ten weeks. Mr Davis had convinced her in the end. He was the person she trusted the most at Selly Oak. He said, 'Why do you want Ben to go to a place that he clearly isn't ready for yet?' He told her Putney had a team of wheelchair specialists who would make a chair to fit my physique. Go there for ten weeks, he said, get a custom-built chair to fit your legs and your back, and then you can think about Headley Court.

The staff at Putney put me in a room on Drapers, which was one of three so-called rehab wards. Drapers consisted of six small dormitories that opened onto a central common room. Each dorm had six beds.

My bed was furthest from the door, by a window that was permanently bolted shut. Opposite me there was an old guy in a wheelchair who was always arguing with himself and asking for crisps. He collected his piss in bottles that he stored on his bedside table and if anyone tried to remove his piss he would scream and shout, so the nurses let him keep them for days and days at a time.

Next to the piss-bottle bloke was a great big Ghanaian guy called Leo. Leo didn't seem to move much, apart from when he was fed. He was fed by a machine that shot food into his stomach once an hour, which made him rock and choke. Leo's family were lovely. They were there almost every day, and a real source of strength and comfort to my mum.

Next to Leo was a fella in his forties who used to shout 'Help me! Help me!' really, really loudly about ten or twelve times a night.

A couple of days after I got there a man in his fifties arrived in the bed next to mine. He had suffered a stroke, which had damaged his brain, but something else was killing him and whatever it was it made him stink. This poor man was rotting from the inside out. His stench filled our room and it made the nurses gag when they came to bathe him. At least they could leave the room. I had to eat next to him.

Putney was a place for some of the unluckiest people on the planet and I did not belong there. It is not that I am better than those people. Far from it. There is no rhyme or reason why one man's mind recovers and another man's decays. But I did not belong on a ward of incurables because I was getting better. I was a wounded soldier who needed rehab. I belonged at Headley

Court – so Putney, hellish as it was, would be a staging post to get me there.

Mum saw the other patients. She heard the mooing and the moaning and the screaming. She saw the staff in purple shirts and knew that meant she must not make eye contact with the patients they were escorting because they could turn violent. She met the teenage girl with a perfect mind trapped inside a useless body. She saw the postman who was knocked off his bike and reduced to a hollow smile. She saw the man with Huntington's who always used to salute when my friends turned up in uniform. She saw the old boy from the Royal Tank Regiment who had lost the top of his head in a car accident and called out for his mother and ate his own shit.

Mum couldn't bear the idea of her soldier son being stranded in a mental asylum. She thought I would be forgotten.

'Ben belongs in the military. He should be with other soldiers,' she said.

There were no other soldiers who were like me at that time. No one else had survived with these kinds of injuries and the system wasn't ready.

'I'll end it for both of us,' Mum sobbed to Andy. 'If we can't get out of here, I'll just go. I'll end it and I'll take Ben with me.'

Mum tried everything she could to get me out. At the end of my first day there, she wrote to the most senior generals and begged them for their help. General Sir Richard Dannatt and Lieutenant General Sir Freddie Viggers were supportive, but to no avail. They seemed powerless to help.

And then we learnt an important lesson: sometimes not getting what you want is no bad thing at all.

36

Putney was a kind of hell but it was run by legions of angels. The people who worked there were among the kindest, most caring people I have ever met.

There was a European guy who cleaned our dorm. I can't remember where he was from, but he got to know that I liked boxing and cars, and he used to bring me the TV guides each week with all the shows he thought I would like marked out.

There were two Filipina nurses, Leena and Gilsa, who were like a comedy double act. They called me Benji Boy and they couldn't do anything without trying to make me laugh.

'Where are you from?' I asked.

'Ah. Too many immigrants where we're from, Benji Boy,' they would joke. 'Had to come to London.'

Anne was the sister in charge of Drapers. She had been a military nurse but she left the army to specialise in neuro-disability care.

'How do you do it?' Mum asked.

'It can be hard,' Anne said. 'But when it works it is the most rewarding work.'

Anne was probably the first person we had met in almost five months of treatment who didn't think we were completely mad to think that one day I could have a normal life. But her optimism came with a sobering warning.

'When a brain starts getting better you don't always get what you want,' she told us. 'You might go from being silent to being unbelievably abusive or screaming. You might start swearing, or rocking, or eating your own faeces.'

Anne decided it was time to do something about the sores on my back and bum. She put me on an air bed, which left the wounds exposed to help them heal. 'If we do not address your skin you cannot function. You cannot lead a normal life and you may die. Make no mistake, sores can be life-threatening. If they get infected, they could kill you in a matter of days,' she said.

She was a realist, but her overriding message was one of hope: 'You must never despair,' she said to me. 'I can see that you are engaging with people. I can see you are looking at things. I can see some very promising signs.'

One positive outcome of Mum's attempts to get me moved was that Putney agreed to give me my own room. I was spared the stench of piss and decay and the other patients were spared the sound of my rasping, hissing breath. The medics at Selly Oak had removed the valve in my crike hole, once I was well enough to breathe unaided, but it had left a hole in my throat the size of 2p piece, which turned my neck into a whistle.

Those first three weeks were deadly boring, waiting for my skin to heal. The army gave Mum a flat in a local accommodation block. Andy took the decision that he needed to be at Mum's side, so he wound down his business and moved to London with the dogs.

The two of them arrived each morning at 8 a.m. and stayed until 8 p.m. We quickly settled into a routine. They days would start with Leena or Gilsa getting me up to wash and shave. Andy would turn up with the newspapers and read me stories from the sports pages. Mum read me more Clarkson books. And we started to play cards. I still wasn't strong enough to hold them, but if Mum held my hand I could point to the cards. We played a lot of blackjack. And in between I would snooze.

Just before lunch, Andy would walk back to the flat, take the dogs out for a walk. Then he would cook some lunch and bring it in for me to eat. (Mum had decided that I would not eat the hospital food when they offered me fish with meat gravy on my first night.) In the afternoons I would usually have visitors, or watch telly, or Mum would read, or we would play more cards. Mum or Andy would walk home and collect a home-cooked supper in the evening and then I would usually be asleep by the time they left.

The level of care at Putney was amazing. At Selly Oak Mum washed me all the time. The nurses were so stretched it was the sort of job that often had to go undone, and so Mum took it upon herself to do it. At Putney, the Leena and Gilsa double act were too quick for her and had it covered with a smile.

'Benji Boy! Look at your food. So lucky, not eating that other rubbish,' Gilsa would grin.

The angels at Putney had seen my potential from the start. They knew what they could do to help me. They were determined to make the most of the time we had together – and so was I.

37

At the start of my fourth week at Putney I started physio with Christian, a Dutch therapist from a military family, and Marvin, his cockney boxer colleague.

Christian and Marvin were miracle workers. What Anne had tentatively called positive signs turned into tangible gains. Because my skin had healed, I was in less pain than I was at Selly Oak. I could concentrate on the training. Instead of dreading physio sessions I looked forward to them. It was the first time I could really show my determination to get better.

At the end of the fifth week my new wheelchair arrived. Putney had a specialist complex posture team, which had taken one look at the wheelchair Selly Oak had given me and thrown it out. They told me it was worse than useless. They X-rayed my hips and saw that my pelvis had been broken and had fused back together in the wrong position. They were surprised it had never been put in a brace.

My new wheelchair was totally custom built. There was a hole in the back for the lump in my spine and the seat was deliberately twisted to match my warped back and crooked hips. When I sat in it, my left stump poked upwards, so they built an eighteen-inch wedge to support it.

Almost every week there was more good news. Now that I could sit in a wheelchair, I was signed off to start speech therapy.

'Now Ben,' the speech therapist said, 'I want you to put your hands on your tummy. Take a deep breath and do what I just showed you.'

I was so excited. I sucked in the deepest breath I could manage.

I put my hands where she had shown me, then I opened my mouth, and, for the first time in six long months, I let out a loud 'Aaaah!'

It was amazing. I was finding my voice again.

All of these breakthroughs came with warnings about not getting overexcited.

'We have to be careful,' the therapist said to Mum. 'This may never develop into actual speech. We are just working on Ben's breathing at the moment.'

One of the side effects of a brain injury is a condition called dysarthria, when you lose control of some of the muscles that you need for speech and swallowing. The therapist explained that because I had been unconscious for four months the muscles I needed for talking had atrophied. The challenge was compounded by my brain injury, which meant there was no guarantee that I would ever be able to control them. She explained that with most of the muscles in your body you can massage them to stimulate responses externally. But with the muscles you use for speech that is impossible, so there was a chance I would never speak again.

But each week I made small gains. Inch by inch, Christian and Marvin managed to lower the block beneath my left leg as they manipulated me into a more normal shape in the wheelchair. Together we were redefining the limits my injuries had once seemed to set for me. At one time it looked like the best I could hope for was sitting up in bed for short periods at a time. And all within the first six months of my accident. It made us believe that plenty more might be achievable in the future.

38

I loved being in my chair. When I wasn't in one of my therapy sessions Mum or Andy, or whoever was visiting me that day, would push me round the gardens and I would breathe fresh, cold air for the first time in months. It was early spring, and the trees were in bloom. For most of my time at Putney the weather was amazing, but my trips outside weren't without their perils.

I remember one day Dad and Dan and Philip had come down to see me, so it was probably a Sunday because Dad had to work in the week.

Philip took me out for a walk in the grounds. Suddenly I heard him shriek and the wheelchair started rolling down the hill until I crashed into a flower bed and flipped face-first into the soil.

Poor old Philip thought he had killed me. He'd been trying to swat a bumblebee and let go of the wheelchair. I just couldn't stop laughing. It was the funniest thing that had happened to me since Rudy's puppet show.

Another afternoon we were sitting in the sunshine and Mum was taking a picture of me when General and Lady Dannatt appeared.

'May I have a copy of that photograph?' General Dannatt asked me. 'I would like to keep it on my desk.'

You don't say no to the head of the army.

'I keep a picture of a young lad who lost his life and I am going to keep a picture of you as well, Ben. I should never be allowed to forget the consequences of my decisions.'

In those days I lived for two things, visits and therapy sessions. With every day that passed it felt like I had more of both.

My son, Blake, was born while I was still in a coma. 7 Para bent the rules a bit so that Holly and Blake could move into married quarters, even though we weren't married. The lads had really rallied around Holly when I was hurt. Having her on base meant it was easier to keep an eye on her and help out.

Every week the 7 Para welfare officer would drive Holly and Blake down from Colchester to see me. Blake was so tiny. He was only a few months old. I desperately wanted to be a good father, but I still wasn't strong enough to hold him.

On Thursdays it was regiment day. There was always a bunch of lads who came down together and they would push me around the garden, talking shit and laughing.

Pippa, Jane and Sarah-Jane – the generals' wives – would usually visit once a week, and we started to see more of the London welfare officer, Major Hall. Our first meeting had been quite frosty, but we came to realise he was a kind-hearted man who was looking out for me. There were so many visitors that at times it felt like Piccadilly Circus.

At the start of week seven I was finally given the all-clear to start hydrotherapy. Getting the green light was quite a process. First I had to wait for the sores on my bum and my back to heal. Then Anne had to satisfy herself that I was totally clear of MRSA. She took swabs from my groin and my nose every week.

The last thing before I was allowed to take the plunge was that I had to plug my holes. For a man who hadn't been shot I was doing a good impression of a human sieve. I had a hole in my stomach for my food and a hole in my throat from the crike. Anne capped off the feeding tube with something like a bottle top, then she covered the crike hole with a large watertight dressing. The crike hole had shrunk from a 2p piece to roughly the diameter of a biro, but it still made an awful hissing noise when I sucked air through it. The last thing I needed was to flood my lungs with chlorinated pool water.

Mum had brought a pair of bright pink flowery board shorts from a box of old clothes that she had found in the attic back in Doncaster. They looked a bit like clown trousers on what was left of my legs, but I didn't care. I was so excited that I was going swimming!

I went down to the pool in my wheelchair, and went right to the water's edge, then they hoisted me out of the chair and lowered me into the water.

The therapist who ran the hydrotherapy was a South Asian Muslim woman. She was brilliant. She wore a wetsuit in the pool and a neoprene cap as a hijab. It's really weird: people always worry that I'll have a problem meeting Muslims. I could not care less. I might be brain damaged, but I'm not stupid. I thought this woman was awesome. All that mattered to me was that she was patient and kind and she helped me get better.

She always had an assistant in the pool and they would stand either side of me and help me build up my strength. My arms had completely withered. In six months, with almost zero exercise, the muscles had wasted away. In those first sessions I had almost no movement in my left arm. With my right arm I could make small circles, but I was still too weak to lift it above my shoulder. Gradually my limbs got stronger and more flexible.

The only session I didn't much like was music therapy. Someone told the woman who ran it that I liked cars, so she asked me if there were any cars I could remember from my past.

'L-a-n-d R-o-v-e-r,' I said, by pointing at the letters on the alphabet board.

'And who do you know who has a Land Rover?' she asked.

'A-n-d-y.' I replied.

The next thing I knew, she had written me a little song called 'I Remember Andy's Land Rover'.

I guess it might work for some people, but not me. I thought she belonged in that loony bin more than I did.

It wasn't just the therapy that was making me better. After about three weeks at Putney I was ready to be weaned off more of the drugs I was taking. I had been on a massive cocktail of painkillers, antibiotics and anti-depressants.

It was a strange, drawn-out process, a bit like clearing your head of a really terrible hangover. Slowly, life became clearer. It was easier to listen and respond. At the end of my seventh week I was formally reassessed. I was no longer in a state of low awareness. For the first time since the blast I was officially recognised as fully conscious.

39

It could not have come at a better time. It was a few days before I was due to transfer to Headley Court. Colonel Mistlin brought two colleagues for a meeting with my care team. Doreen Rowland was the bed manager at the Peter Long ward, where I would be admitted, and Wing Commander Simon Paul, a consultant rheumatologist, would be overseeing my treatment when I arrived.

'Ben is making marvellous gains,' Colonel Mistlin said. 'We are very pleased with what we are seeing.'

He paused.

'But I am afraid we will not take him at this time. We still do not believe that we have the facilities to look after him.'

'But . . . ' Mum faltered. 'Hasn't he met the requirements? Ben's a wounded soldier. He should be in Headley Court.'

'Mrs Dernie, Headley Court is not a right,' Colonel Mistlin said.

Mum was devastated, both for her and for me. It was as if the light at the end of the tunnel had been snuffed out.

Andy was trying to console her when Christian came into my room. He was a general's son and spoke with typical Dutch candour.

'I am glad Ben is staying,' Christian said. 'We are working miracles and I don't want it to stop.'

Then he turned to me. 'You're moving mountains, Ben. We're doing the impossible. If you stay for another eight weeks you won't believe what we can achieve.'

Christian was right. I wasn't getting what I wanted, but I was getting the help that I needed.

40

On the first weekend in May the army and the navy play a rugby match at Twickenham, which usually attracts a crowd of around eighty thousand people. But to me, the Army-Navy game was always just a sideshow.

Less well known, but far more important, is the Adi Powell memorial game between 7 Para and the SAS, which is played on the same day about half a mile away at the Harlequins' ground, the Stoop.

The match is a charity fundraiser in memory of one 7 Para's finest, Bombardier Adi Powell. Bombardier Powell was an awesome rugby player and a superb soldier. He passed special forces selection and joined the SAS, but he was killed in Kenya on a training exercise in 2000, when a lorry he was travelling in overturned.

His memorial game was one of the biggest social events in the 7 Para calendar. It was a massive reunion of serving and former soldiers. Unbeknown to me, my commanding officer, Lieutenant Colonel Hammond, had asked my mum if I was well enough to come – if I was allowed, it would be my first trip out of hospital since I was injured, which was seven and a half months ago. Mum asked the doctors, who said I could probably manage a half hour. The Stoop was seven miles away from Putney. It was only a thirty-minute drive if the roads were clear, but the traffic was bound to be terrible on Army-Navy day. Mum explained our dilemma.

'Well, if you want to take him for longer we cannot stop you,' the doctor said.

I couldn't believe it. I started laughing when Mum told me

and whenever someone mentioned the match my face was a lop-sided smile.

Putney had a small fleet of ambulances that patients and their families could borrow for trips like this. On the morning of the game, Mum got me dressed in a 7 Para rugby shirt and a pair of bright orange shorts. It was really hard to find clothes that fitted because of my crooked hips and spine. Andy wheeled me into the car park and pushed me up the ramp at the back of the ambulance. There was a bit of faffing as he worked out how to strap me down inside, and then we were off.

It was awful. The drive was absolutely horrific. What no one had told me about brain injuries was that one of the side effects is terrible motion sickness. I don't know how we managed to get there without me throwing up, but the moment we arrived I instantly felt better.

All my mates from 7 Para were huddled around in the car park. Everyone was there: Pagey, Rudy, Phil Armitage, Amina Ragamati, Martin Cartwright, Taga Vakatini, Gavin Waddington, Adam Duncan, Phil Greenway, Matty Norman, Adam Crossley, 'Skip' Hopper, David 'Benny Chang' Bentley, Sam Chick, Lee Soper and Rob Steele. We were all in civvies but it felt like I was back in the military. I was back where I belonged, surrounded by my airborne brothers.

Everyone got very drunk. Captain Dan Chapman was so overcome with emotion he was bawling his eyes out. 'Parky's gonna be OK! Parky's gonna be OK!' he said. He was wearing flip-flops, so everyone said he was crying because his feet were cold, but he just kept on saying, 'Parky's gonna be OK!'

He was right. I was going to be OK.

It felt like everybody's best day ever.

I was still on a massive high from Twickenham when I was felled by some very sad news. It became clear that my relationship with Holly was not going to survive.

The truth is that Holly and I hardly knew each other. We met a few months before I went on tour. She told me she was pregnant when I was in Afghanistan and I was excited. I couldn't wait to be a father. I desperately wanted to be a good dad, but I couldn't raise Blake from my hospital bed and Holly needed more than I was able to give.

She came down to Putney with her father one last time, to say goodbye, and then I never saw her again.

'W-h-a-t a-b-o-u-t B-l-a-k-e?' I asked Mum, when Holly had left.

'He will always be your son,' she said.

'I l-o-v-e h-i-m,' I said.

Blake is still my son and I do love him. Unfortunately, I am unable to see him, but Holly sends me photos of Blake and of course I send them child support. I never forget I have a son. I will not discuss it too much here, but Blake, if you read this, I want you to know that I love you. You will always be my son and I will always be your father. I will always love you.

One of the few advantages of my memory loss is that it is easy to put things out of my mind. When Holly broke up with me I did not grieve long for the life I had lost. My twin Dan was more upset than I was. He saw it as my last chance of having a normal family life.

I couldn't see that far ahead and I couldn't think that far backwards. Right then I was focused on my short-term goals. I was making real progress and I wanted to cement those early gains. I had to focus all my strength on getting better, one small step at a time.

41

Christian and Marvin were true to their word. Those two really worked miracles. In that second stint at Putney we started to make the breakthroughs the doctors had believed were impossible.

At first they built up my strength by getting me to throw a beanbag. Then, when I was strong enough, they introduced a banana board: a flat board in the shape of a banana which they used to help me transfer from my bed to my chair without the need of a sling. The way it works is you position the wheelchair next to the bed. As long as they are at the same level, you can place one end of the banana board on the seat of the chair and the other on the mattress. Then I would shuffle across.

To start with, Christian and Marvin would stand either side of me and support me, but it was a huge improvement on the hoist and much quicker. Most importantly, it was a step towards independence.

At about the same time my speech therapist gave me a Lightwriter. Looking back now, the Lightwriter seems unbelievably old fashioned. But this was 2007. Smartphones were only just coming in. At the time this clunky old keyboard bolted on to the side of my wheelchair felt hi-tech. The therapist said it was expensive. She was excited. She said it would revolutionise the way I communicated.

The Lightwriter was a voice synthesiser. It looked like an ordinary keyboard with a small digital screen along the top and it had a built-in speaker. If I typed out a sentence and hit 'speak' an American Dalek voice would say what I wanted to say.

'I AM HUNGRY' was the first thing I said. 'BREAKFAST WAS SHIT.'

I sounded like Stephen Hawking.

'MORE FOOD PLEES.'

I was never very good at spelling.

'CHRISTAN AND MARV AMAZING.'

'I WATCHED TOP GEAR. WANT A MAZERATI.'

The voice was awful and the typing took ages. I was much quicker with the alphabet board. I only had to get the first couple letters on the alphabet board and the person could usually guess the word.

But the problem with the alphabet board is you can't go to a café and expect the waiter to wait while you tap out c-a-p-p-u-c-c-i-n-o.

It took me a while to get used to it but once I did, the Lightwriter was a game changer. For the first time since I was injured it gave me the independence to say what I wanted to say, more or less when I wanted to say it. I didn't need someone else to cooperate. I could go to the hospital canteen and ask for a cup of tea.

It was also a lot of fun.

'You sound like Stephen Hawking,' Pagey said when he visited with Phil Armitage.

'Definitely an improvement,' Phil agreed. 'People might think you're clever.'

'Give it here,' Pagey said.

They must have been mucking about with it for a little while. I wasn't really concentrating. When Leena and Gilsa came in a few minutes later, one of them pressed 'speak'.

'MY BALLS ARE REALLY DIRTY.' The Dalek voice filled the room. 'PLEASE CAN YOU CLEAN MY BALLS.'

42

The next breakthrough came from Italy. One day Anne arrived in my room with a little black box with a couple of dials and a small speaker.

'It's a new kind of treatment,' she said. 'It's a sort of ultrasound and is still in the trial stage. We don't know if it will work because it's supposed to be done straight after the injury, but it can't hurt.'

The Botox treatment that I had at Selly Oak had started to wear off, which meant the tone had returned to my arms, twisting my hands into claws.

'There's an Italian company that has developed this machine that fires sonic pulses at your tendons,' Anne explained. 'We've got one on loan.'

Before she started, Christian came into the room holding a protractor, which he used to measure how far I could extend my elbows and my wrists. Then they held the box over my arms and turned it on. The session lasted about twenty minutes. They ran the machine up and down the length of my arms. At the end of it Christian brought out the protractor again.

My right wrist had started off at a right angle. Its maximum extension was 90 degrees. After that first session it moved to 120. By the end of my second stint at Putney the sonic beam box had totally unlocked my arms.

Not only that, my left leg was almost level again. Christian's physio sessions had reduced the size of the block that I had to put under the stump from eighteen inches to six. The sonic beam dropped it to zero. I didn't need a wedge at all.

One day someone from wheelchair services arrived in my room

with a motorised chair. The lady was wearing a long white coat and said it was just a familiarisation visit. She wanted to see whether I was mentally with it enough to use the chair.

Compared to my custom-built wheelchair, this electric thing was massive. There was a small joystick at the end of the right armrest. The woman spent about half an hour explaining how it worked.

I used the banana board to shuffle out of bed and she buckled me in with a lap belt. It was quite uncomfortable. It hadn't been adapted for the lump in my back and my twisted hips.

'Ben, don't be disappointed if you can't move it. Or if you find that you can't get it to go in the direction that you want,' she said. 'It might be too early.'

She turned the power on and I raced straight out of the door. I couldn't believe it. It was like driving a go-kart. I barged through the common room and hit the double doors at the end of the ward, swinging them open. I zoomed over the glass bridge that linked my ward to the old bit of the hospital. The corridor sloped downwards and I picked up a bit of speed as I went down. I was aiming for the café.

At the bottom of the slope I swung through the doors and saw my commanding officer, Lieutenant Colonel Hammond, sitting at a table with a couple of doctors. They were having a meeting about my progress. I crashed straight into the table and spilt the colonel's coffee in his lap.

'Ben!' someone panted from behind me.

It was the lady from wheelchair services.

'Ben! You aren't supposed to be able to do that,' she said.

'Oh well, nurse. Let's just add it to the list of things Bom Parkinson's "not supposed" to do,' Lieutenant Colonel Hammond said, laughing. 'I'm afraid he's not very good at being told he can't get better.'

Not every rung on the ladder to my recovery was quite as dramatic as that, but others were just as important.

Once we realised I was stuck in Putney, Gilsa suggested that I try to toilet train. Ever since I was injured I had a catheter coming out of my knob which took care of the pissing, but I couldn't control my bowels. When I had to go, I had to go, and I would shit myself in bed. Mum used to clean me up at Selly Oak because sometimes you had to wait hours for a nurse, they were so busy.

At Putney it was better. Gilsa and Leena were there in a flash and always cracking some daft joke. They helped me to laugh at the grimness of it all. But I wanted to be able to look after myself.

There is nothing very glamorous about potty training. It's done through persistence and hard work and it is humiliating when it goes wrong. But in order to get better, I had to be prepared to fail. I had to ask the nurses to remove my catheter, which meant I risked pissing myself.

Anyone who remembers me from F Battery will probably tell you I was never very good at bladder control in the first place. There was one weekend, when we were based in Colchester, that my roommate Keith 'Fish' Fisher came back on a Sunday and found me sleeping in his bed. It was a three-man room but there were only two of us living in it.

I had been there on my own for the weekend because Fish had gone home. I went out on the Friday night, got absolutely wrecked, came back and wet the bed. I went out again on Saturday night but when I got back my mattress was still soaking, so I slept in the spare bed – and pissed in that one as well – so I moved into Fish's because it was the only one still dry.

There are so many things that able-bodied people take for granted. How many times have you been to the toilet since you started reading this book? How many times did you have to tell yourself to hold it in? You do it without thinking.

I had to relearn those triggers, just like a toddler does. I had to rebuild the muscles I had forgotten how to use. But when I got it wrong, I took the same approach as when I pissed myself at Colchester. I laughed at myself and cracked on.

At some point towards the end of June another soldier arrived at Putney. He was the only other patient I could really talk to, because he was the only other patient who could talk.

Lance Corporal Martin 'Ed' Edwards was a sniper in the Rifles. We had overlapped in Selly Oak, but I was too ill to really meet him. Ed was on his third tour of Iraq when he was blown up by an IED in Basra. He was driving a Warrior at the time. It's a massive tracked vehicle that looks like a tank, but which is used to transport soldiers in the back.

Ed wasn't supposed to be driving. It wasn't his job, but he had stepped in for a mate at the last minute. The driver's hatch was open and his head was poking out when the bomb went off. A piece of shrapnel flew under his helmet and cut the top of his head off.

One of the weirdest things about Ed's injury was that he was never actually unconscious. He lost the top of his head but he never passed out. He still had all of his limbs. He could eat and he could speak, but one of the consequences of his injury was that his voice was reduced to a whisper.

'RIFLES' I said with my Lightwriter. 'BUNCH OF CRAP-HAT BLANKET FOLDERS.'

My synthetic voice blared out.

'You only joined the Paras because you can't fucking read,' he'd whisper back.

Ed was a great bloke. It was good to have a soldier around.

The doctors had put Ed in a six-bed dorm with the guy who ate his own shit, calling out for his mum all the time.

Whenever he could, Ed would come and hang out in my room. We played a lot of cards (Ed could hold his cards but, even though I now had more range of movement, I couldn't because I had the shakes. It was a condition called ataxia that comes with brain injuries – so Mum would have to hold mine for me) and we watched a lot of DVDs.

One of the toughest things for Ed was that his regiment was based in Paderborn, in Germany, so it was much harder for his mates to visit. He was also in constant pain, which meant rehab sessions were a real struggle.

One day Lieutenant General Viggers came to visit. Viggers was the spitting image of Mr Bean in uniform. He had the same dark eyes and slightly startled expression.

He went to see Ed in his dorm room.

'How are you doing, Corporal Edwards?' Lieutenant General Viggers asked.

Ed was pretty glum. He shook his head and whispered something the General couldn't hear. He leant closer to the bed.

'Get me a gun,' Ed repeated.

'What?' Viggers asked, surprised.

'Get me a gun. Please, get me a gun.'

'Don't be daft, lad. You're getting better,' Viggers said.

'It's not for me,' Ed said. He nodded over to the patient shouting and eating his shit.

'I want to shoot that fucker.'

When Viggers came into my room Mum was feeding me a Waldorf salad she'd bought from M&S that morning.

'Goodness me, Bom Parkinson! You must be the only soldier in the British army who eats salads with a name.'

I always tried to salute him.

'Not bad. Not bad,' he would say. 'Six out of ten. Room for improvement.'

It wasn't until the middle of August, five and a half months since I first arrived in Putney, that we had our next meeting with the Headley Court team. I was in a good routine at Putney by then. I was getting better. I was getting stronger. I was off the catheter. I was on the Lightwriter. The sonic beams had straightened my arms. I loved the pool and I loved my physio sessions with Christian and Martin. In Ed, I had made a new friend.

I wasn't really thinking about Headley Court that much. Mum tried not to mention it because she didn't want me to get my hopes up.

It was always the same people at these meetings. On my side there was Mum and Andy, Christian and Anne, Lieutenant Colonel Hammond and a consultant from Putney. From Headley there were Colonel Mistlin, Wing Commander Paul and Doreen Rowland.

'Right, Ben,' Doreen said at the end of this particular meeting. 'You are coming to Headley Court. Your bed's ready. We'll see you in a week.'

I couldn't believe it. After almost six months of hating Putney, of thinking it was hell, now it came to crunch time I didn't want to leave. Mum had wanted to kill herself when we first got here in February. Now, part of me wanted to stay. Putney really had been a lesson that good things can come from not getting your own way, so long as you make the most of the opportunities in front of you.

Putney had pushed me to achieve what no one thought was possible, but I think I knew deep down there could be no turning back. Headley Court was the promised land. I had to take the plunge.

BATTLE 6

Go After
What You Deserve

vs

Settle for
Less Than It

43

How much are your legs worth? What price for one, what price for two, above, below, or through the knee? What price would you sell your spleen for? And what do you think is more valuable, a broken back or a damaged brain?

There are faceless grey men who can tell you. Legions of form-fillers from a sub-branch of a sub-branch of the Ministry of Defence, in a building you have never been to, whose job it is to cost survival. I do not envy them. These people have to put a price on everything. They were the ones who calculated what my injuries were worth, and how I would be compensated.

Dan found the letter on the doormat in Doncaster. He was staying at Mum's to keep an eye on things while she was down in Putney. He had to read the letter twice.

'You won't fucking believe it!' he raged down the telephone to Mum. 'They're paying nought for . . . '

He paused to catch his breath.

'Nought for his back, nought for his skull, nought for his pelvis, nought for his spleen. Nought! Nought! Nought!'

Mum couldn't understand.

'It says they only pay for the first three injuries. That's legs, brain and arm.'

'His arm?' Mum asked, bewildered.

'They say his arm is his third-worst injury.'

The letter was from the Service Personnel and Veterans Agency. The people who wrote the letter were merely administering government policy. They probably had no idea that it would kick up such a storm. To them it was just another file. To me it was my future.

The Service Personnel and Veterans Agency represented neither service personnel nor veterans. It acted for the Secretary of State for Defence and its job was to run the Armed Forces Compensation Scheme.

Under that scheme, the maximum compensation pay-out that any soldier could get was £285,000. We all thought I would get the maximum. I had lost my legs, broken my back and was brain damaged, at the age of twenty-two. The doctors all said I was going to need constant care for the rest of my life. At this stage it wasn't clear if I would ever be able to walk again. And on top of all that, I was homeless. Before I was injured I lived in the barracks at Colchester but I couldn't go back there now. I didn't own my own house, so I had nowhere to go.

The staff at the SPVA had analysed my injuries and decreed that they were worth £152,000.

The letter in Dan's hands listed twelve of my injuries in what they considered was their order of severity. These were my 'accepted conditions'. Then, down the right-hand side of the page, there were two columns that listed how much each injury was worth and what percentage of that value they were prepared to pay.

'The scheme rules say that where more than one injury is sustained in one incident we will pay 100% of the tariff for the most serious injury, 30% of the tariff for the second most serious and 15% of the tariff for the third. No further amount is paid where four or more injuries are sustained in one incident,' the letter said.

For losing both legs above the knee I was awarded £115,000. For the brain injury that they weren't able to even try to relieve because there wasn't a CT scanner at Bastion or a brain surgeon at Kandahar, I was awarded £34,500. For the broken back that had bent out of shape and left me hunched over: nothing.

Of all the injuries I suffered, the Armed Forces Compensation Scheme had decided that my elbow – essentially a broken arm – was the third most serious, and for that they awarded me £1650.

Mum was straight on the phone to the SPVA.

'Look, I think there's been a mistake,' she said. 'It's the

combination of his broken spine and his broken pelvis that are worse than his elbow. Don't you realise how catastrophic that is?'

They agreed to recalculate. We all felt relieved. Two days later their response came back. It was exactly the same.

This time, Mum called Lieutenant General Viggers.

'Diane, this must be a mistake,' he said. 'We can't have someone in Ben's state who doesn't get the maximum. You must launch a formal appeal.'

Mum did as he suggested and the answer came back about a week later. This time the letter said two words: 'Appeal rejected.'

So she called the Ministry of Defence. To this day, she's not quite sure how she did it, but somehow she managed to get through to the private office of the veterans' minister, Derek Twigg.

'He has to come and meet my son,' she said to one of Twigg's aides. 'He has got to come and tell my son why he can't have his own home. Come and tell him to his face.'

Later that day the woman called Mum back, and to her absolute astonishment she said the minister wanted to meet me at Putney.

Mum called Lieutenant General Viggers to tell him the good news and Viggers asked if he could represent me at the meeting.

'Ben would be honoured,' Mum said.

'Twigg is a good man,' Lieutenant General Viggers reassured us. 'He gets it. We send these boys to these places, so it is our duty to look after them when they get back. The problem is that to Whitehall and the civil servants it's all about pounds, shillings and pence. Someone's got to stand up to that.'

Mum was in a panic. She knew we had this extraordinary opportunity. She was about to meet the veterans' minister with the adjutant-general, one of the most senior men in the army, in the room and she wanted to make the most of it.

It was clear to her that the Armed Forces Compensation Scheme wasn't designed for people like me with multiple, complex injuries. We knew there must be dozens if not hundreds of other soldiers in a similar situation. It wasn't just about me, it was about them too. But how could we get things changed?

Mum decided she needed legal advice. She wanted a lawyer to

ask the right questions, so called the first group she could think of who supported wounded servicemen, the Royal British Legion, but they were not able to help us.

Mum had no idea where to turn. Then she remembered meeting some lawyers in Selly Oak. They were from a firm called Irwin Mitchell, who had a special relationship with the Ministry of Defence that meant its lawyers were allowed to meet wounded soldiers and discuss their compensation claims. Mum managed to find details for a solicitor who worked there called Andrew Buckham.

When Mum called him, he was in the middle of investigating the worst single loss of life since the Falklands War. He was representing the families of the fourteen people who were killed when an RAF Nimrod spy plane had crashed in Kandahar a couple of weeks earlier.

He listened patiently as Mum explained her dilemma.

'Would you like me to come to the meeting?' Andrew asked.

'Yes!' Mum said. Success at last. 'Yes, please!'

44

Lieutenant General Viggers collected Derek Twigg and his private secretary from the Ministry of Defence and they drove in his staff car to Putney. The doctors wanted to give Twigg a VIP tour but Viggers didn't want to waste any time, so he brought them straight up to meet me. Twigg was a tall, long-faced man with a neat crop of white hair. He said hello, then they all went to the hospital library for their meeting. Lieutenant General Viggers was in his uniform. Mum and Andy were sitting next to each other. Twigg sat next to his private secretary, a female civil servant, who was acting as his adviser.

Andrew Buckham was there, but he waited in the room next door on Viggers's advice. Lieutenant General Viggers said the minister would clam up if there was a solicitor present, so the best thing was to have the meeting then run next door and brief Andrew on what happened while it was fresh in everyone's minds.

'What we don't understand,' Mum said, 'is how someone with Ben's injuries isn't entitled to the maximum amount.'

'It does seem strange,' the minister said. 'I can certainly see that Ben's circumstances are exceptional.'

Almost as soon as Twigg started speaking his private secretary interrupted him.

'I think what the minister means is that this is a statutory scheme,' she said.

'Ben has made a great sacrifice for his nation,' Twigg continued.

'But, unfortunately, the way the compensation scheme works is set out by law,' she interrupted again.

'But you have seen his injuries!' Mum insisted. 'You have seen his back. You have seen that Ben is bent double. How can you say that his broken arm can possibly be worse than a broken back?'

'It is very difficult,' the minister said.

'There is a possibility for us to review the scheme,' the aide said. 'It is only a possibility, but it is something the minister would be prepared to look at.'

Andy had kept quiet, but now he piped up.

'You've got teenage children, right?' he asked the minister.

'I have,' Twigg said.

'So, it's Friday night, you get a phone call from the hospital. How worried would you be if the person at the other end said your child had broken their back in three different places, versus them telling you they had broken their arm? Which would you be most concerned about?'

Before the aide could answer for him, Andy continued:

'I am asking you, minister, as a father. Back or arm?'

'Well obviously it would be the broken back,' he said.

'Well your scheme says that it is a broken arm. So your scheme's not fit for purpose,' Mum said. 'If the law says that's the way it is, then we have to change the law.'

As soon as Derek Twigg and his private secretary left, Mum, Andy and Lieutenant General Viggers marched next door to update Andrew Buckham.

'We have been waiting for a case like Ben's,' Andrew said. 'I think this is the perfect case to change the law. It's not just for Ben, but for all the lads coming home with these multiple, complex injuries.'

Viggers agreed. 'Ben,' he said to me, 'as a general in the Queen's army I cannot stand in the witness box and testify. But short of that I will do everything in my power to support you. We will get this changed. I promise you.'

Buckham said he would work for free but the only way to change the law was to launch a judicial review.

'What's that?' Mum asked.

'Well, even without solicitors' fees it means we need at least

£50,000 in a war chest to cover the barristers and court costs for a start,' he said.

'We haven't got that sort of cash,' Mum said.

'Don't worry,' Andrew replied. 'I've got an idea.'

45

Andrew Buckham rang a journalist he knew at the *Daily Mail* and explained the situation to her. Andrew's hope was that we could get the media to tell my story and help to crowdfund money for the legal battle ahead.

Sure enough, a couple of days later the journalist came back to him and said they wanted to help, but only if they could have a tell-all interview to go with it. I was still a serving soldier, so I was forbidden from speaking to the press, and in any case I could barely string a sentence together. I wasn't coherent enough for a newspaper interview.

So it was down to Mum: Mum who was so camera shy she hadn't been photographed since her wedding day. But as she'd already proved, she'd do just about anything to get me the help I needed. She agreed to a full sit-down interview and the pictures to boot.

On Monday 28 August 2007, the *Daily Mail* ran a front-page story under the headline 'WHAT PRICE MY SON'S BROKEN LIFE?'

They launched an appeal for cash donations to fund our judicial review and it ran next to a photo of me in Musa Qala a few days before the explosion. In that picture I am tanned, topless and unshaven, wearing just a pair of sky-blue boxer shorts, holding an underslung grenade launcher across my six pack. I looked pretty ally.

The campaign was called the Protect Our Protectors Fighting Fund and they raised £250,000 in seventy-two hours. It went mental. The reporter joked to Mum that most of the donations had come from besotted young girls.

It wasn't just the *Mail*. On the morning the story broke Mum was on every breakfast show in the land. She was on the radio all through the day. By Tuesday there were stories in every single national newspaper and journalists were queuing up outside her flat in the army block in Putney.

Not everyone supported me. Some of the comments under the online articles were quite negative. I was a murderer for joining the army. I knew what I was signing up for. I knew the risks and I still volunteered, so I should accept my fate with a stiff upper lip like the soldiers who had gone before me.

It is true. I signed up of my own accord. I wanted to be a para-trooper. I wanted it more than anything else in the world. I wanted to serve my country and I was hungry to go to war. I took the risk and I paid the price.

But 'the price' of serving my country should not be homelessness and poverty, on top of a lifelong struggle to get better. It was clear I was going to need a lot of care. That care comes at a cost. All I was asking was that the army paid to provide that care.

Overall, the support from the public was incredible. My story had really struck a chord. The *Mail* had compared my case to an RAF typist who had been paid £484,000 after suffering a 'sore thumb' and people were predictably outraged.

Simon Weston, the wounded Falklands hero, and Lord Guthrie, the former Chief of the General Staff, both weighed in on my behalf. A couple of days later Bob Ainsworth, the armed forces minister, appeared on Channel 4 News and formally announced a review of the compensation system.

It was the best we could have hoped for.

46

It was my second day at Headley Court when the *Mail* ran their first story.

People weren't as happy about the attention as you might expect. 'I know you think you're helping,' one of the nurses said to Mum. 'I know you think you are doing the right thing, but you are not. It is totally and utterly wrong.'

Mum was surprised. She wasn't just doing it for me. She was speaking out for all the other wounded soldiers who had been short-changed by a system that wasn't set up to deal with our level of injuries. I was still the most seriously injured soldier to survive, but more and more lads were coming back without limbs.

That put Headley Court under pressure. A few days after I arrived, one of the top officers there gave a radio interview in which he said his centre was getting clogged up with 'unrehabbable boys'. He didn't name me, but he didn't need to. Headley Court was a place to get soldiers battle fit again. I was never going to fight again and they weren't set up to rehabilitate someone like me.

Luckily I had no idea. In those days I was worried about whether I was going to piss myself, not making friends with colonels. I don't think I felt unwelcome. In fact, it was the opposite. For the first time in nearly a year I was surrounded by other soldiers. I was back where I belonged, with good old-fashioned shit-talking, trouble-making squaddies. Of course they took the piss that I was in the news. There is a tradition in the army that you have to buy the unit a crate of beer if you're in the papers or on the telly. I owed a lot of people a lot of beer. But they also loved the fact that the world was finally taking notice of us. People were beginning to realise what we had sacrificed thousands of miles from home.

My bed was on the Peter Long ward, on the top floor of a Gerry-built modern unit that looked as if it had been put up in a hurry, with the most seriously wounded soldiers. They were men who would have died in other wars but instead, like me, were lucky to have survived.

Ali McKinney was a sergeant in the Royal Irish Regiment who had been shot straight through the head by a sniper. He was based in Musa Qala, inside the district centre when I was on the MOG outside. The bullet hit just above his left eye, travelled through his brain and came out above his right ear.

He was flown to Pakistan for emergency treatment and then on to the Queen Elizabeth hospital in Birmingham. He had got MRSA and tuberculosis in hospital. The injuries had left him paralysed down his left side and he was partly blind in both of his eyes. It was a miracle he'd survived.

He was admitted to Headley Court a few weeks after me because General Richard Dannatt had been lobbying behind the scenes to force them to accept more men like me, who had head injuries.

Chris Ashton was a logistician attached to the Black Watch in Iraq when he was shot in the face with an underslung grenade launcher. Chris was lucky. He was crazy lucky. He was standing too close for the grenade to arm itself, which meant it didn't explode when it hit him. But it was still a lump of lead that hit him in the eye at about 1500mph.

He lost his right eye and part of his head. He suffered brain damage and had a series of strokes, and was left paralysed down his left side. Another lad, Chris, was a TA rifleman who had been shot in a friendly fire incident when someone let off a jimpy by mistake.

Warren Ward, a Geordie, had been hit by bits of a mortar in Iraq. The shrapnel had punctured his lungs, he had brain damage and was paralysed from the neck down. But somehow the nerves had recovered. He could walk and talk but he had no feeling below his elbows.

Harris Tatakis was a Royal Marine who was left with brain

damage and tinnitus when an IED went off under his Snatch Land Rover in Afghanistan. Aaron Shelton was another one hurt in a Snatch. We called them mobile coffins. They were phased out of Iraq from 2006, but still widely used in Afghanistan despite concerns they were death traps. Aaron was serving with Mercians when the Snatch he was travelling in hit an IED outside Lashkar Gah. Two other men were seriously wounded and Aaron's mate Thomas Wright was killed. Both of Aaron's legs were seriously injured but the surgeons used metal splints to screw the bones together. His legs hadn't been amputated when I first met him in August 2007, but he was in constant pain and he'd been told he would probably lose both of them later.

A Fijian lad called Derri had gone through almost exactly the same thing as me. He was standing in a gun turret when his vehicle hit a mine. He lost both his legs at the scene and broke his back in exactly the same place as me.

The big difference was that Derri didn't suffer any brain damage. He was conscious the whole time and he remembered all of it. Everything. He told me what happened and in a strange way I think some of his memories became mine.

Derri was very religious. He told me God wanted me to survive and I agreed with him. I was never very religious before. I can't remember going to church or praying. But ever since I woke up I have had a very strong feeling that someone wants me alive. There has to be someone up there and I know he is on my side.

These were the guys who looked after me. Especially Chris and Warren. When I was stuck in my bed they would come and sit with me and chat. I had gone from being the healthiest patient in a place of extraordinary care to being by far the most seriously injured patient in a place where you were expected to look after yourself.

The whole ethos at Headley Court was totally different to Putney. It was a military camp and that is what I had wanted. Most of the guys at Headley were expected to do their own laundry and run up and down the stairs. There were signs on the lifts which said 'For wheelchair users only'.

The main building at Headley Court is a big old country house in Surrey that was requisitioned by the War Office during the Second World War and used to prepare for the D-Day landings. Most of the paths round the buildings and the grounds were laid with fine gravel, which was beautiful – but terrible if you're trying to get down one in a wheelchair.

But that's jumping ahead. The first problem I faced was going to the toilet. At Putney, when I needed to go I could call a nurse to bring a bottle or a bedpan. At Headley I went back to wearing a catheter. They put me on Conveens, which are like condoms attached to a big plastic bag. They were easy to get on and off, but they always leaked.

The second problem was the food. The dysarthria in my throat meant I had massive problems swallowing. I was constantly at risk of choking, which was made worse by scarring from the crike the medics performed to save my life in the desert.

The scarring had affected a tiny flap of skin called the epiglottic vallecula, which sits at the top of the windpipe. It's supposed to act as a spit trap to stop saliva running down your windpipe. But because mine was scarred, bits of food got stuck there, which would block my windpipe and make me choke.

Choking wasn't the only risk. If food or drink gets into your lungs you end up with pneumonia, as had happened in Selly Oak when the nurse put my feeding tube down the wrong hole by mistake.

To mitigate all these risks I was on a strictly soft, moist diet. Vegetables had to be overcooked, potatoes had to be mashed, pasta had to have sauce, meat had to have gravy and cakes had to have custard. Things like nuts and lettuce were absolutely banned. Even peas and beans were off limits because the mixed textures of the tough skin and the mushy inside could make me choke.

Almost every hospital in the world will have patients on a soft, moist diet, but Headley Court seemed to struggle with it.

They insisted on putting thickener in my drinks. Thickener is disgusting. It looks and tastes like wallpaper paste – but it was a labour-saving device so the busy nurses didn't have to keep an eye on us while we were drinking. The more thickener they put in my drink the less supervision I needed from the nurses. I remember they used to use so much it turned my tea into jelly. I could turn my mug upside down and it would just sit there.

The result was that I stopped drinking. At Putney I used to drink twelve brews a day, but at Headley Court I hardly drank a thing. There was so much thickener in my drinks I didn't drink them. The nurses threw so much thickener down the sink that one day it blocked the drains and the whole building had to be evacuated while they fixed the plumbing.

Headley Court couldn't cope with the soft, moist requirement when it came to my food. You couldn't make it up. My wets were too dry and my dry food wasn't wet enough. (Yes, I was basically Goldilocks. I wanted everything just right.) When it came to liquids, they had completely overreacted but when it came to solid foods, they didn't react at all. It felt like every mealtime the food would arrive on trolleys from the kitchen in the officers' mess and the orderlies would lay it out on two tables at the end of our ward.

There was one table for the lads who could walk and one table, slightly lower, for those of us in wheelchairs. All of the 'self-carers' would rush up to help themselves. It was standard army scoff – sausages, burgers, drumsticks, that kind of stuff. There was hardly ever anything soft and moist – unless everyone was having lasagne or something like that – so the nurses could only respond in one of three ways. Either they would wait and wait for my food to come. When it didn't arrive, I would eat what was left, sitting at the table on my own because everyone else had gone. Sometimes they would say, 'There's nothing here that you can eat, so just have a treacle pudding with custard.' I didn't mind that. I would have three portions of pudding.

Or thirdly, I would have nothing to eat at all.

We realised this was what Colonel Mistlin had been trying to tell us all along. Headley Court just wasn't set up to cope with a soldier as injured as I was.

Soon after I arrived, I was asked to swap my custom-built wheelchair for an electric one. This was great in one sense, because it meant I could move around on my own. More independence was what everyone wanted. But sitting in it was painful. The nurses would try to customise it by rolling up towels to wedge under my back, but it was never really as good as my custom-made chair.

After a while, I worked out that there was a vending machine on the ground floor that I could drive myself to in my wheelchair, which sold crisps. Crisps were one of the most dangerous things I could eat. Their sharp, dusty texture meant they could easily catch in my throat and make me choke. But I couldn't help myself. I was a glutton before I was injured, but now I had even less self-discipline. Left unsupervised I would regularly risk choking to death for the sake of a packet of Wotsits.

One day I was sat next to the vending machine and I dropped the coins on the floor before I could get them in the slot. I leant out of my chair to try to pick them up and I fell flat on my face on the floor. I did the only thing I could do. I started laughing.

47

It wasn't all bad at Headley Court. Far from it. After meals on the Peter Long ward, when the nurses weren't about, the amputees in better shape than me would borrow the office chairs from the shared computers and use them to joust with each other, using mops and brooms as lances. Two amputees would sit in the chairs clutching brooms and two people with legs would stand behind them and launch them towards each other.

I also started physio sessions with a really popular therapist called Jane. She was blond haired, medium built but really strong and athletic and she worked one on one with a lot of the soldiers. The first thing she promised was to work on my ataxia. 'Starting with your legs, we'll work our way up your body, working on each muscle as we go. Hopefully it will get better,' she said.

Sure enough, my shakes came under control. They didn't go away completely, but they started to get better. We did lots of throwing as well, to build up my strength. The stronger I got the more physio sessions I was allowed to do, although I wasn't considered well enough to attend the group sessions. They did let me go to the group speech therapy, but I didn't speak. They advised me to practise using my Lightwriter instead.

If it hadn't been for Chris and Warren, who came and chatted at my bedside almost every day, I still might not be talking today. They would hang about for hours encouraging me when all I could do was make baby sounds.

That autumn, 7 Para invited me to the inter-battery boxing championships. It was always a massive night at the regiment, held in the main gym at Colchester. My old roommate Martin Cartwright was fighting, and Mum could tell that I was desperate to go.

The problem was the barracks were a hundred miles from Headley Court. It had been hard enough surviving a seven-mile trip to the rugby ground at Twickenham without throwing up. This journey was going to be more than ten times as long.

Headley Court lent us a black Mercedes people carrier with a wheelchair ramp to get me in. Mum and Andy drove down to collect me.

I was dressed in a set of Number Twos. It was a year since I had been blown up and this was the first time I had worn any kind of uniform. I had a khaki shirt and tie, and a khaki tunic with my airborne wings stitched onto my shoulders. We hadn't had time to sort out the trousers, so I just folded them underneath me. In my hands I was holding my most treasured possession. My maroon beret.

It was going to be the first time I had seen my friends since I moved to Headley Court. When we set off I couldn't stop grinning. But by the time we pulled up at the guard hut on the edge of the barracks in Colchester, the blood had drained from my face and I was on the cusp of vomiting with carsickness.

We had just gone through the barrier when we went over a speed bump and the nausea overwhelmed me. I felt a surge of sick erupting up my throat. I didn't have time to think. I brought my hand up to try to catch the sick, to stop it going all over my clothes. But my hand was clutching my maroon beret. By the time I realised what had happened it was too late. I had puked in my beret.

Rudy Fuller was waiting to meet me. He swung open the door of the people carrier.

Mum was still cleaning my face with some baby wipes and Andy was dealing with the beret. Rudy must have realised what had happened, but he didn't say a word, at first. It was very unlike him, because he was normally a gobby shite. He just lowered me out of the people carrier.

Then he took his beret off his head and slapped it onto mine.

'Looking good,' he said.

It might be hard for a civvy to understand how important the beret was to me, but being part of 7 Para RHA was my entire identity. I was still only twenty-three years old but I had been in the army for seven years, which was nearly a third of my life, and wearing the beret meant I was still a soldier. I might have lost my legs, my mind and my independence – for now – but I was still a member of 7 Para. It was everything to me. It was the reason I kept on fighting.

The gymnasium was packed, with raked seats around the ring.

'Sirs, ma'ams, ladies and gents!' bellowed a sergeant major. 'Welcome to tonight's inter-battery boxing championships. We are lucky enough to have the assistance this evening of three very lovely ring girls. I don't need to remind you to be on best behaviour. No filth from anyone. So please give them all a warm 7 Para airborne welcome.'

The room erupted into roars as a trio of beautiful women in bikinis strutted into the ring and danced around like cheerleaders, waving pom-poms. I was so focused on the girls I hadn't noticed that Phil and Pagey had pinched my Lightwriter.

These guys were professional pranksters. They waited for a hush to sweep over the crowd and then suddenly I heard my Dalek voice shouting at full volume, 'GET YOUR TITS OUT PLEASE!'

We were soldiers being soldiers and it meant the world to me.

48

Wednesday 12 September 2007 was my first 'survival day' anniversary. It was a year since I had been blown up. I had spent five months in Selly Oak, six months at Putney and almost a full month at Headley Court. Mum brought a massive cake to the Peter Long ward and she doused my slice in custard so that I could eat it without choking. Chris and Warren helped us dish the rest out to the other lads and the nurses.

Everyone celebrated their survival days – or their alive days – at Headley Court. They were always days of black humour and defiance. I remember one survival day, it must have been a few years later, when I met the wounded veteran Ricky Fergusson. Ricky is a pint-sized loon with no fear of booze who lost both his legs, his right eye and bits of the fingers of both hands in an explosion in Afghanistan. He also suffered some fairly serious facial disfigurement.

'Fuck! What happened to you?' I asked him when we met.

'What do you mean?' He sounded surprised. 'This is an improvement.'

Ricky was part of 4 Rifles in Sangin. They had one of the worst tours of any British unit in Afghanistan. He won a Military Cross for repeatedly rescuing pals who got blown up on patrols, before he was blown up himself. Four of his men had walked over the IED that got him.

I remember staring at his hands. He had still had both his thumbs and two good fingers on one hand and three on the other.

'It's all right,' he said. 'There's nothing you can do with all your fingers that you can't do with two.'

That's what survival days were all about. We celebrated being alive. We focused on the things we had, not on what we had lost. We celebrated the things we could do and the skills we had regained. Ricky still had fingers and he still had a filthy mind.

By the time I reached my first survival day, I had taken my first breaths, I had opened my eyes and emerged from a coma. I had beaten MRSA and Acinetobacter. I had started to move my fingers, then my arms. I could sit up in a wheelchair and play Connect 4. I had found different ways to communicate, first with finger taps, then nods, then with the alphabet board and most recently with my Lightwriter. Most important of all, I had remembered how to laugh and I had remembered how to fight. The laughing made the fighting easier.

As I entered my second year as a survivor there were two clear targets on the horizon. The first was that I wanted to walk. The second was finding a place for me to live once I left Headley Court, so that I could have a normal and fulfilling life. I didn't want to spend the rest of my life in a hospital.

The British army relies on a principle known as commander's intent. It is a military doctrine, also known as mission command, that was first developed by the Prussians in the early nineteenth century and is supposed to keep forces agile and dynamic on the battlefield. Once the commander has made clear what his or her objectives are, their subordinates are free to take decisions within certain boundaries in order to achieve those goals. In order to succeed, every soldier in the order of battle must understand their commander's intent and everything they do must be in order to achieve it.

My intention was to walk again and have a normal life in my own home. When it comes to your life, you are your own commander. In my mind I was the commander of my own recovery. I didn't know, nor did I need to, exactly how the medics and technicians would help me achieve those goals. All I needed to know was that we were pulling in the same direction.

A couple of weeks after my survival day party, when I wheeled myself into the gym for my regular session with Jane I noticed the room was different. There were ropes hanging from the ceiling over a low set of parallel bars. Lying on the padded floor, next to a parachute harness, I saw a pair hollow metal frames that looked like old-fashioned leg braces.

Jane announced, to my delight, that it was time to try to walk.

The metal frames were PPAM Aids: Pneumatic Post-Amputation Mobility Aids, and if Fisher-Price made prosthetics this is what they would look like. They were super-basic prosthetic stumps designed to get me used to bearing weight through my legs again. The pneumatic part referred to a pair of inflatable cuffs that cushioned my stumps where they sat in the metal sockets.

Getting them on took forever. First Jane pulled two elastic stockings over my naked, scarred stumps. Then she covered the socks with the inflatable cuffs. Taking one leg at a time she pulled on the metal frame and inflated each cuff inside it, like an inner tube inside a tyre, until the rubber was tight against the metal. Finally, she attached the tops of the frames to my body with a series of Velcro straps that went diagonally over my chest like bandoliers.

I sat on the gym's foam floor with the PPAM Aids protruding in front of me. Jane grabbed the parachute harness and began to strap me in. She threaded it under my legs and over my shoulders. Then she clipped the harness to the ropes hanging from a metal track on the ceiling.

Most people who use PPAM Aids have only lost one leg so they can put their weight through their good leg and gradually transfer more and more weight through their stump as they get more confident. Patients with a good leg are also blessed with being the same height as before they were injured. Therapists can adjust the length of the PPAM Aid to make it the same length as the uninjured leg.

I had none of those advantages. So I shuffled on my bum over to the parallel bars.

'Ready?' Jane asked.

I gave her a double thumbs-up and I felt the harness lines start to tighten as Jane pulled out the slack. My hands were on the parallel bars and I started to push myself up. The PPAM Aids dragged gently across the crash mats until they were underneath me. I locked my arms and held all of my weight on the bars. At first I did not dare lean on my legs.

Jane was at my side, encouraging me. She had the harness lines in one hand. They ran through a belay on her waist, so she could constantly adjust them, keeping them just tight enough to stop me falling but slack enough to let me sink into my stumps.

I felt the cuffs tighten as they squeezed against the frames beneath my weight. My cheeks were aching from my smile.

'You're standing up!' Jane said.

It was true. For the first time in over a year I was standing. I was actually standing. Ben Parkinson, the most wounded soldier to survive Afghanistan, was not a bed-bound vegetable after all. He was standing.

I wanted that session to last forever. I wanted to go from standing to walking to running in one day. But Jane knew not to push it too far. The excitement was exhausting. My arms were getting tired. All I did that day was stand, then it was time to sit down and rest.

I lived for those sessions with Jane. The next time I learnt to lean to one side. I still held most of my weight on my arms but when I leaned to one side I could lift up a leg and swing it back and forth. Then I did it on the other side.

It took every ounce of concentration I could muster. And just thinking about it tired me out.

On the third or fourth session I put the movements together, holding myself up on the parallel bars and swinging my stumps in turn. Then, maybe ten days or so after I had first donned the PPAM Aids, I put it all together. Lean one way, swing leg, lean the other. Jane held the harness lines tighter than usual as I transferred my weight onto the forward stump and then pushed myself forward with my arms. I had moved about a foot, but I had done it. I had taken my first step.

I could see Jane's eyes were welling up.

'Ben,' she said, 'we have never taught anyone with your injuries to walk before and it may never get beyond this. But we are going to give it a go. We are going to give you every chance.'

The doctors thought I would die in Afghanistan. In England

they warned me I would probably be a vegetable for the rest of my life. The chances I would walk were minimal. I had beaten the odds. I had confounded the science. I had taken my first step. It was a tiny step on tiny stumps. I was wearing a harness, holding parallel bars, with a therapist at my shoulder. But that small step was a giant leap for me. I didn't know how long the path to recovery would be, but I was both figuratively and literally taking steps along it.

I settled into life at Headley Court quite quickly. I could only have been there a month or so when the in-house prosthetics team made me my first pair of stubbies. They were a similar size and shape to the PPAM Aids, but the cups were moulded to fit my stumps. I didn't need the inflatable cuffs. They were much quicker to get on and off, so I spent much more of the physio sessions taking baby steps and less time getting dressed and undressed.

Once I was used to the stubbies, I moved from the parallel bars to a Zimmer frame. They were small, unsteady steps. I would take one step then pause to catch my breath and get my bearings. I had to let my brain catch up before I planned the next step, and the next one, and then I might need a rest.

I was quickly tired, but I never wanted to stop. Those sessions with Jane were the best morale boost. So when Headley Court wanted to cut them short, because they felt I should concentrate on wheelchair independence, it was just one more thing we were ready to fight for.

49

The first inkling of trouble came from my occupational therapist, who was known as an OT. OTs are trained to help injured and disabled people cope with everyday life. One of their regular tasks is visiting someone's home or work, in the wake of an injury or illness, to make sure it's set up in the best possible way for their needs. I am sure there are plenty of excellent OTs, but my experience has not been positive. I think OT stands for oxygen thief.

When Mum met my first OT she spelled out my intention to buy a house in Doncaster, where I could live when I was discharged. It couldn't be any old house. It would have to be a bungalow and it would have to be adapted to my needs. We hoped the OT – as the medical specialist – would give us some advice.

'We don't think Ben will ever be well enough for that,' the OT told Mum. 'When Ben leaves Headley Court, he should probably move into a brain injury unit.'

Mum wasn't having that at all; she was still haunted by the memories of human storage at Putney. But my social worker also wanted me to move into a care home. He told Mum about a specialist neuro-physio centre in Goole, which he said would be perfect for me.

'Please just check it out. Just treat it as a fact-finding mission,' he implored her. 'Nothing has been decided. But we think Goole would be perfect for Ben. They will be able to tailor a programme precisely to his rehab needs.'

Goole was another home for incurables. It was Putney all over again. The first thing Mum heard from the car park was the screaming and wailing from inside locked rooms.

The gym had a single set of parallel bars and an exercise bike that looked like it came out of Argos. On the noticeboard, posters for the week's entertainment offered cake baking and a day out to an allotment.

Mum thought Goole wasn't right, but she was torn. She felt that Headley Court didn't really want me, or at least that it wasn't really set up for me. She remembered how wonderful the staff had been at Putney. At the end of her tour she was introduced to the consultant who would oversee my care. He was a kind, weary American man, who was clearly under the impression that my transfer was confirmed.

'Why would you bring him here if you don't have to?' the doctor asked. 'Headley Court is the Cadillac of rehabilitation. There is nothing we can offer him that Headley Court can't. We can't possibly compete.'

So Mum set about finding me a home. She gained power of attorney over my affairs and used my compensation, together with the bits of salary I hadn't touched since I was hurt, and some generous loans from family, to buy me a bungalow in Doncaster, a few miles from the Donny Dome water slides where Danny and I had our sixth birthday party.

The house was amazing. I couldn't believe that I was twenty-three and I owned my own home, with a garage and a garden. It was a 1930s-style building with white-washed walls and a steep red-tiled roof, which almost gave it a Mediterranean feel. The red-brick driveway ran a hundred feet from the road to the front door, next to a lawn with four or five old trees.

Mum asked the OT at Headley Court to come and visit the property to see what needed changing for a person with my needs. But as Headley Court still believed I was better living in a hospice the OT was not able to visit. The relationship between my mum and my carers started to break down.

Mum called the local NHS hospital in Doncaster and got through to their OT team. She explained my situation. I was a wounded war veteran who wanted to come home to the town where he was born. The first thing they asked her was, 'Who is going to pay for it?'

Mum had no idea, but before she could answer there was more bad news.

'It doesn't matter anyway. The OT list in Doncaster is closed,' the lady on the telephone said. 'There is currently a nine-month waiting list and we are not taking any more referrals. When the list re-opens we can put you on. Is that OK?'

It was not OK. As you know by now, my mum is a fighter. So she called Blesma, the British Limbless Ex-Servicemen's Association. They filled the gap where the government had failed. Pete Shields, who had been thirty-four years in the army, and Keith Meakin, one of the charity's senior welfare officers, came round to the house immediately.

'There's a lot of work to do,' Pete said. 'But this place is going to be about as perfect as you could have found.' Pete said they would arrange for an OT to visit the house at Blesma's expense. They made an appointment for the following week, but when the time came no one turned up. Pete said Headley Court had told them not to come. Headley Court said that was nonsense. I don't know what the truth was, but the OT never came.

The first time I saw my new house was when I came home for Christmas at the end of 2007. It was my first trip home, and the first time I had spent a night outside of a hospital since I was injured. I was so excited when I got there. But I couldn't get through the front door!

I was still in my electric wheelchair, which weighed about seventeen stone on its own, so couldn't get over the doorstep, and even if it could have, it was too wide for the front door. Luckily the house had a conservatory at the back, with a set of double doors that opened on to the garden. Danny had built me a temporary ramp to get in.

The house was even better than in the photos. Andy said he thought the conservatory could be my gym. The conservatory led through to a lounge where Mum had put in a Christmas tree and a massive leather La-Z-Boy chair.

The chair was a gift from Brownie, the mate I had adopted the stray dog with in Iraq. We had talked for hours on that tour about how we were both going to buy ourselves La-Z-Boys when we go got home – like Joey and Chandler in *Friends* – and sit there together drinking beer and watching telly. Brownie had remembered. I couldn't believe it. It was the best welcome home present I could have wished for.

The lounge led through into a kitchen which Danny had agreed to totally rebuild, making the surfaces lower and the gaps between the units wider so I could spin a wheelchair. There are perks of having a twin who is a master cabinet maker, even if he is ginger.

I drove my electric wheelchair through the kitchen to the middle of the house, and Mum showed me my bedroom. It was a big oblong room. She had managed to get hold of a hospital bed with safety rails to stop me falling out and a hoist to get me in and out.

I just couldn't believe it.

But it wasn't all plain sailing. On that first visit home there wasn't a bathroom that I could use on my own, so I needed help washing and going to the toilet. At Headley Court I'd been on the Conveens – the sheaths – for peeing, but I needed help getting them on and off and there are just some things you don't want your parents doing. So to start with I kept a bottle by the bed and if I needed to go in the night I would pee in that instead of waking someone up. It would have worked fine, but I still had bad ataxia, which made me clumsy. I kept on knocking the full bottles over. Usually all over me – and sometimes it was three or four times in a night. Each time Mum and Andy would have to get up, hoist me out of bed, change my clothes and change the sheets.

Then the district nurse told us about VernaGel. It was a total lifesaver. They were little sachets of powder that turned my piss into a gel as soon as it hit the bottle. That way, when I knocked it over it didn't matter. Not quite the Christmas gift Mum had asked for, but hopefully a good one all the same.

50

When soldiers get back from a war-fighting tour they are routinely awarded a campaign medal. These aren't the same as gallantry medals for bravery. But they are a way of recognising your sacrifice and experience. I had been in a coma when my mates from F Battery had been awarded theirs. Then in the chaos of my movements from Selly Oak to Putney and on to Headley Court there had always seemed like something important that had to be dealt with. But once I was settled in Surrey, 7 Para decided that they wanted to put that right.

By this point the regiment was run by a new commanding officer, Lieutenant Colonel James Learmont, and F Battery had a new OC, Major Andy Thomson. They knew, from conversations with Mum, how worried she was that 7 Para would see me as a burden, a problem from a different era. The medal ceremony was their way of saying absolutely not. You are one of us.

My goal was to make sure I could stand when the medal was pinned on my breast. I trained as often as I could on my new stubbies. They were simple white casts which slotted over my stumps with stainless steel 'feet' that protruded about three inches from the bottom. I had practised for weeks to make sure I could pull myself up on a Zimmer frame and balance on my stumps with my hands on the frame.

All the lads from F Battery had driven down from Colchester. Mum and Andy, Philip and Dan had all come down for the day. Major Thomson and Lieutenant Colonel Learmont were there. They had brought Brigadier Colin Tadier, director of the Royal Artillery, to award the medal. We were in a large oak-panelled room in the old country house part of Headley Court. All the lads were lined up behind me. I pulled myself up and held on to the Zimmer frame while the officers said a few words. Major Thomson made a joke about me driving too fast in my electric wheelchair.

Lieutenant Colonel Learmont handed the medal to Brigadier Tadier.

'Bom Parkinson,' Brigadier Tadier said, 'you deserve this medal more than any of us.'

I was only four feet tall on those stubbies, but when Tadier pinned that medal on my chest I felt like I was 6' 4" again and fully part of 7 Para.

'I WANT TO STAY IN 7 PARA,' I told Lieutenant Colonel Learmont on my Lightwriter. It felt important to say it because most soldiers who get injured are medically discharged sooner or later, which feels like being thrown on the scrapheap. Being discharged would also mean I'd no longer be entitled to stay at Headley Court and I would be at the mercy of the NHS. I am a massive fan of the NHS and the tireless, selfless people who work there, but I didn't want to wait nine months to get on a waiting list for an OT to visit my house.

'Absolutely,' he said. 'Bom Parkinson, you are my soldier. You are part of 7 Para and you are my responsibility.'

Unfortunately, Headley Court weren't as keen to keep me as I was to stay there. In February 2008 I was admitted to Frimley Park hospital in Camberley with a blood clot on one of my lungs. I spent two nights in ICU. When I got back to Headley Court, the language of my care team had changed.

Instead of words like recover, rehabilitate and walk, they used words like plateau, manage and maintain. They were using the language of acceptance. The language of defeat. The sort of words that crap hats used – words I didn't want to hear.

When Headley Court looked at me they saw a problem they didn't think they could solve. They saw a drooling, crippled, brain-damaged wreck who was never going to fight again, so I wasn't part of their core mission. They saw a life laid out for me in overheated care homes, with cake days and bingo nights where no one took part. That was not how I saw myself. That was not the life I wanted. I was twenty-three years old, I was learning to walk and I had my own home. I wasn't going back to Putney. I kept my morale up with my physio sessions with Jane and some good old-fashioned soldier humour.

One day the Peter Long ward was suddenly full of hairdressers. They had been sent by some celebrity salon to offer us all free treatments and makeovers – which is what soldiers yearn for.

One of the fellas flounced into my bay.

'Hello Benny, oooh aren't you handsome? What can I do for you today?'

He waited while I typed on my Lightwriter.

'I WOULD LIKE A FOOT MASSAGE.'

No amount of jokes, though, could solve the fact Headley Court was under pressure for beds. The number of seriously wounded soldiers was doubling every year and it felt like everyone apart from Jane had given up on me.

The army wasn't set up for soldiers like me with multiple, complex injuries. Before the wars in Iraq and Afghanistan, Headley Court did traffic accidents and sprained ankles. Not brain-damaged amputees with broken hips and twisted backs. People like me weren't supposed to survive. It was only because of the incredible advances in battlefield medicine that we were still alive.

That presented Headley Court with a conundrum. They needed to adapt their rules and ambitions to meet the needs of Britain's twenty-first-century battlefield casualties. General Dannatt, the head of the army, saw the problem for what it was. He was the one who promised me I could stay in the army because he knew if I was discharged there was very little chance that I would get the care I needed in the NHS. General Dannatt put huge pressure on Headley Court, behind the scenes, to accept more patients like me and Martin Edwards, who had suffered head injuries. But change takes time.

Soon after I got back from Frimley, the staff at Headley Court sent in an expert to assess the progress I was making with walking. At that stage I was still using the white stubbies with a Zimmer frame to take a few steps at a time. I was still reliant on my electric wheelchair for getting around. When I walked on the Zimmer frame I relied a lot on my upper body strength.

I can't remember this expert's face. I wonder if he remembers mine, or if I was just another case to him. He concluded that unless I could put my prosthetic legs on myself they should discontinue the therapy, and instead focus resources on what they believed would be a more achievable outcome. I couldn't put my legs on by myself, so the sessions with Jane came to a sudden end. She was told she could no longer work with me.

Then in one of the regular meetings where all my therapists got together with Wing Commander Paul, the consultant and my parents, we started to hear observations such as, 'Ben doesn't initiate conversation,' or 'Ben doesn't understand the difference between a shop being open and closed.' That second comment came from a trip to Leatherhead. We had arrived before the shops opened and I was just impatient to get inside.

Mum always attended the meetings to speak on my behalf. She never stopped believing in me. She was adamant I would walk again.

'You're being cruel,' one of the nurses told her. 'I know you think you're doing the right thing, but it's unfair on Ben to put his expectations so high. He's only going to be disappointed.'

Everyone at Headley Court believed I had peaked.

'If you put together all the minute gains that Ben will make in the next twenty years they won't add up to a single significant thing,' one of the social workers said.

Challenge accepted.

51

In a way, Headley Court becoming icier towards me gave us more energy to fight for what I needed. And towards the end of 2008, what I needed was a green light for a back operation.

My back had been getting worse for ages. The kyphosis caused by the broken vertebra was folding me further and further forward. It was a constant source of pain and it made everything more difficult. Chairs were agony. Eating was awkward. I had to crane my neck forward to get my face upright. It wreaked havoc with my balance and made walking ten times harder.

The doctors at Putney could see the damage that my spine was causing and they believed I should have an operation. Putney had a relationship with the Royal National Orthopaedic Hospital (RNOH) at Stanmore, in north London, and they had suggested referring me there. But Headley Court had a relationship with Stoke Mandeville and they sent me there instead. When we got to Stoke Mandeville it was the usual story with the slings. They couldn't find the right one for a double amputee. We waited for two hours before they could hoist me out my chair so the surgeon could examine me. By that time the surgeon was impatient and annoyed.

He asked me to sit up. I took my T-shirt off and he spent about five minutes examining me.

'A lot of my patients would be glad to have a back like yours,' he said. 'I am recommending no further action.'

It was not what we had hoped to hear, so Mum asked Headley Court if they could get a second opinion.

In late 2008, Mum pressed the case with Wing Commander Paul. 'What do you think Ben's worst injury is?' he asked.

'His back,' Mum said. 'If he has to stay in a wheelchair for the rest of his life, he at least has to be comfortable. At the moment he's in agony.'

'We can fix that with a cushion,' the occupational therapist chipped in.

Mum glared at him but said nothing.

'He needs an operation,' Mum said.

'If you honestly believe that, then we'll refer him to Stanmore for a second opinion,' Wing Commander Paul said. 'But we don't think it will make any difference. You've already been to Stoke Mandeville.'

The surgeon we met at Stanmore was a solid, smiling man who exuded a quiet sense of self-assurance. Stewart Tucker had been a consultant spinal surgeon for nine years and he split his time between the RNOH and Great Ormond Street Hospital for children in central London.

We sat in his consulting room while he studied a fresh set of X-rays. Then he asked me to take off my top and he studied the shape of my back as I moved from side to side. He explained the risks: if the operation went badly, I could be paralysed. The risk of failure was something like 0.7 per cent. He asked me some questions about the pain and about whether it was getting better or worse.

'Ben, I think it's a no-brainer,' Mr Tucker said. 'We'll do the operation. It is not just because you are hunched over and uncomfortable. The kyphosis is getting worse and eventually it will crush your lungs.'

I gave Mr Tucker a double thumbs-up and grinned my lopsided grin. Mum had once again proved that if you keep on pushing, eventually something's got to give.

I was still on a high from Mr Tucker's diagnosis when I got back to Headley Court. Andrew Buckham called to say that our campaign had worked. The government had made a complete U-turn. They had rewritten the compensation rules to recognise complex injuries.

'It's amazing, Ben,' Andrew said. 'It's just about the best result we could have wished for. Well done.'

'NOT ME,' I said on the Lightwriter. 'MUM.'

The next day the *Daily Mail* ran a front-page story with the headline 'JUSTICE FOR OUR INJURED HEROES'.

There was a party atmosphere on the Peter Long ward. The government had scrapped the multiple injuries rule (the one which meant you only got paid for the first three injuries and nothing for the rest) and said they were dishing out an extra £10 million to more than 2700 men and women who had been injured in the line of duty. All of us were going to benefit.

My compensation was going to increase from £152,000 to £546,443.

Martyn Compton, a lance corporal in the Household Cavalry who was horrifically burned when a bomb hit his wagon in Helmand, saw his pay-out quadruple from £98,837 to £393,538. Royal Marine Ben McBean, who lost an arm and a leg in a landmine blast in Afghanistan, saw his compensation almost double from £161,000 to £281,150. It was the most amazing news.

52

The MoD had timed the announcement to coincide with the Millies, a new national awards ceremony like the Oscars for the armed forces. I had been nominated for one of the awards and I hardly had time to absorb the news about compensation before I was dressed up in my Number Twos and whisked off to Downing Street to meet the prime minister.

There were thirty-three people nominated in eleven categories and all of us had been invited to Number 10 before the big gala event at Hampton Court Palace in the evening.

Gordon Brown was there with his wife Sarah. I remember their two-year-old son Fraser made everyone laugh when we were all lined up for an official photo because he was the one who shouted out 'Smile!'

I had been nominated in the category for overcoming adversity, alongside Royal Marine Mark Ormrod and a gunner called Anthony Makin. I didn't think I stood a chance.

Mark had been at Headley Court with me. He was the first triple amputee to survive an IED in Afghanistan and an all-round brilliant bloke. Anthony was a Headley Court legend because he had done what we all wanted to do. He had overcome his injuries and gone back to Helmand.

Ant did the same sort of job as me. He was part of 29 Commando Royal Artillery, who took over the light guns from us in 2006. He had been travelling in a Snatch Land Rover two days after Christmas when they hit a landmine near Garmsir. One of his comrades, James Dwyer, was killed. Ant was thrown clear and his right leg was shredded. He had to have it amputated. But now, less than two years later, he was back on operations in Afghanistan.

The Millies were Prince Charles's idea but the *Sun* had made it happen – and they had really gone to town. There were red carpets and celebrities everywhere. We started off in a medieval banquet hall with tapestries on the wall. Prince Charles was surrounded by Page 3 girls and Camilla didn't seem to mind. John Terry, captain of the England football team, and his Chelsea teammate Frank Lampard were chatting to a group of awestruck soldiers.

'All I do is kick a ball,' Terry said. 'You guys are the real heroes.'

David Cameron was there with his wife Samantha. Martin Johnson, World Cup-winning captain of the England rugby team was there with his teammate Laurence Dallaglio (they were easy to spot because they were head and shoulders taller than most of the other guests). There was Dame Kelly Holmes, the double Olympic gold medallist, and Bruce Forsyth holding court with Ross Kemp, the *EastEnders* star turned war reporter who had spent time with the Royal Anglian regiment in Helmand.

They had Alexandra Burke, the winner of that year's *X Factor*, kick proceedings off with a live performance of Mariah Carey's 'Hero'.

Esther Rantzen was on my table. When we sat down she noticed a big plate of hors d'oeuvres already on the table.

'Those hors d'oeuvres are bad news, Ben,' she said. 'I've done a lot of these things and that tells me it's ceremony first. We won't be fed for a while. If I were you, I'd dive in.'

I didn't need to be told twice.

My category was supposed to be one of the last awards of the night, so I took Esther's advice and started to tuck in. Phillip Schofield, host of *This Morning*, and Tess Daly from *Strictly Come Dancing* were up on stage with Jeremy Clarkson.

'This is a prize which will have a special meaning to many of you here. It had a special meaning to me, because I have been lucky enough to meet the three extraordinary men who have been shortlisted for overcoming adversity,' Clarkson said.

My face was firmly in the trough. Mum poked me in the ribs and told me to pay attention.

'Your Royal Highnesses, my lords, ladies and gentlemen, the inaugural Millie for overcoming adversity goes to . . .' Clarkson opened the envelope. 'Lance Bombardier Ben Parkinson from 7 Para Royal Horse Artillery.'

The room erupted. It was like the roar in a football stadium when someone scores a goal. Everyone was standing. Camilla started sobbing. Everyone looked at me. I wiped my face and grinned. They played a short video of me recovering at Headley Court. Then David and Victoria Beckham appeared on screens all around the room, saying how they had followed my story and apologising that they couldn't be there in person.

Major Andy Thomson, my new battery commander, was sitting opposite me. He walked round to escort me up. (He was especially pleased that in all the shots of me at Headley Court I was wearing a 7 Para T-shirt.)

I wheeled up the ramp on to the stage on my electric wheelchair. I stopped in front of Clarkson. I couldn't say anything. I couldn't speak. All I could do was smile. He handed me my award and I stared out into the darkness beyond the stage.

I hadn't prepared anything to say – I was so sure I wasn't going to win I hadn't plugged an acceptance speech into the Lightwriter. So I thanked Clarko and went back to my seat.

The room was still roaring when I got back to my table, clutching the award beneath my right arm. Mark Ormrod was already there, standing next to my chair.

'Let me be the first to say it, Parky. Congratulations! It's absolutely right you won,' he said.

As everyone settled back down into their seats, I realised there was something I wanted to say, so before we left that night I found Tom Newton Dunn. He was the journalist from the *Sun* who had organised the whole event.

'I WANT TO DEDICATE TO CAPT JIM PHILIPPSON AND CAPT ALEX EIDA,' I said. They were the 7 Para officers who had been killed on the same tour as me. 'AND ALL THE LADS NOT AS LUCKY AS ME.'

Then I typed another sentence.

'I WANT TO STAY IN THE ARMY.'

*

That night, when I got back to Headley Court one of the nurses came up to me. She had been watching the awards on telly and she was in tears when she saw me.

'You mustn't ever stop, Ben,' she said. 'Don't let anybody stop you.'

Looking back now, I think something changed that night. I didn't realise at the time, but that was the first time I had stepped, or rather wheeled, out of obscurity and into the public domain. All the work we had done to change the compensation scheme through the newspapers had been old pictures of me, when I was fit and healthy, and interviews with Mum.

The Millies were different. I was there in person. I had gone on stage in front of hundreds of people – in front of our future king – to collect the award myself.

Most importantly – and this bit always surprises me – I had started to inspire other people. Back then, when people told me I inspired them, I didn't really understand. I used to say, 'Why? I'm a cripple. You don't want to be like me.'

But they would tell me that I encouraged them to keep going. If they could keep going then so could I. It was a virtuous circle. We can all encourage and inspire each other. We can make each other stronger. I'm really happy I did that, especially because it's not rocket science. It's something everyone can do. One foot after the other (whether you've got feet or not), and as cheerfully as you can manage it until you can manage it cheerfully.

53

I was counting down the days until 31 March. It was my birthday, and it was also the date of my back operation: the only present I wanted.

The care team at Headley Court tried to talk me out of it, citing the downsides of the operation.

'You know, even if it succeeds, you will need a protracted period of rehabilitation afterwards,' one of the social workers kept telling me.

He just didn't get it. Protracted rehabilitation was exactly what I wanted. It was what I needed. I knew the road ahead was long and the journey would be tough, but that had never stopped me before. Somebody should have told him I'd taken P Company seven times.

They weren't the only people not listening to me. At home, Andy had ignored my requests to buy a Maserati supercar. He had bought us a Kia Sedona instead, with money that was raised by our local paper.

The Kia wasn't exactly ally, but it was exactly what we needed. It was much better than the ambulances because Andy had installed the Stannah stairlift of the car world. It was a hydraulic passenger seat called a Turny Orbit, which allowed the passenger seat to swivel 90 degrees out of the car and then lift up and down on a hydraulic arm so that I could transfer from my wheelchair. It was a total game changer. For the first time since I was injured I could travel in the front seat of a car (with a bean bag in the footwell to stop me slipping forwards), instead of sitting in my wheelchair in the back. It was like riding first class instead of cargo all the time, and it meant I felt a lot less carsick.

Mum and Andy collected me on 30 March and we drove to Stanmore together (Andy at the wheel, obviously – I didn't drive). It looked eerily like a Second World War barracks. Rows and rows of wooden huts were built down the side of a hill overlooking London. It was the cleanest hospital I have ever been to. I had a room on my own and it had double doors that opened onto a little terrace.

Dr Kofi Agyare, the consultant anaesthetist, came into my room the next morning and talked me through the risks of the operation. I was lying in bed, with the back slightly raised, in a blue hospital gown. Mum and Andy were sitting in the room. He emphasised this was a big operation with risks and he talked us through all the drips and pain relief that he would give me. There was a junior doctor in the room, from the surgical team, and he gave me the consent form, which I signed and handed back to him.

Just at that moment there was an urgent knock at the door. A military doctor rushed in.

Dr Agyare was posher than any Guards officer I've ever met. He looked at the little intruder with the patience of a weary father.

'We've just spoken with Headley Court,' the military man said. 'Are we sure we have consent for the operation? They believe Ben is not competent to give his consent and his mother, Mrs Dernie, can't consent on his behalf.'

The consent form was attached to the anaesthetic record. Dr Agyare showed it to the intruder.

'We are satisfied the operation can go ahead,' his colleague added.

They wheeled me out of my room and down the hill to the last row of huts, which contained the operating theatre. I spent six and a half hours in surgery. They removed part of a damaged vertebra, fused broken vertebrae together and bolted a pair of 52-centimetre titanium rods to hold up my spine like scaffolding.

Three hours after it had finished, Dr Agyare summoned my mum.

'Diane, we're having a bit of trouble waking Ben up,' he said. 'We hope it's nothing to worry about. It's probably a result of his brain injury. We were wondering if you could come and talk to him. Sometimes talking helps.'

She followed him back down the steep central avenue and into the Nissen hut that served as the recovery wing. When he opened the door and ushered her in, Mum let out an involuntary gasp.

'He's ... He's ...' she stammered. Mum saw me plumbed and piped and drained, wired to a computer screen.

'He's lying flat!' she said.

'Yes,' Dr Agyare said. 'Ben has grown nearly six inches during the operation.'

Dr Agyare reached down and double checked the notes at the foot of my bed. '152 millimetres, to be precise. That is how much height he had lost from the curvature of his spine. Now he has got it back.'

Mum's eyes welled up.

'Ben, they fixed your back,' she said to me.

Just as Dr Agyare predicted, my eyes started to open soon after and they wheeled me out of the recovery room and into intensive care. But the next day, I caught pneumonia.

I knew nothing of this, because I slipped back into unconsciousness, but Mum and Andy were terrified. Not for the first time, and not for the last time, they thought I was going to die. Mum phoned my dad and my brothers to warn them.

'Ah,' said Dr Agyare when he came in later that morning. 'Minor setback. Nothing to worry about, it is not unexpected.'

I was stuck in ICU for a week. Major Gary Wilkinson, my troop commander in Helmand, came up to visit with Brownie and Stapes. They were like three wise men bearing gifts. One of them stuffed a fistful of porn under my mattress, another came with a tiara and the third brought matching diamanté earrings. Just what I needed.

'So you can dress up, mate,' Stapes said.

'And knock one off in the mirror, now you're fixed,' Brownie added.

'They made you six inches taller, Bom Parkinson,' Major Wilkinson said.

'Yeah! Shame they didn't make him six inches longer where he really needs it, sir. Next time, eh?'

Every bed in the intensive care ward at Stanmore had its own set of double doors that opened directly onto the grass outside. The ward was always bright and airy and after about a week the pneumonia had cleared.

They wheeled me further up the hill to a general in-patient ward. The nurses adjusted the bed so that I could sit slightly more upright, and as soon as I was, I started trying to talk. It was extraordinary. I can't say why.

Apart from that first 'Aaaaaah!' that I let out when I was in Putney over a year ago, I had hardly made any sounds since I was hurt. Now I was sitting straight-backed in bed for the first time and trying to make words. It was really hard to form my words clearly, but it was an important start and it felt amazing.

And I wasn't drooling. Before the operation drooling had been a regular annoyance and embarrassment, but I just thought there was nothing I could do about it, so I got on with it. I never thought for one second that my back op would fix it.

Straightening my back had transformed me. We tried to call Headley Court to tell them the good news, but nobody answered the phone.

Before the operation Stanmore had been very clear that while they took referrals from all over the country, they only offered rehab to patients who lived in their catchment area. The plan was for me to go back to Headley Court. At least that's what we thought.

'It's the best place you could be,' the surgeon, Mr Tucker, said.

Mum and Andy called Headley Court to ask them to arrange an ambulance because I couldn't travel in a normal chair while my back was still healing. We couldn't get through. It was a problem, because Easter was approaching and Stanmore were eager to have me out before the long weekend. Eventually, Andy managed to get hold of someone at Headley Court.

'Ben's come through the operation,' Andy said. 'And Stanmore are ready to discharge him.'

'Ben isn't down to come back to Headley Court,' the social worker said. 'We've discharged him.'

It took a while to understand what had happened. It was only later, when we got home, that we found the letter on the doormat. Headley Court, the promised land of military rehab, had discharged me at 11 p.m. on 31 March 2009, while I was still unconscious after surgery. But somehow we hadn't known.

'Well, we've got no choice,' Mum said. 'We'll take him home.'

'What's your discharge package from Headley Court?' a therapist at Stanmore asked.

'We haven't got one.'

'No, I don't think you understand,' she said. 'Are your carers in place at home?'

'We haven't got any.'

'Who is going to look after Ben?'

'That's me and Andy,' Mum said.

The therapist said she'd call Headley Court for us, but they confirmed it to her: there was nothing in place. Headley Court said I was now in the care of the Doncaster health services. Doncaster said they were not aware of my existence.

Still, more pressing at that moment in time was how to get home. I had to travel flat on my back, so the Kia was out. Mum started calling around to hire a private ambulance, but she wasn't having any luck. Eventually the ward sister came up and said the hospital had issued a call for volunteers. A crew from Leeds had agreed to drive down that evening.

That crew were angels. So often, in my darkest times, I have been saved by the kindness of strangers. I don't know their names. I'm not sure how I could find them. But the people who drove that ambulance made a four-hundred-mile round trip that evening, after they had finished their day shift.

They pulled into Stanmore, which is just off the M1, at 10.30 p.m. on Maundy Thursday and it was after 2 a.m. on Good Friday by the time they got me home.

They chose to give up that time at home with their families to come and help a perfect stranger for no obvious reward or gain. In the last chapter I said some people are kind enough to say I've inspired them. It is people like the volunteer crew of that ambulance who inspire me.

54

The first morning at home, I woke up with a lot of challenges. I had no legs for a start. My prosthetics were still at Headley Court. I had no access to a gym, I had no physiotherapist, I had no speech therapist. I didn't even have a GP.

As I lay in bed that morning, I tried to remember how far I had come. It was two and a half years since I had been injured and almost written off as dead. I had survived. I was breathing independently. I was fully conscious. I could understand what people said. I could laugh. I could swallow. I had learnt to use an alphabet board and a Lightwriter. I had beaten Acinetobacter once, MRSA and pneumonia twice. I was making sounds and trying to talk. The drooling was much better. I had taken my first steps on a Zimmer frame. I had collected the first-ever Millie for overcoming adversity. And I had grown more than six inches on the operating table when the doctors undid the curve on my spine.

But you can't get anywhere if all you're doing is looking backwards. It was encouraging how far I had come, but I had to concentrate on what was left to do. They was still a very long way to go. If you had come round to my place that Easter, in 2009, you would have seen a cripple with no legs, weak arms and a flabby face from lack of exercise. The noises I made when I tried to talk were totally unintelligible. I peed in a tube and I tired very easily. People used to talk about me as if I wasn't there and that really pissed me off.

My goals were clear: I wanted to walk on my own and I now also wanted to talk so I could be understood. Those goals were my guiding stars.

The district nurse came every day to change my dressings, but

Doncaster Primary Care Trust behaved as if they had never heard of me. No, I wasn't on any lists, they said. No, there wasn't help available.

For the last two and a half years Mum and Andy had immersed themselves in learning the army system, working out who to ask for what and how to get things done. Technically, I was still serving. But I was held at arm's length and my salary had been reduced because I was deemed 'no longer fit to face the enemy'.

So Mum and Andy had to navigate the new maze of austerity NHS and Doncaster social services. It took six months of mixed messages, cancelled assessments and false starts before I restarted any kind of meaningful therapy. That was six months when my physio sessions – the key to walking again – came to a complete halt. For whatever reason, Headley Court didn't send my prosthetic legs, and Doncaster could not get hold of any for me.

I was stuck in my wheelchair.

I am lucky that life doesn't get me down, but these were difficult days. For the first time I shared Mum's fears that perhaps I had been forgotten. For those first six months at home it felt like we were in a dead zone. I was waiting for my back to heal. I couldn't exercise and I was bored. I just watched Andy mow the lawn.

'Don't worry, Parky,' Brownie used to say when he came to visit. 'There's someone out there who can teach you to walk and there's someone out there who can teach you to talk. It's just a question of finding them.'

For everything else, it was a case of just cracking on and making the most of the opportunities that existed. Our army liaison officer, a top bloke called Neil Davies, helped me get a multi-gym from the Army Benevolent Fund so I could work out at home once my back was better.

The multi-gym was great for building strength, and ideal to have in the house, but I also wanted to do some cardio. Andy suggested we go to the gym together at the Donny Dome; he was recovering from a hip replacement and wanted to use the exercise bikes.

I could hear the splash and squeal of children on the water slides as we arrived, but it didn't distract me from worrying about what people were going to think. I hadn't been to a public gym since I was hurt. I had never seen an amputee in a regular gym before. I wasn't even sure if they would let me in. I half expected them to say 'Sorry, mate, you're not allowed. Insurance doesn't cover it', or something rubbish like that.

I needn't have worried. The guy behind the counter greeted me like a long-lost friend.

'Aaah, aaah anga oa ow,' I said.

'He wants to work out,' Andy translated.

'Too right, mate. Let's get you sorted.'

If he was worried about my lack of legs he didn't show it. This was the first of many times that Doncaster embraced me. Strangers often stop to talk:

'Eh up, mate!'

'All right, Parky?'

'All right, Ben, how's it going?'

When the mayor heard I was using the gym he issued a decree that I could use all of the city's municipal facilities for free. At the end of 2009 they made me Yorkshire Man of the Year and many years later, in 2017, they gave me the Freedom of the Borough. It means I can drive my sheep over North Bridge.

The receptionist showed us into the gym. I wanted to use a hand-bike to build up my arms. Andy wanted to use a normal bike to build up his hip. They were at opposite ends of a long row of machines. The gym attendant saw our dilemma and wheeled one of the exercise bikes to the far end of the room so that Andy and I could work out together.

'Shout if you need anything,' he said. Then he left us to it.

It must have been on our third or fourth visit that I clocked a giant skinhead eyeballing me across the room. I had seen this guy there before. At 6' 4" with a bushy beard, a thick silver chain and fluorescent purple nails, he was difficult to miss.

I was sitting at a weights machine doing a set of pull-downs. Andy was holding my hips to stop me slipping off the seat.

'Hello Ben,' the skinhead said when he reached us.

The laces on his trainers were undone. 'My name's Dr Aidan Robinson. I think I might be able to help you.'

'Ay oo airing ail aa-ish?' I asked.

Andy translated. 'He said, "Why you wearing nail varnish?"'

Aidan let out an enormous laugh.

'Why not?' he said. 'People like to pick fights with me because I'm a big bloke. Purple nails put them off.'

Aidan explained that he was a chiropractor and he thought he might be able to help me.

'You need to work on your core,' he said.

In those first few months that I knew Aidan I thought he walked on water. He was the first person who told me what I could achieve instead of what I couldn't. I would meet him at the Dome and he would make me lie on my back with him lying across my stumps while I did sets of sit ups. He got me into a proper weights programme. Then he introduced me to the grappler, the machine that changed my life.

Ten years later, the grappler is still my best friend and my worst enemy. It is an exercise machine with a long loop of thick rope that runs up and down between two pulleys in front of where you sit. You reach up with your hands, one after the other, and pull the rope down towards you.

It was agony. At first all I could manage was to grab the rope in front of my face and pull it down towards my waist. I was too weak to reach any higher. Little by little I started to reach higher, until I could stretch both arms over my head and heave the rope down towards me.

Aidan transformed my social life as well. After we finished a workout, he would take me out in the evenings with two gorgeous girls, a mother-and-daughter combo called Sharon and Sarah, to Zest, a Mediterranean grill on the high street, which fast became my favourite restaurant. I wasn't just getting fit. I was starting to have a life again.

55

There comes a point in any battle when you have to have something to fight for. In a war you fight for your country and for your mates, for the guys to the left and right of you. When you are fighting for your own recovery you still need that sense of purpose.

Charity work gave me purpose. Sometimes I raised money, sometimes I raised awareness. In June 2009 I travelled to Normandy to lay a wreath at the Pegasus Bridge as part of the annual D-Day commemorations. That August, General Dannatt invited me to attend the Norfolk Dog Day – a massive charity dog show that was more like a country fair in the grounds of a stately home – to raise money for Help For Heroes as a representative of wounded servicemen.

It's not a role I would have chosen for myself when I joined the army all those years ago, but it's a role I relish and I've embraced it because it's a chance to turn what happened to me into something really positive. When people first look at me they probably subconsciously think I'm disabled and not much more. But even back then I was almost always smiling, and if you had the patience to understand my ill-formed words I would have tried to crack a joke and show that I was still fighting.

There's a more active side to my charity work that I'll get to soon, but often my job is just being there. It is turning up. You might think it's not very hard and perhaps there are times you are right. But just being well enough to get in a car and go to a place and talk to people at a dog show was a massive victory for me.

It created a virtuous circle. Invitations to events like the Norfolk Dog Day gave me a target and a deadline to work to. They encouraged me to get fit. They made me want to speak more clearly. Once

I got to the event, I usually achieved two things. The first was to make people think about all our soldiers' sacrifices. The second, which follows the first, was to encourage people to dig a bit more deeply when the collecting tins came round. I was more than happy to play that role if it meant the public took more notice of the armed forces.

And from a selfish point of view, it made my life more fulfilling. Being well enough to travel was a huge victory for me. Being part of these events was its own reward. Everyone needs fulfilment and purpose to keep them sane and happy. If I can find those things, so can everyone else too.

56

The leaves had begun to fall by the time I finally started physio at the Tickhill Road hospital. It had taken that long for the NHS and Headley Court to agree a treatment plan. But if you thought Headley Court were done playing the pantomime villains, they were still lurking behind me. My new physiotherapist Dawn Brookman, a kind woman in a blue hospital uniform, had been in touch with them for my treatment notes and had asked them to send up my prosthetic legs. They never arrived. They also told her their view was that I was too badly brain damaged and therefore she should discontinue my therapy, presumably to focus on what they considered more achievable aims. But Dawn was a hero, and I am a grafter.

'From what I've seen, I'm prepared to give you a chance,' she said.

Dawn focused on neuro-physio and she said I could start with two sessions a week. To begin with she would massage and manipulate my muscles to try to get them working again. Her colleague Sarah, who specialised in amputees, would work on getting me walking again.

Around the same time, I had my first session with Dawn's daughter-in-law Nina, my speech therapist. She was a bubbly Yorkshire lass with a shock of bright red hair whose first loves were her dogs. She had also been discouraged by Headley Court.

'We'll give it a try,' she said. 'Headley Court have said we shouldn't bother. They said you won't make progress talking and that you prefer using the Lightwriter. Do you want to talk, Ben?'

I nodded and made a strange baby sound from the back of my throat.

'Press your lips together and explode them,' Nina said.

We worked our way through the letters, starting with the plosives. They are the easiest sounds to relearn, letters like B and P, T and K, which you say with a sudden release of air.

The first word I said was 'banana'. It came out clear.

'Typical,' Mum said, 'that your first word would be food!'

After that I stalled. I could say 'bee' but I couldn't say 'bed', 'pee' but not 'peg'. Some sounds came easily and others seemed impossible. Stringing words together was even tougher and progress was slow. But that had never stopped me before and it wasn't going to stop me now. I knew I had to keep practising. The only people who could really understand me were Mum, Andy and Nina. That was usually because they could guess what I was trying to say. It was frustrating. Even now, my speech is clearer but it's not perfect. Children understand me better than adults. I think it's because adults need to hear every word and if they miss one they get stuck. Children go on the sense of the sentence. People who can't understand me often make the mistake of thinking I am the one who is stupid.

BATTLE 7

Find Purpose

vs

Feel Sorry for Yourself

57

Even though Headley Court had discharged me, I was still technically under their care so they were being billed for my physio. I was getting two forty-five-minute sessions a week. They were supposed to be hour-long sessions but it always took about fifteen minutes to get started.

When we spoke to Headley Court to ask them to pay for more physio time, they sounded surprised. They thought I was getting eight hours a week, which was ample. The NHS was billing each session as four hours, because there were four staff in the room: two physios and two physios' assistants.

Part of the problem was that Tickhill didn't have any of the same facilities as Headley Court. They didn't have the parachute harness and ceiling track, which meant they had to surround me with people all the time to catch me if I fell. If one of those four people was ill or busy or otherwise engaged my whole session would be cancelled. If there was a bank holiday, my session would be cancelled. If I carried on like that for ten years, I wouldn't have made any improvements. So we decided to try to buy Tickhill a harness.

In early 2010, I launched Ben's Challenge. It wasn't a charity in itself. It was a fundraising vehicle to support other causes and our first goal was to raise £25,000. We pledged some of the money to Tickhill to buy a treadmill and a harness, like the ones they had at Headley Court. The rest would go to Blesma, the British Limbless Ex-Servicemen's Association.

On 11 April 2010, a year and a day after I came home to Doncaster, we held our inaugural event at Doncaster Lakeside.

It was a kayaking competition on the fifty-acre man-made lake between the shopping centre and the Donny Dome.

Seven teams took part. We had the fire brigade, the local bill, three local canoeing clubs, the Doncaster Knights rugby club and a crew from 7 Para, who turned up with a 105mm gun. It was a great day and all the local news channels came down to cover it.

I wasn't racing, but I was taking part. I remember banks of cameras in my face as I heaved myself out of my wheelchair and on to the Zimmer frame, which had wheels and handles at shoulder height.

Andy was standing next to me as I walked down a path lined with people towards the waterfront. Everyone was cheering. I looked down at my legs and then up to the water's edge. It was probably only thirty metres but it felt like a marathon. In my head I repeated a simple mantra: 'The doctors said you would never walk. Where are those doctors now?'

At the bottom of the path Andy was there to lift me into a two-man inflatable kayak. He handed me a yellow paddle, someone climbed in behind me, and we set off.

People took my story and used it to inspire their own initiatives. Soon after the Lakeside kayaking event, we were approached by pupils from a private school in Surrey, called Cranleigh, who wanted to raise money and awareness to help my recovery. Harry Adolphus and Morgan Roberts, who were sixth formers at the school, launched a programme called Back Ben Parkinson and together with six friends they cycled nine hundred miles from Fort George in Scotland to Fort Blockhouse in Portsmouth, stopping in at as many military bases as they could along the way. Aidan volunteered to be their team chiropractor and I joined them on the route, including a great night with 7 Para in Colchester.

But charity work doesn't always go to plan and I had some lessons to learn. Around the time that the Cranleigh lads were finishing their ride the NHS informed us, very nicely, that they didn't want the money we had raised for Tickhill hospital. They said they didn't want a treadmill or a walking harness because they didn't have the space or the staff to use them.

So we gave that money to another charity. It was a charity I had only heard of a few weeks earlier. It was a charity that more than any other has transformed and enriched my life. Enter the Pilgrim Bandits.

58

My first contact with the Pilgrim Bandits, the charity that changed my life, was a short message they sent me on Facebook.

'Alright Ben,' the message said. 'Fancy doing the Fan Dance with the Pilgrims?'

There was a telephone number, so I showed it to Mum and asked her to call them, but she thought it was a prank. I got a lot of messages from online weirdos in those days. I still do. It's mostly men with amputation fetishes asking me for naked pictures. Mum looked at the sender's profile picture and frowned. He was a grizzly-looking bald bloke with a beard.

What Mum didn't know, and I did, was that the Fan Dance is not a dance. It is a hill. A legendary hill in Wales which is used for the SAS selection course.

I still had no idea who the Pilgrim Bandits were, but I wanted to find out more.

'Please call them,' I said. 'The answer is yes.'

A gruff man called Mike Witt answered the phone.

'We don't do sympathy,' Mike said. 'And we don't do cotton wool like some of these other charities. Lads like Ben are squaddies at the end of the day. We give them challenges. We give them a chance to have fun, and a chance to sing and swear and take the piss out of each other like they used to.'

'Right,' Mum said.

'Why don't you bring him down to Netheravon for a parachute jump?'

*

The Pilgrim Bandits were formed by a group of his friends who played golf together at charity tournaments to raise money in memory of Mike's son Darren, who had died in a car accident in 1998. Darren had just signed his papers to play professional football for West Ham when he was killed. Pilgrims is a nickname for the SAS, where some of Mike's friends had served. Bandits was the accusation levelled at them by the other teams when they won the charity tournaments.

By the time I met Mike in 2010, the Pilgrim Bandits was a charity in its own right, focused exclusively on helping injured servicemen.

A lot of its staff were ex-special forces and their mantra was 'always a little further'. It is a quote from a poem, 'The Golden Road to Samarkand' by James Elroy Flecker, which is engraved on the SAS memorial in Hereford. It is the same poem that gives the SAS their nickname:

> 'But who are ye in rags and rotten shoes,
> You dirty-bearded, blocking up the way?'

> 'We are the Pilgrims, master; we shall go
> Always a little further . . . '

It was late September 2010, when we drove past the long lines of Second World War barrack huts that mark the edge of Netheravon Airfield in Wiltshire. The land was flat for miles around and in front of us was a vast hangar strewn with men and women in brightly coloured jumpsuits. There was a burger van off to one side, selling brews in little polystyrene cups. Two planes that looked like flying vans waited next to rolled-grass runways. A Tannoy called out people's names when it was their turn to jump.

Mum was absolutely terrified. She had been getting more and more nervous on the four-hour journey down from Doncaster.

'Are you sure you want to do this, Ben?' she said as Andy helped me out of the car.

I got comfortable in my wheelchair – or as comfortable as I could – then looked up at her and shrugged.

'What's the worst that could happen?' I asked.

Mike met us in the car park. He was in his late fifties, short and solidly built, with white stubble on his chin and close-cropped white hair. He was dressed in Crocs and shorts.

With him was a man called Major Al Macartney. I looked him up and down. Al was in his early thirties, tall and slim with dark curly hair and dressed in a bright red jumpsuit.

'This is who you'll jump with,' Mike said.

Al was the national skydiving champion. He had made thousands of freefall jumps and founded the British Legion's skydiving team. That year he finished ninth at the world championships, and he'd just got back from the Swiss Alps, where he leapt off the north face of the Eiger in a wingsuit.

'He knows what he's doing with a parachute,' Mike said to Mum, to reassure her. 'But he's still a hat,' he said to me.

For a man who loved jumping out of planes I was surprised Al hadn't joined the Paras. He was an army linguist who spoke Pashtu, the language of the Taliban, and served in the Royal Logistics Corps.

Mike grabbed the wheelchair and whisked me off towards the hangar, leaving Mum and Andy slightly lost. Today wasn't about them. Mike had made that clear. For him, it was always about the injured lads.

There were a couple of other amputees there to jump that day. Mike took us to a quiet corner where we put our jumpsuits on. Al explained the rules of tandem jumping while Mike went round us one by one and folded the empty cloth back over our stumps and strapped them up with silver duct tape. That was his style. No fuss, no sympathy. Just get on with it.

'You ever done a freefall before?' Al asked.

'Once,' I said. My words were still very soft and it was hard for them to understand me. 'In Afghanistan. I flew out of my WMIK.'

When it was our turn to jump Al and I shuffled forwards, to the edge of the open plane door. The air beat our faces. Down below were patchwork fields and cars the size of bugs on roads no wider than a matchstick. I folded my arms in front of me while Al held on to the frame of the plane.

'Let's go!' I shouted to Al over the sound of the wind whipping past along the fuselage. I was leaning forward with excitement.

'Steady!' Al shouted. 'Wait for it. 3 ... 2 ... 1 ...'

And we were freefalling towards the earth. Al spun me round so I could see in every direction and he pointed out Stonehenge. I could feel the skin on my face being pushed backwards and it was hard to breathe because of the force, but I couldn't stop grinning. Then Al pulled the cord and the parachute yanked us upwards. The roar of falling was replaced by the silence of the sky and we floated this way and that, in whichever way Al pulled the strings.

As we got lower, the drop zone came into focus. It was clearly marked out, and I could see someone pushing a trolley into the middle of the lush, grassy field. As it got bigger I realised it wasn't a trolley, it was Andy pushing my wheelchair. We were heading straight for him! I thought we were going to crash into him, but right at the last minute Al slammed on the brakes. I think he could have landed with his arse in the wheelchair if he'd wanted, but instead we hovered for a second and he put us down gently about three metres away.

'How was that, Ben?' Andy asked.

When you get injured you think your life is over. You think, That's it, I'm done. I've got no legs. I'm an invalid stuck in a wheelchair. I am not going to do anything. I am not going to achieve anything. Then all of a sudden you're tumbling out of a plane at fifteen thousand feet with the national skydiving champion strapped to your back. You have just spent the morning with a bunch of shit-talking, piss-taking squaddies who are all missing limbs, who are all in pain, and who are all finding ways to crack on. For a few hours in that aircraft hangar I was Parky again, not a patient. That's when you know it isn't over. It was moments like that when I knew there was a difference between simply being alive, which was one thing, and having a life. That was something else.

Mike had changed my life. At the time I didn't realise how important that parachute jump was. It was the start of a new chapter in my life. Up until that point no one really gave me the time of day. Mike was different. Mike believed in me and if it wasn't for him, there is absolutely no way I would be where I am today.

'How do you feel about going skiing?' he asked a few minutes later, as he helped me out of my gaffer-taped jumpsuit.

'Well, that's just not going to happen, is it? Not for Ben,' Mum said.

I had never been skiing before in my life.

'It is going to happen,' Mike said bluntly. 'If Ben wants it to. Just because it hasn't been done doesn't mean it can't be done.'

'Where?' Mum asked.

'Colorado.'

There was silence.

'We're going in December and there's a space on the trip if you want it.'

'Yes!' I said. 'Let's go.'

59

By September 2010 Sarah, my amputation physio at Tickhill hospital, confided to Andy that she thought I had gone as far as she could take me.

She said I still had scope to improve, but she and Dawn were working at the edge of their knowledge and resources. Most of Dawn's work was with elderly patients struggling with their balance. Sarah had never dealt with a double amputee before. They could see I was hungry to go further and they recommended we call in some specialists to plot a new course forward.

Dawn contacted a woman called Mary Lynch-Ellerington, an expert in a branch of neuro-physiotherapy known as Bobath.

Bobath is based on the principle of nurturing the brain's ability to adapt and reorganise itself into new neural pathways to overcome the effects of damage. Mary was one of the world's leading authorities on Bobath. She had a private practice in York and a part-time teaching role at a specialist hospital in South Korea.

Someone in Dawn's team called in Robert Shepherd, an amputation specialist who ran a private clinic that manufactured its own prosthetics on site. Shep started life in the merchant navy but he retrained as a physio in 1984 and specialised in leg amputations a few years later.

At the same time Mum contacted a consultant neuro speech and language therapist, Judith Scholefield, who specialised in cases of traumatic brain injury.

Between them, these three people had more than ninety years' professional experience in precisely the areas that I needed help. They all came to the same conclusion.

'There's no limit to what you can achieve,' Mary said. 'As long as you're prepared to keep trying and there is someone prepared to keep working with you, then you will keep improving.'

Judith advised me to keep trying to talk and Shep said he was convinced that one day I would walk. It was the best news I could have hoped for.

The first time I went to Shep's clinic it felt like walking into an aircraft hangar. It was on an industrial estate in Colville, on the outskirts of Leicester, about seventy miles from my home. The offices were at the front, then down the left-hand side were the workshops where Shep's business partner, Gordon, made the moulds and sockets. The rest of the space, which was most of the warehouse, was an enormous rehab gym. You could probably walk seventy or eighty yards in a loop.

I had first met Shep when he came up to Tickhill to assess me. He took one look at the legs the NHS had issued and said, 'These don't fit. It's like trying to walk with a pair of plant pots on.'

A problem with prosthetics is that your stumps keep changing shape. Prosthetics never fit for long. When I first started wearing legs my stumps were flabby and swollen with fluid because they hadn't been used. It's the same reason your feet swell on an aeroplane. When I started to move my stumps, the swelling went down and the stubbies came loose. The NHS solution was to pad out my stumps with layers of stockings and socks, but this was like playing the piano with gloves on. It just made everything harder.

The first thing Shep did, when I got to Colville, was ask Gordon to cast me a new set of stumps. That made a huge difference. They were thinner, lighter and a much better fit. Walking became immediately easier. Three days a week, Andy would heave me onto the Turny Orbit and into the Kia, and we would drive down together. The sessions were three hours each.

At first I worked on the parallel bars while I got used to the new set of legs. Then I moved on to the Zimmer frame. It was almost as tall as I was. A few months later we started working on crutches and by summer 2011 I had ditched the frame for ever.

Shep had endless patience. We worked on moving my weight from my hands to my stumps. I was using my upper body strength to hold myself on my crutches. We set goals, like walking a hundred yards in under a certain time, or getting to the end of the parallel bars in seven seconds instead of twelve.

One of the hardest things was recalibrating my brain to the length of my legs. Deep in my subconscious, in the part of my mind that governs movement, my legs were as long as they always were. A small movement of my thigh would mean a big movement of my foot. Now everything was different. Everything had to change, every little movement. It's not just the length of the stride, it's how much you swing your hips, how much you roll your shoulders, where you look to stay balanced. It is when you breathe.

It was hellish tiring. The sessions started out as three hours long, but they normally finished when I couldn't work any more. Something I learnt from Shep is that the window at the limit of your exhaustion is the most precious time to learn. When you're ready to give up, just push that bit more because that's the time the lesson is imprinted in your subconscious. It's surprising how you will always have a bit left in the tank; you think you're done, but your brain is underestimating your body. Your body can do anything.

I had no idea in those early years what a massive role Shep would play in my recovery. I had no idea what an amazing friend and supporter he would become. I had no idea that three years after we first met at Tickhill hospital, after countless hours of exhausting work in his warehouse in Colville, it would be Shep at my side on one of the greatest, proudest moments of my life. You'll find out about that later.

60

Learning to speak again started with learning to eat again. My first session with Judith was a lunch of egg mayonnaise and pasta salad at home. It was Judith's idea. She wanted to watch me eat.

There were four of us round the table. Me, Mum, Andy and Judith. Mum put on my apron and laid the table with my big-grip knife and fork. I manoeuvred my wheelchair into position.

Judith had studied copies of the video-fluoroscopy tests that were done at Headley Court. Video-fluoroscopies are a type of X-ray where the doctors film you chewing and swallowing various different types of food and drink, then a dry swallow, to assess if your swallow is working. I had had two of them done about eighteen months apart, and both showed that my oesophagus was significantly paralysed. I had no peristalsis, the wave-like contractions that pass down your gullet to move food in the right direction.

Judith gave me a series of exercises, which I hated – but then nothing that's worth it is easy. Two of them were particularly bad. They both involved home-made lollipops of frozen cotton wool.

In the first exercise, either Mum or Andy would run one of these freezing woolly ice lollies over my lips. The cold was supposed to stimulate my tongue by triggering a reflex that makes you lick your lips. The tongue is a muscle and like everything else it can atrophy with lack of use.

I had gone so long without eating and even longer without speaking that my tongue had withered. To start with I couldn't even stick it out. I couldn't even lick my lips. We had to do the freezing-lips exercise five or six times a day and I absolutely dreaded it.

The other exercise was even worse. It was the same principle of using cold to stimulate a reflex, but instead of my lips it was on my soft palate. I had to open my mouth and they rubbed the ice on the back of my mouth. Next time you're pushing through a gym session because you want to lose weight and you think you can't do it, picture me being tortured by my parents. If I can do that, you can do anything.

Judith said she thought I should have thickener in my drinks, but I was dead against it. I'd had more than enough jellied tea at Headley Court. After a while Judith accepted that I was managing without it and, apart from the few days immediately after my back operation, I was avoiding bouts of pneumonia. Pneumonia is one of the main indicators of problematic aspiration – when food or drink gets into your lungs. People less fortunate than me, with similar swallowing problems, contract it many times a year.

'The most important thing is your position,' Judith said. 'Always eat at a table and always sit close to it to keep your swallowing mechanisms upright. Even leaning forward slightly could mean that you choke. You need to use gravity to help the food go down.'

A lot of it was common sense, but it was good to hear it from a professional.

'The last thing is the apron,' she said. 'I can see why you're using it. It takes away the worry about spilling your food, but we need to harness that worry and make it a positive force. Think of every meal as a training session. You are training to enjoy it without making a mess.'

She banned me from wearing an apron.

'Things will improve, I promise,' she said.

Judith said she wanted clinical evidence about my condition and so booked me in for an assessment at the Charles Clifford Dental Hospital in Sheffield. She asked the dentists there to assess me for a soft palate prosthesis. It is a type of plate that you wear in the roof of your mouth. A piece of soft plastic sticks off the back of the plate and lifts the fleshy valve between your mouth and your nose to close it. Most people's palate closes without them even realising. You do it when you swallow and you do it when you speak to stop the air your voice box needs from rushing out through your nose.

I can't close mine. When I speak the air comes out of my nose, which means I run out of breath. I have to speak in short sentences. I can't make certain sounds. The dentist at the Charles Clifford spent about half an hour wiring up my throat with so many electrodes I looked like the inside of a telephone exchange. Then she plugged them in to various machines to measure which muscles were active when I spoke.

I watched her look at her screens. She double-checked the readings, then she checked the wires around my throat, carefully making sure that each one was fixed securely, and asked me to speak again. Then she called in a colleague to confirm what she was seeing.

'What's happening is impossible,' she said. 'You're not moving your vocal cords when you speak, like everyone else does. You are making minute movements of the muscles in your neck to compensate instead. We can't confess to know what is going on, but it looks like you have taught yourself to do something we don't fully understand.'

As the saying goes, where there's a will there's a way. It's not true for everything – I would never say that if you try hard enough you can get around cancer, because lots of brave people fight it and don't make it. But if you want something and you're committed to getting it, then there's no limit to what you can achieve. I'm living proof of that: I cheat science every day. I shouldn't be able to talk; I shouldn't be able to swallow.

If you want something, you've got to believe you can have it and you have to work for it. Reach for the stars. You might not get there, but you certainly won't end up with a handful of mud.

An NHS speech therapy session with Nina was supposed to be an hour, of which we might get forty minutes if we were lucky. The session with Judith was supposed to be an hour, but it might run on to two. They were almost as exhausting as the sessions in Shep's yard.

To begin with, when Judith couldn't understand me, Mum would sit in with us and act as a translator. After a while that got to be a bad idea. I love my mum to pieces, but there is only so much being told what to do that I can take. Speech therapy was tiring and frustrating work. When I couldn't do something I would shout words no one could understand.

I was better behaved when it was just me and Judith. She gave me plenty of encouragement, but she stopped me whenever I got something wrong and made me do it again until I got it right. If Mum tried that I would shout at her.

Each day followed a pattern. If we had been working on a particular letter, Judith would then give me a passage to read to check that I could use what I had learned.

If we had been working on 'g's in the first half of the session Judith would give me a passage to read in the second half that was full of words with 'g' sounds.

They were from children's books and the text was always in large print, but at first I struggled to read them. My eyes had forgotten how to scan lines of text, so to begin with I was reading word by word, like a child. It was just one more thing to add to the list of mountains I was going to conquer.

One day, when the nights had started closing in, Judith arrived with a shopping bag full of different kinds of whistles and toys. There was a black plastic referee's whistle, a tiny silver dog whistle, a bright red kazoo, a child's toy trumpet and a range of party blowers.

'I've been collecting these for years,' Judith said. 'Each one has a slightly different mouthpiece, so you have to make a different shape with your lips to blow it.'

It was a workout for my mouth. Each shape corresponded to a sound. The more shapes I could make the more sounds I could make.

We also started working on widening my vocabulary. Often there were times when I couldn't say a word because I couldn't make the right sound. In the early days I would just get stuck, or stumble through without making sense. What Judith taught me to do was to use an alternative. For example, in recent years I have been invited to hand out prizes at quite a few school speech days. When I started, I could never manage to say congratulations because the 'k' sound comes from the back of your palate, so I would say well done instead.

It was all about rebuilding the links inside my brain that connect ideas with words. The only way to repair it was to use it. Judith encouraged me to express ideas. We would talk about football or cars or the army.

'The Paras are the best of the best,' I would say. 'The MoD are rubbish. Really, really rubbish.'

Judith always recorded our sessions on a little black voice recorder and just before the end of each session she would rewind the tape and play it back, to let me hear what I really sounded like.

It was a shock. The voice I heard was nothing like the voice I heard in my head. It wasn't me. It was nasal, monotone and higher pitched than I was used to. When I hear myself in my head, I speak as clearly as I always did. When I heard my voice played back on tape, I couldn't understand a word I said. There was no definition. My words were blobs of gobbledegook. If we had been working on 'd' that day then the 'd's might be clear, but everything else would sound like I was talking underwater.

The first time I heard it I wanted to punch something. It felt as if Judith hadn't pressed play. She had pressed reset. I was back at zero, at the start of an unimaginably long journey.

Of course, she hadn't pressed reset. Judith had done me a favour. She had given me a milestone. Hearing my own voice was a marker in the sand. Now I had a way of measuring progress. It would be two and a half years before I dared to speak in public in any real sense. Even then, when I saw myself on television my first reaction was always 'my voice is crap' – but maybe everyone thinks that!

I kept the Lightwriter until 2013. I'd been using it for six years by that point and the Dalek voice was like an old friend. It might have been a premature thing to do, but it had become a crutch and I knew I had to force myself to face the world without it. I had to try to talk.

I spent five years with Judith, and I did more than seven hundred hours of whistles and ice pops and gruelling speech therapy to get to where I am now. I'm still learning, and I know my speech is far from perfect or as clear as I would like it to be. But I've come a long way from where I started, and some fights are worth the slog.

61

I had never seen so many amputees gathered in one place as I did in Colorado that first winter. There must have been six or seven hundred of us. We were all staying at the same massive ski-in, ski-out resort on the edge of an old gold rush town in the Rocky Mountains.

There was every kind of injury there. Single, double, triple and quadruple amputees, and all the latest prosthetics. If you strolled through the lobby of the Beaver Run Hotel during Wounded Warrior week it looked like a cyborg convention in the snow. In a way, that's exactly what it was.

For two weeks every year the town of Breckenridge hosts the Hartford Ski Spectacular, the largest event in the world for disabled skiers of all backgrounds. It was organised by Disabled Sports USA, a charity founded by a Vietnam vet who had lost a leg to a grenade in 1969, and the whole thing was paid for by a massive American insurance company as part of its corporate social responsibility.

Americans do things on such a massive scale compared to the Brits. And they treat veterans like gods.

Everywhere you went, strangers would stop you and say, 'Thank you for your service.'

The ski week at Breckenridge wasn't only for wounded soldiers, it was open to anyone who was disabled. But there was a link-up with an organisation called the Wounded Warrior Project, which meant it was free for injured servicemen, whether you were serving or retired, and hundreds of them seized the chance.

The whole resort was given over to disabled skiers. Everyone on the slopes was either maimed or blind, or helping someone else who was. Instead of feeling self-conscious about our injuries or embarrassed about falling over, we encouraged and inspired each other. We didn't give each other sympathy. We saw the different ways people had learned to adapt. When I saw someone with no legs carving through the snow, my immediate reaction was *I want to have a go.*

The Pilgrim Bandits group was small. This was their first year and there were only five of us on the trip. I shared a room with Aidan, who had come with me from Doncaster to act as my carer. Mike shared a room with John Sandford-Hart and Johno Lee. John was a long-time amputee who had come along to help out. Johno was a young Afghanistan vet I knew from Headley Court. We had been put in a room together there because both of us had suffered from Acinetobacter. Johno had been serving with the Yorkshire Regiment when his Snatch Land Rover hit an IED near Gereshk in central Helmand in 2007. He lost his right leg below the knee.

On the first morning in Breckenridge we collected our ski passes from one of the hotel conference rooms, then Mike took us to the ski hire, where the Wounded Warrior delegates linked me up with two professional ski guides. I can't remember my guides' names, but they were legends. These guys normally charged rich clients hundreds of dollars an hour to guide them in the Rockies, but everything they did in Wounded Warrior week was free. They introduced me to the sit-ski.

The sit-ski was a chair mounted on a pair of skis. I had a pair of short poles which had little skis the size of shoes on the bottom so that I could lean on them as I turned.

That first morning, the sun was shining and there was fresh snow on the mountains. To start with, when I was learning, one of the guides would ski behind me, holding the back of the chair and guiding me down the mountain, while the second would ski slightly further behind, a bit like a rear guard to stop other skiers crashing into me or cutting me up by mistake. The weather was amazing and we skied on great wide-open pistes and narrow, winding tracks through pine forests.

As I got more confident they tied a pair of nylon straps to the back of my chair, like the reins on a sleigh, which let me ski more independently. It was amazing. I could steer by leaning left or right. The only problem was I couldn't stop – but I didn't really care. The guide on the reins would have to put the brakes on every now and then. I kept on wiping out, I kept on face-planting in the snow, and all I would do was grin and laugh, and ask to go again.

'You're a madman,' Johno said one lunch. 'We've all got to watch out when Parky's about.'

I was out every day from when the first lift opened, and I skied until it closed with a short break for lunch. At the end of one of the days I found Mike waiting for me at the bottom of a run.

'You know something, Ben,' he said to me. 'The smile across your chops was wider than a fucking milkshake. That tells me we're doing the right thing.'

I nodded and pushed myself towards the chairlift for one last run of the day.

'You don't seem to mind the cold,' Mike said.

I shook my head.

'That's given me an idea,' he said.

There was silence. Mike is rarely one to elaborate unless you push him. I looked at him to say, 'Are you coming on this lift, or not?'

He replied, 'Always a little further, Parky. Always a little further.'

62

In September 2011, about a year after I started my first physio sessions with Shep, a letter landed on the doormat from the Organising Committee of the London 2012 Olympic and Paralympic Games. It was the organisation run by the double Olympic gold medal winner Seb Coe – now Lord Coe – that was laying on the games. It was known as known Locog for short.

The letter said that my name had been put forward to carry the Olympic torch when it toured the British Isles in the build up to the opening ceremony in summer 2012. There were thirty thousand people on the list and only eight thousand places so I didn't pay it much attention. I knew a few people had put my name forward. I had nominated Harry Adolphus, the lad from Cranleigh who founded the Back Ben Parkinson campaign, and he had nominated me straight back. I think the Bishop of Doncaster had nominated me as well.

It wasn't until December that the second letter arrived, to say I had been successful. People assumed I was over the moon to have been selected, but I wasn't. All I could think about was walking.

The first thing I said was, 'I am not doing it in a wheelchair. I want to walk it.'

If I was going to carry the torch I was going to walk. The torch relay would last ten weeks from start to finish and it was scheduled to come through Doncaster on 26 June 2012. That would be my day. 26 June 2012. It was less than eight months away.

I could tell Mum and Andy were nervous. They were my biggest supporters but they didn't think I could do it. I would have to walk three hundred metres carrying the torch. It was ten times further than I had ever walked before, and that was always with crutches or a frame.

The day after the letter arrived Andy drove me down to see Shep. We didn't speak much in the car. If I wanted to do the torch walk – which I did – we had to reply to the Locog letter and accept their invitation. But I was only saying yes if I could walk. And I was only saying yes if Shep was ready to back me. It was like Shep was my coach and I was a boxer on the cusp of a title fight.

'It's not just a question of walking,' Shep said nervously. 'You'll have to carry the flame as well. That means you can't use crutches.'

I hadn't thought of that.

'I want to do it, Shep,' I said. 'I really want to do it.'

'Then we'll find a way.'

From then on, our sessions had a new sense of urgency. I had a distance and a deadline that would soon be fast upon us. There was a lot of work to do.

Shep had just got me a new pair of Ottobock C-Legs, worth about £60,000.

The C-Legs were the best prosthetics in the world. They had an 'intelligent knee joint' designed to imitate a human knee. Sensors in the joint detect when you're swinging the leg or when you're leaning on it. If there's weight on the joint it's supposed to lock, and when you take the weight off it swings. They were amazing, but it meant I had to learn a new way of walking.

At the same time, Shep devised a system where he could support me by putting his arm under my armpit when we walked together. Meanwhile Andy googled everything he could to find out about the size and weight of the Olympic torch. Then he made a replica with a bamboo lantern from a garden centre. He chopped it down to size and filled it with sand until it weighed exactly 850 grams.

In the workshops at Colville, Gordon stitched me a sash with a pocket at the bottom to put the end of the torch in. It meant I could wear the sash over my chest and rest the weight of the torch in the sash. Then all I had to worry about was holding it steady in the crook of my left arm.

Back at home, Mum was on the phone to Locog to try to find out

where I would be walking. No one got a choice. You were just given
your route, and much nearer the time. Luckily, the man from the
Locog branch in Doncaster was also a local councillor. He knew
about my story and he said he thought it would be fitting if I started
opposite the cenotaph.

At the beginning of May, when we had two months to go, Shep
started coming up to Donny for our Friday sessions. He would park
at our house and Andy would drive us into town, and we would
walk the cenotaph route together.

It was one thing walking in Shep's gym, but I had to get used
to the pavements, to the cracks and the slope of the road. I had to
get used to the gusts of wind. Like any good training package, we
tried to make the exercise as realistic as possible. If anything, we
made it harder. That's the army's mantra: train hard, fight easy. We
practised again and again and again.

The problem was I was doing so much walking that my stumps
started changing shape again. The more I walked, the slimmer my
stumps got and the looser my prosthetics. About a month before
the big day I sat down with Shep, Gordon and Andy. We had a
dilemma. Did I risk a new set of legs at such a late stage? Or did I
tough it out with the ones I had?

The slimmer my stumps got the more painful it was to walk. If
my flesh didn't fill the moulds it meant all my weight was transferred through the tip of the bones in my stumps. But new legs
always took a bit of bedding in. I decided to stick with the legs I
had. I would battle through the pain.

A week before the big day, we received another letter from Locog.
This one contained a surprise. It told me I was to walk a totally
different stretch from the one I had been training for. It was uphill,
over a flyover.

I was struggling to make it to three hundred metres on the flat.
There was just no way, at such a late stage, I would be able to cope
with the hill.

Mum called Locog straight away. The lady on the other end
was helpful but astonished. She said our local Locog office never

had any authority to promise me a particular route. For a while it looked like the whole thing might be off. I was adamant I wouldn't do it in a wheelchair.

Mum went back to Locog and explained my situation. The lady promised to see what she could do. Half an hour later she called back to say she had solved it. Amazingly, the person slated for the cenotaph had agreed to swap with me. I don't know who that person was, but thank you. You changed my life. My plan was back on track.

63

From the moment I woke up on 26 June there was a news crew in the house. It was a bright sunny day and it already felt hot. They filmed my breakfast, they filmed me pulling on the white tracksuit uniform that Mum had shortened for my legs. They filmed Shep and Andy strapping up my stumps with stockings and pulling on my stumps.

The Locog rules were really strict about branding and things like that. You weren't allowed to wear anything that constituted advertising. But I had decided to wear two wristbands for good luck.

One was for the Pilgrim Bandits. The other was in memory of a soldier called Tay Cheeseman. It said 'May angels lead you in'.

Tay had been a soldier in the Green Jackets and was only twenty-one when he fell very suddenly ill with cancer in Afghanistan and died a few days later in England. His mum had sent me the wristband and asked if I would wear it. For some reason that message, 'May angels lead you in', really struck a chord with me. I wanted them there with me too.

Locog had ordered all the Doncaster torch-bearers to rendezvous at the School for the Deaf, which they had commandeered for the day as their logistics hub.

It was a massive operation. The Olympic flame had been lit six weeks earlier in the temple at Olympia in Greece. The flame was flown to Britain on a specially modified British Airways plane – BA 2012 – and it landed at the Royal Naval Air Station Culdrose, near Land's End.

Since then it had been to Wales, the Isle of Man, Northern

Ireland, Dublin, right across Scotland to the Shetlands and the Outer Hebrides. If everything went to plan it was due to finish up at the Olympic stadium in London on the night of the opening ceremony, on 27 July. It seemed like everything was planned down to the minute.

On 26 June the flame was just over halfway through its journey. At the morning briefing at the Deaf School, the lead in charge of the Doncaster leg said it was travelling seventy miles that day, from Sheffield to Cleethorpes via Donny. It was already on its way. They said 130 people were taking part and I was number 50.

They gave each of us a torch. It was the first time I'd held it. It was a slender brass cone with the London 2012 logo near the top. It was exactly the same size as the bamboo lantern that Andy had made me, but it was easier to carry because the weight was the fuel reservoir at the bottom. The bamboo lantern I had been training with was top heavy.

While we were in the briefing I got messages from my mates outside that crowds had already started to line the streets. A whole bunch of lads from 7 Para were among the first ones there.

The woman in charge said all of us had to board a coach that would follow the route of the flame. When one person finished their leg the next one would get off the coach and take over. This was Locog's way of making sure everyone was in the right place at the right time. It made sense for them, but straight away I knew it would be a massive problem for me. There was no way I could get my wheelchair on and off, and the last thing I needed before the biggest day of my life was to sit cramped and uncomfortable in a coach seat for two hours, letting my back and my hips cramp up.

'When it's your turn, you will each have a maximum of three minutes to complete your three-hundred-metre walk,' the woman said.

That was impossible. It was absolutely impossible. Once she had finished the briefing Andy called her over for a word.

'It'll take me twenty minutes,' I said. But she couldn't understand me, so Andy had to translate.

'Well,' the Locog lady said. 'I'm afraid that's too slow. You'll have to do it in your wheelchair, but you can still carry the torch.'

'He can't hold the torch and push the wheelchair at the same time,' Andy said.

'Can you push his wheelchair?' she asked Andy.

'I want to walk,' I said.

'But you only have three minutes,' she insisted. 'If you can't walk it in three minutes you'll have to do it in your wheelchair. I'm sorry, but there are hundreds involved and we have to keep to a very strict schedule.'

'Well you can have this back then,' I said. I lifted the torch off my lap and held it out for her to take. If I couldn't walk there was no point.

Matty Norman, the same seven-foot-tall Matty Norman who told a crap-hat nurse where to get off at Selly Oak, was standing next to me at that moment. He called our CO, Lieutenant Colonel David Walker, who was on the street outside with the rest of the 7 Para lads. Walker called his predecessor, Colonel Gary Wilkinson, who had left 7 a few months earlier to take command of the Olympic Games security operation.

Within in a few minutes Colonel Wilkinson was on the phone to the local Locog organiser, warning her she risked a public order issue. It was true. By now the crowds were almost fifteen deep on either side of the road. Every vantage point was taken. Families with kids were waiting with their flags to wave me on.

'Listen,' Colonel Wilkinson said. 'Just let Ben get on with it.'

'We're worried he won't finish,' the lady in Doncaster protested.

'That's rubbish,' Colonel Wilkinson replied. 'I know Bom Parkinson. He'll finish.'

Andy pushed me in my wheelchair from the Deaf School to the spot where I would start my walk. And we waited for the flame. We could tell when it was close from excitement in the crowd. The noise was rippling towards us like a Mexican wave.

I stood up, out of my wheelchair, and Shep put his left hand underneath my right armpit. Shep, like me, was dressed from head to toe in white. The unlit torch was in my right hand, its base firmly in the sash. The shouting in the crowd grew louder.

The lads from 7 Para had formed up in a rank behind me. Andy was on my left shoulder. He had the wheelchair in case something went wrong. There was a squad of plain-clothes policemen, in grey Olympic uniforms, in a box around me to stop the crowd surging in.

One of the policemen came over with a torch that was already lit and touched it to the top of mine. There was a soft *whoosh* as mine caught fire and I heard the children shouting my name.

'Go Ben! Go Ben!' How do they know who I am, I think.

I look straight ahead and take my first step. Suddenly the world goes quiet and I feel a familiar stabbing pain shooting through my stumps. I am carrying the Olympic torch.

Step. Lean. Step.

I am totally in the zone.

Step. Lean. Step.

The pain is easy now.

Step. Lean. Step.

And the crowd are roaring again, waving flags.

Step. Lean. Step.

Remember to breathe. Deep breaths.

Step. Lean. Step.

'That's it, Ben,' Shep says. He is standing at my shoulder. 'You've got this.'

People are screaming my name.

Step. Lean. Step.

Where are the doctors who said I would never walk?

Step. Lean. Step.

It is a sea of Union Jacks. People are waving them over their heads. They are hanging off the lampposts.

Step. Lean. Step.

'Go Ben!' the crowd chants. 'Go Ben!' I must not let them down.

Step. Lean. Step.

I walk towards the cameras. The police hold people back.

Step. Lean. Step.

The weather is red hot. I feel like I'm in a furnace.

Step. Lean. Step.

The stump is twisting in the socket. I feel more pain.

Step. Lean. Step.

A mother in the crowd is crying. I would do it all again, I want to tell her. I would do it all again. Every bit.

Step. Lean. Step.

I have no regrets.

Step. Lean. Step.

I wonder if Shep's OK? I look across. He might be welling up. Ha!

Step. Lean. Step.

'Shoulders back,' Shep says. 'Keep doing what you are doing.'

You are an absolute legend, Shep.

Step. Lean. Step.

I think my stumps are bleeding now.

Step. Lean. Step.

Just suck it up. It's only pain.

Step. Lean. Step.

'Airborne!' someone shouts.

'Airborne!' I murmur back. Those men from 7 in the maroon berets, those men are my brothers. I am doing this for them.

Step. Lean. Step.

It is nothing compared to P Company.

Step. Lean. Step.

A copper comes and takes my torch. Are we there already?

No. My torch was running low on fuel. The copper has replaced it with a fresh one.

Step. Lean. Step.

Ten minutes later he is back again.

Step. Lean. Step.

Another fresh torch. Another ten minutes.

Step. Lean. Step.

'You're doing amazing,' Andy says. He is behind me with the chair. There is no way I am sitting down, and he knows it.

Step. Lean. Step.

The pain has gone away now.

Step. Lean. Step.

I am doing this for the guys that didn't make it back.

Step. Lean. Step.

For Captain Jim Philippson, for Captain Alex Eida, for Tay and all the rest.

Step. Lean. Step.

May angels lead them in.

Step. Lean. Step.

I know they are up there, in Heaven. I know they are willing me on.

Step. Lean. Step.

I am one of the lucky ones.

Step. Lean. Step.

God wanted me to survive.

Step. Lean. Step.

The crowd are going mental. I am doing this for them.

Step. Lean. Step.

There's a lady with another torch.

Step. Lean. Step.

She's not a copper, she's a torch-bearer like me. The cops in grey tracksuits help her take the flame from mine. Hers is alight. My job is done.

I have made it.

'How was that?' shouts a reporter.

I have collapsed back into my chair. I am gasping for breath, but I have made it. It took twenty-seven minutes to cover three hundred metres. I took 798 steps.

'How was that?' she shouts again.

'It was nothing,' I say, panting. 'Just another walk.'

Shep tells the press it was the equivalent of running a marathon, with three times my own weight on my back.

Lieutenant Colonel Walker is there with the 7 Para lads. 'We'd have crawled over broken glass to see you do this, Ben,' he says.

Mum is next to me now. She is sobbing. She leans down and gives me a kiss.

'Another one, please,' a photographer shouts.

'Do I have to?' Mum says and everyone laughs. She leans in a second time. 'I am so proud of you, Ben,' she says.

Then it's back to mine for a party.

64

In October 1942, a small team of allied commandos parachuted into Norway on one of the most audacious and successful sabotage missions of the Second World War. Their target was a water plant hidden in an arctic plateau that was making a key ingredient for a Nazi nuclear bomb.

The Norsk Hydro heavy water plant was built into a gorge on the edge of the Hardanger plateau, a vast arctic wasteland about eighty miles west of Oslo.

The allies had considered trying to bomb the plant, but they ruled it out because all the heavy water processing equipment was buried in the building's basement, beneath eight floors of steel and concrete. Bombing was unlikely to succeed and it risked serious harm to nearby civilians if the bombs damaged the massive ammonia storage tanks on site.

Eventually they hatched a plan to drop commando teams on to the Hardanger plateau, one of the most inhospitable places on earth, and they would ski cross-country to the plant and destroy it with explosives. Their missions were codenamed Operation Grouse and Operation Gunnerside, and the men who took part became known as the Heroes of Telemark.

Mike's idea, which was hatched on the slopes of Breckenridge, was to retrace the saboteurs' journey to mark the seventieth anniversary. As far as any of us knew, it would be the first time any wounded soldiers had made the attempt.

'Just because it hasn't been done doesn't mean it can't,' Mike said.

*

The men chosen for the mission were all Norwegians who had fled to Britain after the German occupation and joined the Special Operations Executive, the secret unit formed on Churchill's orders to 'set Europe ablaze'. The Norwegians spent months in the Scottish Highlands, mastering the mixture of survival and sabotage skills and mental resilience they would need to survive on the Hardanger plateau. They were led by a twenty-three-year-old demolitions instructor, Joachim Rønneberg, who had been picked for the mission because of his calmness in a crisis.

Mike was our Rønneberg. His first challenge was to persuade the Ministry of Defence that his plan would work. I was still a serving soldier and I needed their permission to do anything. Mike was summoned to MoD Upavon on Salisbury Plain to explain in more detail what he was proposing. The army was worried it would end in disaster. Conditions on the plateau can be brutal and they were terrified of negative headlines that said 'WOUNDED HERO KILLED ON SKIING TRIP'. Mike didn't care about headlines. He cared about giving wounded veterans a chance to feel normal again, and he had a secret weapon up his sleeve. One of the guides he had enlisted to help us was Glyn Sheppard, a former SO2 senior warrant officer, whose last job in the army was running adventurous training. Glyn spent half his life in Norway, he knew the route, he knew the huts, he knew that we could use a dog sled to get off the plateau in an emergency. Most of all, he knew how to appease the risk-management brigade, and that's just what he did.

About twelve of us flew out to Norway in March 2013. I only knew Mike and Andy, who came to look after me, but we all gelled almost instantly, like any good team faced with shared hardships and shared goals.

I had been training hard for months, ever since Mike hatched his madcap plan. I had spent hours on the grappler and the hand-bike, building up the strength in my arms, my shoulders and my back. Compared to skiing at Breckenridge, where I was going downhill for a few minutes at a time and getting chairlifts to the top of mountains, crossing the Hardanger was a challenge of a totally different magnitude.

The weather would be ten times colder, the living conditions far more spartan. I needed to be in peak physical fitness to cope with the cold, but more than anything, I needed the strength and stamina to make sure I could trek all day without tiring.

There was another veteran called Paul Jacobs. Paul was an amazing man who had been blinded by an IED in 2009. He had had a tough start in life. For a start, he was a ginger. He was a massive, fat gwar who was in and out of foster care. He was always in trouble.

One day, by sheer chance, he was sitting under Nelson's Column, in the middle of Trafalgar Square in London, when he saw a soldier strutting past. Something in the soldier's swagger caught Paul's imagination and he followed him to a recruiting office.

'You give me a chance and I will give you everything,' Paul said.

He joined the army at eighteen and it became his whole life. The army really was his family.

Paul was the guy at the front of a foot patrol who sweeps the ground with a metal detector, looking for IEDs. A bomb went off behind him, killing an eighteen-year-old private who had just been drafted in as battlefield replacement a few weeks earlier.

Paul ran back to recover his body and a second bomb went off. That second bomb killed Paul's sergeant, Paul McAleese.

Paul, my mate, was seriously wounded by the second blast but before he lost consciousness he managed to drag himself to a mine-free area so that his comrades could save him without putting their lives in more danger. He won a George Medal for his actions, but he lost the sight in both eyes.

I think, like me, the thing Paul missed most was being a regular bloke in the army.

The other guys on the expedition were a mixture of ex-special forces, soldiers, Marines and adventurers. Ish and Morgs were both ex-gunners from 29 Commando, Moxy was a former Royal Marines medic, Matt Bennett had been in the Royal Military Police and Geraint 'Taff' Hampton was a Royal Engineer just back from Afghanistan. There was also an ex-policeman called Gary Jones.

It felt like I was back in barracks, living with old friends who constantly took the piss. It made me feel alive.

The first couple of nights, we stayed in a camp about a hundred
miles south of the plateau. That is where we met our guides, who
were all British ex-soldiers who knew the saboteurs' route. One
guide, Brian Desmond, had worked with the TV presenter Ray
Mears when he recreated the Telemark expedition for a BBC doc-
umentary in 2003.

'Down here it's like an alpine resort,' Brian warned us. 'Up there
it's like the Arctic.'

It was snowing hard on the morning that we left camp and drove
north, past mountain fjords. After about an hour we stopped to put
the snow chains on. Two hours later we pulled into a layby. There
was nothing else around but a fleet of skidoos waiting to transfer
us and our kit.

'Wear every bit of kit you've got,' Glyn warned us.

I wore two hats, two coats, a face mask, goggles and down gloves
with liners, and my stumps were wrapped in ski trousers and a sleeping bag. I sat in a trailer, pinned down by the rest of our luggage.
And even then I was freezing! We travelled for two hours through
a gale to reach the first hut at Fjærefit.

The huskies were there before us. They had huddled together
for warmth and were buried beneath a snow drift that sheltered
them from the wind. The drivers of the sled, known as mushers,
were a husband-and-wife team called Olav and Elle. They knew
each of their dogs by name. They called each one in turn to
check they were OK and each time a single snout would appear
through the snow.

The hut was a simple log cabin, a Norwegian version of a Scottish
bothy, at the western end of a frozen lake called Songevatn. The
beds were wooden boards and the loos were long drops in the
woodshed about twenty metres away. There was a solar panel and
a gas hob but there was no running water, so we melted snow to
drink and cook with.

In the build-up to this trip I had felt a nagging fear that I hadn't felt before the other challenges. This was by far the hardest thing I had attempted since I was injured. It was one thing jumping out of aeroplanes or kayaking around a lake in Doncaster; this was totally different. It was a proper Arctic expedition. We were trying to cover sixty-five miles across an unforgiving tundra and there was no guarantee we would make it. But I also felt excited. It was my chance to prove that no one can tell me what I can or cannot do.

The hut at Fjærefit had been built after the Second World War, but it was the closest shelter to the place the first commandos landed in October 1942. It was where we would start our mission.

When we woke up the next morning the storm had got worse. The weather was so bad that Glyn – a real stickler for timings – pushed back the start from 8 a.m. to 10 a.m. to try to let it clear.

When it was finally time to saddle up, Andy and Ish lifted me into my pulk. It was a custom-built fibreglass sledge, a bit like a sit-ski on steroids. Pulks are the sleds Arctic explorers tow behind them with supplies. They are normally low to the ground so they can't blow over, but mine had been raised about two feet off its skis to give me enough space to use my ski-poles.

I had been training for months to build up the strength in my arms and my upper body to propel myself with my ski-poles, while the other guys would take turns towing me as well.

Paul's plan was to make the trek on cross-country skis, with guide lines attached to Gary. The lines were attached to both men's hips, so that Paul could sense if Gary turned, and Gary would also guide him with his voice.

The original plan had been for Andy to ride along on the dog sled but Mike did his back in before we set off and he had to ride with the huskies instead. Andy, who was fifty-five and had never done anything like this before in his life, had no choice but to walk.

'You better get training, then,' Mike said as he handed Andy his snowshoes. Mike was absolutely gutted that he couldn't do the walk, and there was also a concern that Andy wouldn't be up to it and the whole expedition would suffer as a result.

But Andy just said, 'All right. Guess I had.'

Andy is a real trooper.

The first commandos to jump on Operation Grouse were part of a four-man team led by Captain Jens-Anton Poulsson. Poulsson was a pipe-smoking mountain man who was born on the edge of the Hardanger plateau and learnt to hunt reindeer there as a boy, with his father.

The word plateau might suggest that the landscape was flat, but as Poulsson well knew, it was anything but. When the weather finally cleared we could see the terrifying scale and beauty of the terrain we were planning to cross. The Hardanger looked like a vast arctic Dartmoor, blanketed in snow and ice, riven by fissures and ringed in the distance by jagged mountains. At more than 3500 feet above sea level we were twice as high as Dartmoor, and many, many times larger. It is one of Europe's last and largest uninhabited wildernesses.

The first day was a short day. We were only trying to cover nine kilometres to the next hut, at Berunuten. As we set off into a headwind gusting at 60mph, it was easy to see why Norway's greatest explorers – men like Fridtjof Nansen and Roald Amundsen – had come here to train for their historic expeditions.

The snow felt sticky. Conversation dwindled until the only sounds were our breathing and the rhythmic shush of skis and shoes on snow. Occasionally I could hear Gary telling Paul which way to go.

'Left a bit. Straight,' Gary would say. But when the wind picked up they couldn't hear each other. They had to rely on the ropes.

After about an hour I had to stop to have a drink, eat a snack and take a piss – all of which is harder than it sounds in minus 40 degrees Celsius. It is surprisingly easy to get dehydrated in arctic conditions, so it is vital to keep drinking. That also means you have to keep pissing. If you spill your piss on yourself – easily done when you're shaking with cold, your hands are in mittens and you don't have any legs – then suddenly you're looking at a risk of getting frostbite. It gets so cold so quickly on Hardanger that according to Norwegian legend it freezes the flames in a fire.

Glyn had a second guide working with him, called Steve Kelly, but known as Ned. He was a former military medic. A couple of hours after we set off he drew level with my pulk.

'You all right, Parky?' he said.

I shook my head.

'What's up?' He was worried I might be cold. Everyone was worried that my stumps would freeze because I wasn't moving them.

'Piss,' I said.

'What?' he shouted over the wind.

I pulled my face mask down.

'Piss!' I shouted back. 'I need a piss.'

'Oh,' Ned said. 'Thank fuck for that.'

Ned called everyone to stop.

'Get some hot drinks down,' he shouted to the rest. Then he squatted next to my pulk and started unclipping the red snow valance, a waterproof awning like the spray deck on a canoe, which was designed to keep me warm and dry.

'Mate,' Ned said, 'it's probably quicker if I just help you do this, all right?'

'All right,' I said. 'But if you hold my cock too long it counts as a wank.'

'No wanks on a first date, mate,' Ned said. 'Not unless you buy me flowers.'

Andy had prepped a piss bottle with a sachet of VernaGel. Ned undid my trousers and put my knob into the bottle. I leant back with my hands in my mitts while the other lads stood round in a semi-circle to try to make a windbreak.

'What's the matter, Parky? Why you not smiling?' Paul shouted. 'Ned, if Parky's not smiling, you're not doing it right!'

'Are you done?' Ned asked me.

I took a deep breath in.

'Nearly,' I sighed.

His face was about a foot from my cock.

'Are you done?' he asked again.

'Nearly.'

He was about to let go.

'Wait. Not yet.'

'What?'

'Give it a shake,' I said.

The windbreak cheered.

'You enjoyed that way too much,' Ned said. 'Next time, you piss on your own.'

We started to think about lunch as soon as we finished our mid-morning snack. That's when we saw a lone red dot on the horizon.

When the Telemark heroes made this journey in 1943, Rønneberg's men had to hunker down in a hut for three days to let a storm blow through. When they emerged on the third day, miles from civilisation, they were astonished and slightly alarmed to see a lone skier in the distance, approaching their position. They were worried he would give them away.

When the skier finally reached their hut he was far more scared than they were. He was a local hillbilly out poaching and had run into six heavily armed men in uniform. The hunter swore blind that he was a Nazi collaborator because he was convinced that Rønneberg and his men must be Germans. Rønneberg realised the poacher was lying and so, unwilling to kill in cold blood and unwilling to set him free, he ordered his men to tie the poacher to a toboggan and take him with them.

As we slogged forwards, the red dot got larger, until we could see it was a tent, pitched next to a pair of skis standing upright in the snow. We wondered what kind of crackpot would be out here on their own in these conditions. It was the only sign of human life for miles in any direction. Perhaps it was the poacher's ghost? We were almost on top of it when a heavily gloved hand unzipped the front flap and a man dressed in arctic kit stepped out.

'All right, Ben?' he said.

I had never seen him before.

'Fucking hell,' Ish gasped. 'Leighton Clarke! Of all the people. What are you doing out here?'

Ish and Leighton hadn't seen each other since they served in Bosnia together in 1995.

'Well I heard you were coming through,' Leighton said. 'Thought you might like a bit of hot scoff.'

Leighton lived in Norway because he had fallen in love with a Norwegian woman. He'd heard on the army grapevine that we were attempting the Hardanger crossing. He knew the plateau well and he thought we were mad, but he was the sort of person who liked a madcap idea. He also knew that there was a place where he could intercept us. The route that we were tracing ran from west to east. Leighton had driven to a point on the southern edge of the plateau and trekked north for a day to cut us off. To see a friendly face in the middle of the wilderness was mind blowing. It didn't matter that most of us had never met him. He was Ish's mate and he was an ex-soldier, which made him one of us. Inside his tent he had a pot of slow-cooked wild boar stew. His friend had shot the boar in Sweden, he had cooked the meat at home and hauled it out here on his sledge. That was enough to make him everyone's best friend.

Leighton had left the army after the Iraq War and worked in private security. He had just got back from Basra, where he was nearly killed in a mortar attack, and he was about to go to Mogadishu. He had pitched his tent about two hundred metres in front of the hut where we were due to stay that night.

'And I brought a bit of warm kit as well. Got a load of extra jumpers in case anyone's feeling cold,' he said.

We were all in high spirits. That first day was really a test to see if everything worked and it had. We had made it to Berunuten.

The hut was really old – the saboteurs had stayed in it on their journey. It was built on a slope overlooking a small frozen lake and it had a weird feeling about it. Olav and Elle said the huskies refused to go near it. The dogs would growl and fight if you tried to take them inside. Brian said his dog was the same.

According to local legend, the hut had belonged to a Norwegian farmer who used to bring his cattle there in summers in the nineteenth century. One year, something went wrong and he was facing ruin. Instead of driving the cattle south to Denmark, which was what he usually did, he lost his mind and murdered his wife and three small children with an axe. Their ghosts were said to haunt the place.

The long drops were in the woodshed and Glyn said that sometimes the shed door locked itself from the outside.

'I don't believe in ghosts,' he said, unconvincingly. 'But Brian refuses to sleep in this hut and his dog won't cross the threshold. If you're shutting the woodshed door, just make sure there's no one left inside.'

The first thing we did was to get a fire going to warm the place up. Ish filled a pan with snow and put it on the fire to boil for drinking water.

Andy was always there for me, always making sure I was warm, clean and dry, and as comfortable I could be, but it was frustrating not being able to help, not being able to do more for myself. When the rest of the team were chopping wood, building fires, cooking or packing, Paul and I would sit on the bunk beds chatting because it was hard for us to help.

He told me how he had woken up in Selly Oak after three weeks in a coma and they had to break the devastating news to him that Sergeant McAleese had died.

Paul met a nurse at Selly Oak, called Louise. They fell in love, got married and had a son together. It was the most amazing love story, but the romance had soured after a while. Paul told me how he struggled with depression and PTSD. He had just got divorced when we went on that trip and was in quite a dark place. He suffered flashbacks and mood swings.

'Sometimes it's the invisible wounds that are the worst,' Paul said. 'Though, mate,' he went on, 'they're all invisible to me.'

That afternoon we played spoof and drank tea. Spoof is a simple game where you have to guess how many coins people are holding in their hands. If you guess the right number you get out. The loser is the last man in. We decided they would have to do a forfeit.

There were three of us left in when Ish leant over and whispered a plan to nail Morgs. 'Parky, you say three next time, I'll do three and we'll get Morgs.'

When it was my turn to call, I said two.

'What was that?' Ish said. 'Did you say three, Parky?'

'No,' I said. 'I said two.'

I opened my hand to reveal two coins inside. Ish gawped as he realised what I had done. Morgs burst into laughter. Ish, the last man in, stripped down to his underpants and ran down to the frozen lake, where he had to do twenty press-ups while the rest of us looked on and cheered.

We woke the next morning at 6 a.m. to the sound of the wind battering the timbers of our ancient haunted hut. Glyn had warned us that day two would be the toughest. It was twenty-four kilometres to the next hut. This was our longest day by far, and it included a brutal nine-kilometre uphill climb.

Outside was a blizzard. I could barely see the man in front of me and the wind was so loud it drowned out all the sounds apart from my heaving lungs and the crunch of snow. I swung my arms forward, punched the ski-poles into the ground and pulled myself forward. All I could think about was the pain. All I could do was keep going.

At the top of the hill we stopped for drinks and snacks. It was at least minus 20 degrees Celsius and the wind was gusting up to 80mph. It felt like we had been travelling into the wind all morning.

'Right, lads, let's get moving,' Morgs said after a couple minutes. 'My toes are going down.'

Morgs was a mountain of a man. He was barrel-chested 6' 2" but it didn't take long for the cold to bite.

'Wanna borrow my socks, mate?' I asked.

It was always an easy laugh.

'You got socks?' Moxy chipped in.

I nodded. Not on any feet of course, but I had them for my hands, for my stumps and to keep my water bottles in to stop them freezing.

'Go on then,' Moxy said. 'I'll have 'em.'

I dug a pair out of my daysack and threw them over to him. Moxy pulled down his pants and bared all to the wind. Then he put one of my thermal socks over his cock and balls.

'I'm far more worried about them getting frostbite than my toes,' he said.

Cheerfulness in adversity is one of the tenets of the commando spirit. We had that in spades.

'You can keep the socks,' I said.

The other tenets are courage, determination and unselfishness. I had relied on all of those qualities since I was injured. There was more courage than I will ever know when my comrades risked their lives to save me. The determination was mine to get better and prove the doctors wrong. So many people have shown me unselfishness, from the strangers who gave blood at Camp Bastion to keep me alive on the operating table to when Ned held my knob so I could piss in the pulk. But most of all it is Mum and Andy, who have given everything to look after me, who have shown they've got the commando spirit. I think it's a brilliant set of values to live your life by, and they've proved tenfold that you don't need to be in the army to demonstrate them.

Each morning we woke up slightly stiffer and more exhausted. By day three, my arms, my shoulders, my ribs and my back were aching. Andy helped me with my daily ablutions and the rest of the team cooked porridge or packed kit.

'What's the plan today?' Mike asked Glyn.

'I don't know,' he quipped. 'How about we get up and march nine hours into a headwind?'

Andy hadn't trained for this, but he kept up with the best of them without a word of complaint. Paul couldn't see. He didn't complain. Ish, Morgs, Moxy and Matt were all pulling me each day. Nick was pushing. None of them complained. I didn't complain either.

I thought about the saboteurs.

Poulsson's team had been living on the plateau for a month when a second wave of airborne troops took off in two Horsa gliders from an airfield at the tip of Scotland. Their plan was to rendezvous with Poulsson's men, who would lead them to the heavy water plant.

The gliders were towed by Halifax heavy bombers. Each glider carried fifteen commandos and two pilots. The bombers were to release the gliders high over the Norwegian coast, so that they could fly to the plateau in silence. Poulsson's men had marked out a landing strip about three miles from the plant, but the gliders never made it.

Low clouds blanketed southern Norway that night. Poulsson had a homing beacon, designed to guide the planes to him, but the bombers failed to find its signal and the mission ended in disaster.

One of the bombers crashed into a mountain, killing all on board. Both of the gliders crash-landed, about forty miles apart and more than a hundred miles from the heavy water plant at Vermok. There were twenty-four survivors from the gliders. Some could walk but others were seriously hurt, and the able-bodied men refused to leave their wounded comrades. They were all rounded up by the Gestapo and by January the next year they had all been executed on Hitler's infamous Commando Order, the 1942 Kommandobefehl, which stated that allied agents should be killed without trial.

That evening, in the hut, once the fire was lit and the snow was melting, the conversation turned to food. Each of us was burning around six thousand calories a day, and when we weren't thinking about the cold we were thinking about food.

'What I'd do for a pizza right now,' Ish said.

'A nice juicy steak. I'd kill for steak and chips,' Matt said.

'I'd give my right eye for a steak,' Geraint said.

Andy had been helping me put on my prosthetic legs. My stumps had got slimmer because I was burning so many calories and he was rummaging around in his backpack for some extra bandages to try to make them fit.

'Do you know what I really want?' Moxy said. 'Battenberg. A little loaf of Battenberg cake, with sponge and jam and marzipan. Fuck me, right now I'd suck someone off for a slice of Battenberg.'

There was a silence as we all imagined our favourite foods. There were fourteen of us crammed into a tiny hut that only had four plank beds and two old sofas. I leant back on the sofa, put my hands behind my head.

'Andy,' I called out. 'Get the Battenberg!'

On our fourth day the weather changed almost every hour. Sometimes we could see for miles, sometimes the land blended into the sky, and sometimes we could barely see the man in front.

'Left a bit, right a bit. Straight. That's good.' I heard Gary guiding Paul in the rare moments when the wind dropped.

'You're not missing much,' I said to Paul as he drew level. 'It's another white-out.'

There was a crust of ice on Paul's face mask.

'You sure, Parky?' he said. 'Cos in my mind it's clear blue skies with palm trees.'

That night we stayed in a privately owned hut which, like the previous two, the saboteurs had used seventy years earlier.

It was our final night on the plateau and I was absolutely exhausted. My whole body ached and my stumps were in pain because they had changed shape, they had withered, and the moulds for my prosthetic legs didn't fit any more. They kept falling off and I was getting more and more annoyed. Every time there was a problem Andy stopped what he was doing and came over to help me.

Someone suggested we should have a team photo, outside the hut before sunset. For most of the group it meant nothing more than walking outside. For me it meant getting my legs on, which meant I needed help. The thing that upsets me more than anything about being injured is not being able to do the little things. It is the constant frustration and loss of independence. I had nearly crossed the Hardanger plateau, but I still couldn't get my legs on by myself. I was unable to leave the hut without help. Those were the times when I really felt the impact of my injuries. It's impossible to be positive about life every second of every day.

Andy came over and he grabbed my stubbies, which were lean-ing against the timber wall. He pulled one on, then the other. I was feeling impatient and grumpy. I wanted Andy to work faster because most of the group was already outside and I wanted to be there with them.

When I felt like my legs were on, I hauled myself up on to my crutches, but my left leg just fell away and clattered to the floor. I fell back onto a chair, dropped my crutches and swung my arms in frustration. I caught Andy square on the chin and he staggered back a couple of steps.

Ish – who is a policeman in real life – saw what had happened and he was on me in a flash.

'Parky!' he said in disbelief. 'What are you doing?'

Andy said nothing. He rubbed his chin and walked quietly outside.

'I just . . .' I knew my anger had got the better of me.

'Listen, mate,' Ish said. 'Friends come and go, but Andy is family. He has absolutely stood by you through thick and thin. You need to have a word with yourself and give your head a wobble.'

I was looking at the ground. Then I looked up at Ish.

'Yeah. I'm sorry,' I said to him.

'Not to me. You need to apologise to Andy.'

He was right. He was absolutely right. I had let the frustration boil over and taken it out on the person who, like Mum, has done more for me than anyone else since I was injured. Andy is a legend and I am only where I am today because of his tireless love and support.

I did exactly what Ish said. I had quiet word with myself then I went outside to find Andy.

'Sorry, Andy,' I said.

'Eh up, Ben, don't worry about it,' he said. 'You'll forget about this in half an hour, and so will I.'

Andy has done so much for me over the years that there is no way I could ever thank him enough or repay him. He and Mum see a side of me that very few others ever do. They see me when I am tired and frustrated and fed up with being injured, and because they are the people closest to me, sometimes I take it out on them. They have always forgiven me and they have never borne a grudge. It's strength of character that the most fearsome army general would be proud of.

*

After the disaster with the gliders, the allies decided to send in Rønneberg's six-man team by parachute on the night of 16 February 1943. They waited three days for a storm to blow through then skied south to meet Poulsson's crew. Together, they set up a forward base, which they staffed with two men and a radio. Then the rest of them – Poulsson with two men and Rønneberg with four – skied down towards the plant. They reached it at about 8 p.m. on the night of 27 February.

I got my first glimpse of Vermok as we crested the edge of the plateau on the afternoon of 26 March. The massive concrete building has long since been torn down, but an older part of the plant still stands. It is a grand old building, built on a rock shelf halfway up the side of the gorge. These days it's a museum.

When the glider crews crash-landed, local Norwegians had tried to help them burn all their maps before they fell into German hands, but not all the papers were destroyed. The Germans realised that Vermok was the target and they increased security.

Poulsson's men had been watching the plant for months. They told Rønneberg that there were three ways in. They could descend from the mountains above, following a line of water pipes that fed the hydroelectric turbines, but that route took them directly past the Nazi barracks where the garrison was sleeping and Poulsson feared the slopes around the water pipes had been mined. They could attempt a full-frontal assault, but that meant crossing the only bridge across the gorge. It was a single-track suspension bridge that was heavily guarded on both sides. Their third option was to descend to the bottom of the valley, ford an icy river and scale the cliff on the other side.

Poulsson's team took an overwatch position in case anything went wrong. Rønneberg and four saboteurs dropped into the valley with their bergens full of explosives, crossed the river on an ice bridge and began to make their way up the cliff. Luckily for them, the sound of their ascent was masked by the rush of the river and the hum of the turbines.

They were armed with detailed plans of the plant which had

been smuggled out of Norway by members of the resistance. Based on the drawings, they had planned to creep in through a tunnel. But the plan nearly came a cropper when they found the tunnel's entrance blocked by a heavy padlocked metal gate that wasn't on the plans. The SOE had given Rønneberg a hacksaw for such a scenario, but it would have taken too long and made too much noise.

By good fortune, Rønneberg had packed a pair of bolt croppers that he had bought on a whim when he walked past a hardware store in Cambridge, on his way back from a trip to the cinema during a rare break in his commando training. He cut the padlock and they snuck inside.

At this point, all of them believed it was probably a one-way mission. They made their way to the basement undetected and placed two strings of explosives on the key parts of the heavy water machinery, including a large storage tank. The fuses SOE had issued were designed to burn for two minutes, but at the last moment Rønneberg decided to cut them down to just thirty seconds, to give them just enough time to get out but still be close enough to hear the bangs.

He needn't have worried. The explosions echoed through the mountains and by the time the sirens started to wail his men were back across the river on the far side of the gorge. The mission had been a complete success. No one died on either side and the plant was out of action for months while it was rebuilt. Even General von Falkenhorst, the commander of the Nazi forces in Norway, conceded that the operation had been a 'brilliant coup'.

The saboteurs hiked back to the place where they had stashed their skis and skied back to the forward base so the radio teams could transmit a report of their success. Then they all split up. Rønneberg went east to Sweden. Some of his men skied west and returned to Scotland by sea. Some of Poulsson's men stayed behind to train up the resistance.

When we reached the plant we weren't fearing for our lives. The future of humanity was not hanging in the balance, but we had achieved something great nonetheless. I was elated, exhausted and relieved. We had made it.

'Paul! Parky! You two,' someone called out. 'Let's get a picture of you in front of the memorial.'

'What fucking memorial?' Paul asked.

It was a massive stone disc in front of the museum. It was impossible to miss, unless you were blind.

'I'll show you,' I said.

Paul put his hand on my shoulder and I walked over on my stubbies, with him following patiently behind.

'It's like a big millstone on its side,' I said. 'It's got the date and the names of the men.'

'Where is it?' he asked.

'One step forward,' I said.

I felt him squeeze my shoulder, then he reached out and ran his fingertips along the stone and over the saboteurs' names.

We were both silent for a while, just standing in front of the stone.

'Thanks, mate,' Paul said.

For me, these expeditions offer two most precious things. First, there is the challenge. It is real and all-consuming. Battling arctic winds and miles of snow to cross the Hardanger plateau left me feeling cold and exhausted – and inspired and empowered that I could overcome new obstacles.

Secondly, there is the camaraderie. It is every bit as precious, and it will be familiar to anyone who has served in combat and anyone who has embarked on a serious expedition with a team. We were comrades bonded by a common purpose. We shared the same hardships, the same joys, the same risk of failure and the same joy at success.

We sat around the campfire talking shit and we forgot that Paul was blind and I was maimed. We were soldiers in a regiment again.

Perhaps Joachim Rønneberg summed it up best when he was asked about the Hardanger mission many decades later.

'We were a gang of friends doing a job together,' he said. 'It was the best skiing weekend I have ever had in my life.'

65

My best friend is called Roberta. We message almost every day and we see each other about twice a week. We usually go to the gym near home for a swim and a sauna. Then we have lunch together and we kill time in the afternoons.

Roberta is a pretty, petite woman, a couple of years older than me. She has bright blue eyes and long dark hair. We first met at an army reunion – I can't remember which one – and then we ran into each other again at the Army–Navy rugby match at Twickenham. A few weeks after that she got in touch on Facebook. She said she wanted to get involved in supporting a veterans' charity, so she started fundraising for the Pilgrim Bandits. Then we started hanging out.

She used to arrange for us to sit inside local supermarkets with collection buckets. Whenever there was a fair or a show, or any sort of event in Doncaster, she would get the organisers' permission to fundraise there. Over the years we have raised hundreds of thousands of pounds together. I can't do it on my own and it is not often that other people have the patience to sit with me all day, making small talk with strangers.

Starting in 2014, the two of us got to know an old soldier called Rusty Firmin. He was one of the guys who was part of the legendary SAS mission to storm the Iranian embassy in London, after it was overrun by Arab separatists in 1980. It was four years before I was born, but I have seen so many pictures and read so many stories about the hostage crisis, it feels like I was there, watching from on Prince's Gate, watching the men in black gas masks abseil down the building and smash their way in through its windows.

Rusty was an ambassador for the Pilgrim Bandits and he toured the pubs and clubs and British Legion bars of Britain giving talks about the Iranian embassy siege to raise money. To me he was a living legend.

'I'm not a legend, Parky, I'm a leg-end,' he'd always say.

'Good,' I'd reply. 'I need a leg-end. I need two of them.'

Whenever Rusty was giving a fundraising talk he would invite Roberta and me to join him, and we would travel all over the country to see him. I would always sit in the front row and I never got tired of the story. He would tell us how they came up to London from Hereford and how they prepared. They were stood up. They were stood down. A deadline came and the deadline passed. Then, just after 7 p.m. on 5 May – five days after the siege had started – one of the hostages was killed and his body thrown on to the street. That's when they knew the mission was on.

The red team went through the front. Rusty was part of the blue team that went in the back of the embassy. He went into the library on the first floor seconds after the first stun grenade.

I wait until he's at the point in the story where he's standing on a ledge at the back of a building with four other guys. They are poised to smash the window with a sledge hammer and storm inside. Rusty's a brilliant storyteller and the audience are always perched right on the edge of their seats.

'Wait, Rusty! Wait!' I interrupt from my wheelchair. 'You've forgotten something, mate.'

The first time, he looked surprised.

'I was with you, remember? What about me? Don't forget me!'

It always gets a laugh.

'You weren't even born!' he scolds.

I have got to know Roberta's family and she has got to know mine. Her husband Dave is an airline pilot and her kids George and Charles are like an extra set of nephews to me. Roberta is like a second sister.

The last time I saw them together, George, who is fifteen, was dressed up all smart in her house, with a shirt and a belt on.

'What are you dressed like that for?' Roberta asked.

'He wants to get a bird,' I said in his defence. 'George, you are looking great, mate.'

'Ben!' Roberta said. 'He's fifteen.'

'Yeah, but he's still a man,' I said.

Sometimes people who see us think we behave like a married couple, but Roberta's a married woman and I totally respect that. But people think that because we bicker a bit. I don't mind telling her off when she wheels me into a lift at the gym and lets the doors close on my legs.

'Why's it not shutting?' she asks, like it has never happened before.

'Are you for real?'

'What?'

'It's my feet!'

Luckily it doesn't hurt because they are made of metal.

'Oh yeah!'

I think the only time we have argued properly is when she doesn't trust someone. I tend to like everyone. That is just the way I am. Roberta is a bit more cynical of other people's motives and she is protective of me.

But the rest of the time it's just good old army banter. Roberta is ex-military. She was a physical training instructor in the Royal Logistics Corps. She might look slender now, but she's tough as boots and every time we go to the gym she beasts me worse than Rudy ever did. When we go swimming she gets in first and waits for me to get craned in on the hoist, then stands in the water supporting my waist so I can swim without sinking head-first.

She is more than a surrogate sister. She is a best friend and a carer. She sees all my struggles, whether that is getting dressed in the morning without falling out of my chair or trying to shower on a camping trip when the disabled bathroom is out of order. She has seen me get frustrated, when everything boils over and I lose my temper because I get fed up of not being able to do things. Most of the time she sees me smiling, because I love our days together.

She will always message me the night before she comes round, so that I can look forward to whatever we plan. She'll let herself in and make us both a brew while I get into my PT kit. Then we'll drive to the gym a few miles away. We're normally there for four hours. I work out six days a week and I get bored of the gym at home, so it is good to mix it up a bit, with a trip to a gym in town, or a trip to a restaurant or a café. Sometimes we go shopping, we might go to a movie, or while away an afternoon shooting pool together.

A lot of these things could easily seem trivial, but having friends like Roberta is absolutely fundamental to my quality of life. It's fundamental to everyone else's quality of life too. Humans need company, whoever they are. Go get a Roberta if you don't have one already. If you do, then donate your time to be a Roberta to someone who doesn't.

BATTLE 8

Push Yourself
a Little Further

vs

Never Know How
Far You Can Go

66

In May 2013, I was awarded the MBE for my charity work. It's strange to think of all the things that had led me to that point in time – I would never have had time to fundraise, or had the impetus to do it, if I hadn't been blown up. And I'd never have been able to do it if I hadn't fought my hardest to be in a position where practically it was possible. So it was a proud moment recognising just how far I'd come. The oath you take when you join the army revolves around the royal family, so there was also an extra honour in that. I'd never have dreamt when I was sixteen, taking the oath in the Donny recruiting office, that one day I would be standing in Buckingham Palace, being given a gong.

I asked Mike to come with me that day, as he was the man who had made most of the charity work possible. I can't stress enough how much Mike helped me. He's not just the boss of a veterans' charity. Mike is a friend, a mentor and an inspiration, not just to me, but to Mum and Andy and so many blokes in the charity. Mike always believed in me. He had taken me under his wing, and I knew one thing for certain: when I walked up to the stage on my crutches, I wanted Mike to be at my shoulder.

Mum had made me practise how to address the Queen. Every day for weeks.

'Do you remember what to say, Ben?'

'Yes, Mum.'

'What is it when you meet her?'

'Your Majesty.'

'And then?

'Ma'am.'

'Ma'am like ham.'

When we got to Buckingham Palace on a cold, sunny spring day, one of the palace officials informed us that Prince Charles would be handing out the gongs instead. That was even better. Charles was Colonel-in-Chief and honorary head of the Parachute Regiment. He was part of the brotherhood. Technically, I think, he was let off without doing P Company, but he did his jumps in 1978 and he still wore the wings on his shoulder.

Mike and I were ushered into the great investiture hall, and we lined up with the other MBEs in the order that our names would be read out. The palace staff had done the drill a thousand times and they wanted things to run like clockwork. There must have been more than a hundred people waiting for an award and the footmen's job was to make things run as fast as they could.

One of the palace officials, who was wearing billowing black trousers with gold and scarlet embroidery, came over to check if I was going up in my wheelchair.

'Absolutely not,' Mike said.

For a moment it was like the Olympics all over again. I was adamant I could walk and eventually they agreed, and then we waited for what felt like hours. I was just beginning to wonder if I was going to have to get my piss bottle out and take a leak when a footman bellowed my name to the packed investiture hall.

'Lance Bombardier Benjamin Parkinson!'

It was all red carpets and gold trim as I entered stage right. The audience was on my right, on rows of gold and velvet chairs. Charles was centre stage, on a little dais to my left. He was flanked on both sides by a bodyguard of tailcoats. I heard the clack of my crutches as they hit the carpeted floor. One of the footmen walked a few steps behind me, pushing my wheelchair.

Charles was wearing his admiral's dress uniform with a chest full of medals and his wings stitched on to his right shoulder. I was in my Number Ones, the smartest uniform we have, which was specially tailored to fit my longest set of legs, and for the first time in my life I had a pair of polished black brogues on my prosthetic feet.

Charles leant down from the stage so his face was close to mine.

'Lance Bombardier Parkinson,' he said in his usual clipped tones, 'you must be so proud to be collecting this award.'

'Your Royal Highness,' I replied.

Charles pinned the medal on my chest. My left arm was shaking slightly and he put his hand on my shoulder to steady me.

'Ben,' he said, looking me straight in the eye, 'you are an inspiration to all of us.'

I wanted to say thank you, but the words wouldn't come out. I stammered for a second as I tried desperately to reply. Then suddenly the two words tumbled out.

'Cheers mate,' I said.

I heard Mike gasp behind me, and he coughed to stifle a laugh.

'You must keep up your good work,' Charles said. He didn't seem to mind my massive breach of protocol.

'Yes sir,' I said. Then I turned and walked out.

Afterwards we had a massive party, which 7 Para had organised. All of the lads came down from Colchester. My whole family was there; so were all the Pilgrim Bandits, and Caroline Flint, my local MP, had come across from her office in Westminster. It was a good day.

67

I am upside down, underwater. The water is murky and cold. A second ago I was laughing. Now all I can hear is a dull thrashing sound and my thumping heart.

I am wrestling to break free, but I am trapped. I am trapped inside the nose of a kayak and I am running out of air. For a split second I wonder, Is this how it ends? After everything I have been through, is this how it ends – on a training day with Ish, in Poole Harbour?

It is a two-man kayak and I am strapped into the bow, held in place by a spray deck. I feel for the edge of the boat with my hands to rip myself clear, but I can't find it. I want to scream. I want to breathe. I want to open my mouth and gulp in a lungful of water.

Suddenly I feel someone else in the water. It is Ish. He has dived underwater and his arms are working fast. I can see swirling lights on the surface rushing towards my face. Finally I gasp for air and feel its coolness calm my lungs, then I am spluttering and choking and swearing blue murder.

A second or two later, when we are bobbing in the water, I look across at Ish and register the panic on his face.

'All right, mate?' he asks.

I cough.

'You took your fucking time, mate,' I splutter – and we both burst out laughing.

It was at the end of the MBE party when Mike announced his next madcap idea. On the back of the Heroes of Telemark trip to Norway, he had decided that we were going to recreate another iconic commando raid: Operation Frankton, the successful sabotage mission in 1942 that led to the foundation of the Special Boat Service.

Op Frankton is sometimes known as the Cockleshell Heroes raid. It was a British mission to sabotage Nazi shipping in Bordeaux. Much like the Telemark raid on the Norsk Hydro heavy water plant, it was a staggering feat of daring and endurance that dealt a major blow to the Nazis. But the differences were stark. Instead of trekking across an arctic plateau, Op Frankton took place in canoes on Europe's largest estuary. The men had to paddle over open ocean and up the Gironde for more than seventy miles.

Both of the missions succeeded but Frankton came at a terrible price. Unlike the Telemark mission, where everyone survived, all but two of the Cockleshell Heroes died. Two succumbed to hypothermia and drowned. Six were captured and shot.

What Ish and I had discovered on our training days in Poole Harbour was that paddling with no legs makes it much, much harder to balance. The blue two-man canoes we were using for Op Frankton were slimmer and sleeker than the canoes I had used before. That made them faster but less stable.

For most people, when they sit in a canoe the weight of their legs acts like a keel, which helps the boat to right itself between strokes. If you lean out one way, your legs automatically go the other. But without any legs I was dangerously top heavy. It took a lot of practice, some adjustments to the ballast and lowering my seat to make it slightly more stable.

We trained for about a year, sometimes in Poole and sometimes in the choppy waters off the north coast of Devon. Ish and I capsized a lot. And I loved it. It felt good to be alive. But we knew the conditions in France would be much tougher.

The currents in the estuary were deadly. Mike had picked another mission right at the limit of what was physically possible. The men who capsized in 1942 died. It was that simple. We wouldn't be facing Nazi patrols, but the water would be just as treacherous as it was more than seventy years ago.

*

Lord Ashdown, the former leader of the Liberal Democrats and ex-SBS commando, hosted a reception at the Houses of Parliament to see us off in May 2014. He had written a book about Op Frankton, called A *Brilliant Little Operation*, and there was probably no one else alive with his experience and knowledge to fully understand how mad our mission was. I don't think he thought we would make it, but he wished us all the luck he could and he bid us on our way.

In that group of thirty, nine of us were injured servicemen. Five of us were amputees. There was Andy Reid, a former corporal in the Yorkshire Regiment, who lost both legs and an arm in an IED blast in Afghanistan in 2009. He woke up in hospital and said, 'I am a survivor, not a victim.' There was Jimmy Wilson, a Royal Engineer, who lost both his legs. Colin Hamilton and Jay Hare were both single amputees. And there was Hari Budha Magar, a Gurkha, who lost both his legs in Afghanistan in 2010. Hari was born in a cowshed and married at eleven. He grew up in a tiny village in the foothills of Mount Everest, dreaming that one day he would reach its summit. Losing his legs hadn't dimmed that dream. If anything, it had hardened his resolve. Like me, Hari lost both his legs above the knee. He walks on C-Legs with knee hinges, but he climbs in stubbies with crampons bolted to the bottom of the moulds instead of feet.

'This is my second life,' he said to me. 'And I want to make it as meaningful as possible before I die.'

There was only one woman in our group. Sarah Holmes, a Wren, was on a family pilgrimage to honour her great-uncle, George Jellicoe Sheard, who was one of the first commandos to die on the original Cockleshell mission.

Sarah had brought eight large pebbles from the base of the Operation Frankton memorial, at the Royal Marine base at Portsmouth, and painted each of the stones with the names and dates of the fallen. As we reached the place where the commandos were last seen, we would pull all our boats into a solemn huddle. Sarah would say a few words about who they were, and she would drop the pebbles into the sea.

*

In 1942, the men had launched in the dead of night from a submarine called HMS *Tuna*. We didn't have a submarine and we weren't dodging Nazi patrols, so we launched our canoes in daylight from the marina at Le Verdon, the town at the tip of the Gironde.

At first, we were all a bit surprised how calm it was. We thought it was going to be easy.

'Stay together,' was Mike's only order.

Then the tidal race came out of nowhere. Suddenly our boats were corks on boiling water. In the trough of a wave all you saw was thick brown water in every direction. On the peaks you'd catch glimpses of the others below and paddle frantically to avoid crashing on top of them.

Andy Reid capsized. Our safety boat raced alongside and towed Andy and his crewmate into calmer water. But even then, it was a job to haul Andy out, bail the boat and lower him back in. If anyone had any doubts how dangerous this was, Andy's capsize was a warning. He took it well.

'Just fancied a swim,' he said.

The ten men on the original mission were led by Major Herbert 'Blondie' Hasler, commander of the strangely named Royal Marine Boom Patrol Detachment, which was the forerunner of the Special Boat Service. They paddled for an hour at a time with five-minute breaks. We tried to stick to their schedule. I had been training hard for almost a year, but even so, my back was in agony. My hands soon blistered and my arms ached.

There were times when we seemed to paddle for hours without making any progress. But those were the times I would think of the commandos who made their journey in winter, at night, sleeping rough in the reeds on the riverbank and living with the constant threat of violent death. We did it in May, in the daytime, with a well-provisioned campsite which we returned to every night by car. It is always good to have heroes to look up to, to remember there are always people who have had it tougher than you. Feeling sorry for yourself doesn't get you very far.

Having said that, dwelling on the past will only get you so far.

*

It was the Pilgrim Bandits' camaraderie that made those long days in the canoe bearable – everyone doing their English best to stay cheerful in adversity. I looked around at men like Ricky, Andy, Jimmy and Hari. Here was proof of the human spirit.

'Come on, Ish, you lazy gwar,' I said as he slogged away behind me. 'Pull your effing weight.'

'Do one, Parky,' he said. It might have been something worse.

'I'm always in front of you. Always winning,' I replied.

'Aye, but I bet it's not the first time you've had a sweaty bootneck up your arse.'

One night, Sarah had arranged for us to meet a French woman called Jeanne 'Ginou' Baudray, who had helped the original mission. She was ninety when we met her and sadly has since passed away, but she had the most extraordinary story of courage and unselfishness to tell.

Ginou was eighteen when, on 8 December 1942, word reached the French resistance that a group of British men were hiding, cold and starving, on the riverbank. Hasler's men had been spotted by a group of fishermen as the sun rose on the first morning, and they had directed the commandos to a better hiding place.

They had also told Ginou's father, Jean, who ran a little café in the town of St Vivien and was a prominent member of the resistance. Jean gave his daughter a bag of baguettes, two bars of chocolate and a bottle of wine, which she packed into the wicker basket on her bicycle.

To anyone else who might have been watching, Ginou was an innocent young French girl, whistling to herself as she pedalled along a web of canals towards the Pointe aux Oiseaux, where the men were hiding. If anyone had asked, she was just getting some fresh air, with a few snacks in her basket in case she got peckish. The truth was that she was risking her life. The punishment for helping the commandos would almost certainly have been torture followed by death at the hands of the Gestapo.

There were only four men left when she found them. Two of

the canoes had capsized on the first night. A third was missing presumed lost after they were forced to separate to avoid a patrol of German gunboats. Six of Hasler's men were dead or captured and the mission had barely started.

The night we met Ginou, she was driving a bright red sports car faster than we could keep up in the Pilgrim Bandits minibus as she led us to a restaurant near her father's café.

'At first, when I saw those men with guns,' she said, 'I was terrified that they were Germans. But when I got close, when I spoke to them, I knew that they were English. One of them was very handsome. He had the most beautiful blue eyes and bright blond hair, but he spoke French so badly, I knew that he had to be English.'

The same four men who were nourished by Ginou's kindness made it to Bordeaux on the fifth night of the mission. They paddled into the harbour undetected, placed sixteen mines on six vessels, and were gone before the mines exploded. They paddled back to a town called Blaye, scuttled their canoes and split into two pairs for the planned escape to Spain. Only Hasler and his crewmate Bill Sparks made it. The other two were killed.

Blaye was our last stop. When we made it to the port, a small crowd had come to meet us.

They cheered and clapped as Ish and Andy lifted me out of the boat and lowered me into my wheelchair.

Blaye's old citadel had been turned into a hotel and Mike had booked us all in, to spend our last night in France in a proper bed instead of at the campsite. But the way up to the citadel was a steep cobbled road and the stones were glistening and slippery with drizzle. I tried to push myself along, but I couldn't find the strength. After so many days of paddling, my arms were exhausted.

Andy came to help but I waved him away. I was tired and grumpy and I could feel the flush of embarrassment rising up my neck.

'Hang on, mate,' Hari said.

He was sitting on the cobbles, pulling on his prosthetic legs.

'Can you give me a hand?' he asked.

He reached out and grabbed my hand, and heaved himself on to his C-Legs.

'Thanks,' he said. 'I'll push you. I haven't got any crutches and I could do with something to lean on.'

He grabbed the back of my chair.

'All right?' he asked.

I nodded.

Hari leaned into the chair and started pushing me up the hill. It must have been a sight. A man with fake legs was pushing an amputee in a wheelchair.

'Thanks mate,' I said quietly.

'Parky,' Hari said, 'you know, if I have learned one thing, it's that everything happens for a reason.'

68

A couple of months before my thirty-first birthday, when the grounds of Castle Craig Hospital were still blanketed in snow, I heaved my wheelchair up a makeshift wooden ramp and took my place among a group of addicts inside the decompression chamber. The chamber was a large metal cylinder with padded benches down the length of both sides, with bulbous ends and portholes like a submarine.

I was there for my first dose of hyperbaric oxygen therapy. It was Mike's idea. He had heard about this miracle treatment that soldiers were getting in America, which helped with brain injuries.

In Britain hyperbaric oxygen therapy is used to treat the bends. Divers who surface too quickly are bundled into decompression chambers to breathe pressurised oxygen and it saves their lives. Staff at Castle Craig, an expensive rehab clinic south of Edinburgh, were pioneering it as a way of curing patients' addictions, by accelerating the body's natural detox processes.

As I sat inside the chamber that first morning there was every kind of addict with me – sex, gambling, drugs, drink, pills and work were all there. On the bench opposite me was a well-to-do lady who sat down and started knitting. Next to her was a scrawny lad with a strong Scottish accent and tattoos on his throat and fists. Next to him, a smartly dressed man with a bundle of papers to read.

In essence, the treatment is simple. Patients breathe pure oxygen at up to two times normal atmospheric pressure, to increase the amount of oxygen that dissolves in their blood. Each session is called a dive.

The man running the session was Dr Max Volino. He was

a bookish man with steel-rimmed specs and a salt-and-pepper beard. He spoke with a soft lisp that hid the lightning zeal he felt about oxygen treatment and its benefits. He followed me into the tank and helped me fix the oxygen mask over my nose and mouth.

'It's too bad you haven't had a brain scan, so we can see before and after,' he said. 'But we really think this might just work a miracle for you.'

When Mike first called to tell us about hyperbaric oxygen therapy he was really excited, and he said that the Pilgrim Bandits would pay for me to go to America to have the treatment there. But the more we looked into it, we realised that in order to get the most benefit I would have to do it for a prolonged period of time – at least a month and maybe longer – and that would make America too expensive.

The UK's leading expert on hyperbaric oxygen was Professor Philip James, emeritus professor at Dundee University, where he had spent most of his professional life involved with deep-sea divers.

Professor James was a man possessed when it came to oxygen therapy. We had come to Castle Craig at his insistence because he was the lead consultant there. Dr Volino, who ran things day-to-day, was his protégé, and he jumped at the chance to treat me because he wanted to prove to the Ministry of Defence what the treatment could achieve.

It was very clear when we met him that Professor James thought oxygen was a panacea for all sorts of conditions, including brain damage like mine and post-traumatic stress disorder. He said percussion from explosions damaged soldiers' brains and every soldier who came back from war would benefit from treatment.

'It's not expensive. Every time you go up in an aeroplane you are sitting in a hyperbaric chamber,' he told us. 'The problem is that this is still seen as quackery by a lot of the medical establishment. Well, I can tell you, the way that most of the medical establishment treats brain injuries is still stuck in the dark ages.'

The mask was secured with three straps that went over and around my head. Dr Volino pulled them tight to seal the rubber to my face, then he plugged the hose into a valve at my shoulder. Everyone had masks on, apart from Dr Volino. They reminded me of the masks that fighter pilots wear.

Dr Volino went round and checked the other patients. There must have been about thirty of us in there and all of them had done this before. I was allowed to talk to them – when we weren't wearing our masks – but I wasn't allowed to ask anyone's name. That was a rule of the rehab clinic. We had also been given very strict instructions not to bring any alcohol, prescription drugs or painkillers of any description onto the estate. We weren't even allowed to bring Vicks VapoRub.

Dr Volino made sure I was comfortable. When everyone was ready, he turned on a television that was bolted to one of the bulbous ends, said a brief farewell and then closed the heavy metal door behind him as he left.

'OK, Gordon, ready to go,' he called to the engineer, who stood like an old-fashioned railway signalman next to a wall of levers and dials.

'OK, stand by, compresh,' Gordon replied. He flipped a lever down. We heard a faint hiss of gas and our ears started to pop.

I was the first British soldier to be treated like this. It was a shame, Professor James said, because the sooner the treatment is given the higher its chance of success. It was eight and half years since I had been injured.

'Oxygen is a key component in any healing process,' Professor James explained. 'But sometimes, if the damage is too severe, the oxygen in the air isn't enough. All we are doing in a hyperbaric oxygen chamber is giving you a higher concentration of oxygen.'

He said conventional wisdom among the medical establishment was that brain cells damaged by severe trauma were dead and irreparable, but there was now overwhelming evidence that those cells were better described as dormant and could be revived. There was also research coming out of America that showed mice given hyperbaric oxygen therapy had dramatically increased numbers of stem cells, which also help the body to repair itself.

He hoped that, by treating me, the Ministry of Defence might see the error of its ways.

'One day,' Professor James said, 'when the rest of the world catches on, hyperbaric oxygen therapy will define a new era in medicine.'

It is essential to be open to new ideas and to seize new opportunities. I know from painful, personal experience that big institutions take time to catch on, they are naturally risk averse and always thinking about money. In my opinion, that's why we still had Snatch Land Rovers in Afghanistan; that's why the Armed Forces Compensation Scheme took years to catch up with multiple, complex injuries like mine; and that's why the NHS and the MoD don't put wounded soldiers in hyperbaric oxygen chambers. Here was someone offering me something that could make me better. There were zero risks and no known side effects. I wasn't just going to give it a go, I was going to give it everything I had got.

Castle Craig had bought their chamber, on Prof James's advice, from a decommissioned oil rig. It was at least thirty years old and it had been installed it in a wooden shed in a corner of the castle grounds. They used it to treat addicts based on a belief that it increased appetite and improved sleep, both of which could help to break the cycles of addiction. It definitely made me hungry and tired.

For me to get the most out of it, Professor James and Dr Volino said I should stay at Castle Craig for a month and do an hour's hyperbaric therapy every day. In between the sessions they recommended I take regular exercise, of both my mind and my body.

Mum and Andy drove me up there on a Sunday night and we checked into a converted barn in the castle grounds. The barn was basic (there was ice on the inside of the windows the night we arrived) but big. At the time, I had a personal trainer called Paul Hallam who used to visit me at home most days. I had asked Paul if he would come with me to Castle Craig and he agreed.

Each dive lasted for an hour. Then it took another fifteen minutes to decompress before we could get out. As soon as we had finished, I would go to the gym with Paul. There wasn't much there

I could use, but there were weights and a hand-bike. It was enough for Paul to beast me, and I went as hard as I could.

Then we'd head back to the barn. We had games to stretch my mind, like chess, draughts, sudoku and a bunch of brain games that I had downloaded onto my iPad, and we had games to test my coordination, like Connect 4 and Perfection, where you have to fit strange-shaped plastic pieces into matching holes. I even slept with classical music playing in my room all night. I was so desperate for this to work I did absolutely everything I could to squeeze every ounce of possible benefit out of every single session.

And the amazing thing was, it worked. Even on that first day, when I got back from the gym and we were playing board games in the barn I could sense my speech was sounding clearer. Mum and Andy could hear it too.

It is hard to explain how exciting that felt. I could talk by that point, but my words lacked definition and lots of people still struggled to understand me. Now, after just one session in the tank, I really believed I was getting better.

On Tuesday I was first in line for the dive. Then I went to the gym, then we played more board games and I went to bed early with Rachmaninov. On Wednesday morning I noticed that the swelling on my stumps had started to go down. By Friday my scars had started to soften.

The days at Castle Craig were exhausting. I was always doing something. It was gym in the morning or a walk in the grounds, then lunch and a dive. Then back to the gym in the afternoon, board games, brain games, coordination practice, then finally dinner and sleep.

On the Tuesday of the second week something extraordinary happened. I woke up in the middle of the night with a tingling feeling in my stumps. It was a feeling I had never felt before. When I told Dr Volino he was over the moon.

'That means the nerves in your leg are re-growing,' he said.

If the nerves were growing in my legs, what was happening in my head?

On the Thursday afternoon I sneezed. I *sneezed*. I had got back to the barn and was playing Connect 4 when my head convulsed and I sneezed for the first time since 2006. Again, Dr Volino said it indicated that nerves might be re-growing.

I did six dives a week, every day from Monday to Saturday. I was always the first in line and I never missed a session. The only reason I didn't dive on Sundays was because there were no dives on a Sunday. We would drive home for a night, then drive up again on Sunday evening, to start all over again on Monday.

My speech continued to improve. Tiny bits of shrapnel that had been embedded in my arm suddenly worked their way to the surface and for the first time I felt strong enough to walk up to two miles a day. I even took a few steps in the gym without my crutches.

When Mike came up to visit he was blown away by my progress.

'You've got to keep going, Ben,' he said. 'Always a little further.'

We found a place in Rotherham that could offer the same treatment closer to home and I booked in for a second month as soon as I got back to Doncaster.

The chamber in Rotherham was run by a local multiple sclerosis charity. MS is a disease that affects the brain and the nervous system. According to the two big multiple sclerosis charities, the MS Trust and the MS Society, there is no clinical evidence that hyperbaric oxygen therapy does anything for the disease. Yet almost all of the oxygen chambers dotted across Britain that don't belong to deep-sea divers are run by MS therapy centres. Patients consistently say that time in the oxygen chamber reduces their fatigue, and improves bladder function, balance, eyesight and coordination.

The chamber in Rotherham looked more like a diving bell compared to Castle Craig's submarine. There was space for about six people if I was in there with my wheelchair. Most of the other people were suffering from MS. Some had cancer. Quite often there were professional footballers. You could always tell if there were footballers there from the brand-new Range Rovers in the car park. A lot of the clubs subscribed to hyperbaric oxygen therapy as a way of cutting recovery times for injured players. Manchester United had bought their own decompression tank after Wayne

Rooney hurt his foot, but a lot of the smaller clubs relied on their local MS centres.

I never recognised the players, but I remember that one of them turned up with a pair of swimming shorts because his teammates had told him he was going for a dive.

The treatment was so exciting for me that I kept at it for a year. I might have kept at it for ever if it wasn't for the fact that other parts of my rehab had started to suffer. I was spending so much time at the decompression chamber it meant I was spending less time at the gym and less time with my speech therapist.

I believe hyperbaric oxygen treatment worked miracles for me. It didn't cure me completely. I still needed crutches to walk; my speech is not perfect. Some people still struggle to understand me. But the hours in those tanks improved my strength and coordination, they gave me back my sneeze, they gave my words more clarity. They made me significantly better. And that was over eight years after I was injured. Imagine what they might find in the next ten or twenty years that might get me even further down the path of recovery. It's good to have faith, based on proof, that something like that might happen.

69

In the autumn of 2017, I found myself unconscious on an operating table in Preston hospital as a surgeon used a pair of bolt croppers to cut the metal rods that were holding up my spine.

I have grown used to hospitals since 2006. I have lost track of all the times I have had to go in, but a few visits stand out.

In 2014, when I was thirty, I came back from the Cockleshell Heroes trip and needed more than a dozen spiky bone spurs removed from the end of my right femur. At the end of 2019 I had the same operation on my left stump.

The spurs grew backwards, like barbs on a fish hook, protruding upwards from my stumps. The X-rays made my legs look like upside-down umbrellas. The spurs were sharp, calcified spikes. Left alone, they weren't that painful. But when I pushed my stumps into the moulds of my prosthetic legs it was agony.

The operations always knocked me out for a few weeks. The surgeons had to open up the skin on my stumps and chip away the bone. There was always a time when I was healing that I wasn't allowed to walk. Then I would have to get my moulds recast because my stumps would have changed shape. It would take a few months to build up the strength that I had lost and get back to walking again.

But the operation on my back was something else.

It was eight years since the surgeons at Stanmore had made me six inches taller by straightening the curve in my back. They had inserted a set of metal rods that had held my spine in place and transformed my recovery for the better. But over the years I had started slumping sideways.

The Stanmore rods ran the length of my lungs, from the top of my back to the third vertebra above my pelvis. Where the rods stopped my spine had started bending sideways, so my hips were always out of kilter.

I had started seeing a doctor called Nabeel Alsindi, who referred me back to Stanmore. I drove down with Mum and Andy. A surgical team came into my room and asked me to walk so that they could examine me.

'I am sorry, Ben,' the doctor said. 'There's nothing we can do.'

I couldn't believe it.

'This is a holistic result of your injury,' he added. I wasn't sure what that meant, but he carried on: 'This was always going to happen. If we do an operation it will just happen again. There is a weak point at the bottom of your spine. The rods stop your spine moving forward so it always moves sideways instead. If we push it up to the right it will just give out on the left.'

For a while, we thought that was it. But one day I was at the limb centre in Preston, where I went to get my prosthetic legs. All the old soldiers I knew went to Preston because it had a reputation as the best of the new prosthetic centres that had opened since 2011.

Preston was run by Dr 'please call me Fergus' Jepson. I told him what had happened at Stanmore. He said he had a friend in Preston's spinal team who might be able to help.

The consultant, Alex Baker, took on board what Stanmore had said, but his opinion was the opposite. He said I needed the operation.

'The doctors at Stanmore might be right,' Mr Baker cautioned. 'We can do this operation and it might not last for ever. It might only last ten years. But wouldn't you rather have ten good years than no good years? And if it lasts ten years it might last for ever.'

He said there was a risk and an element of uncertainty. He said they wouldn't know what was possible until they opened me up in theatre. I would be under a general anaesthetic, so there was always the risk I wouldn't wake up. It was an operation on my spine, so there was the risk they would damage my spinal cord and I would be paralysed or worse. There was also a risk that, when they inspected the rods, they would have to fix the new ones to my pelvis. That would be a disaster, because it would mean I would lose all lateral movement. I wouldn't be able to twist my torso. It would make everything – especially walking – many times more difficult.

But my slump was getting worse. Walking was getting harder. I felt this was a risk worth taking. You can't let fear of the unknown keep you trapped in a bad situation. I wanted the operation.

When I went to Stanmore they measured my spine and said it was 17 degrees off centre. By the time I saw Mr Baker the slump had increased to 27 degrees. Mr Baker believed that the rods were slipping and feared if we allowed it to carry on then one day they could hit my spine and risked paralysing me anyway.

'It is clearly getting worse,' he said. 'If we don't do this operation now then I can guarantee that there will come a point in the next ten years when you have to have it done. It is better to do it now, while you are younger and when it is not an emergency.'

Just before the operation, one of the nurses came in with an open-backed gown for me to change into, and a pair of compression stockings.

'I'm really sorry,' I said. 'I know it's disappointing, but I don't think I'll need the tights.'

The operation took seven hours. It took two men with both their hands on the bolt croppers to cut through the old metal rods. The BBC filmed the operation and when I watched it back I was amazed at all the tools they used. There were hammers, wrenches, chisels, screwdrivers – the lot.

And when I came round, it was to the news that the operation had been a success.

They were able to keep the original rods in, which meant they didn't have to attach anything to my pelvis. I was still able to twist. They also added a couple more rods to the ones already there, to help me stay more upright. From 27 degrees off centre they had got me back to 2 degrees off vertical.

'You have a long recovery ahead of you, but it's the best result we could have hoped for,' Mr Baker said.

I spent a few days in intensive care and came home as soon as

I could. I was on a lot of painkillers and in a lot of pain. Clear, pinkish fluid kept leaking from the wound. It wasn't a great time, but one of my mates, Phil Newmarch, made it slightly better by bringing me a little bell that I could ring to summon Mum and Andy. I thought it was great. They thought it was awful.

About ten days after I got home I suffered one of the most painful moments of my life. The district nurse had been visiting every couple of days to clean the wound, which kept on leaking, and after a week or so she decided she needed to remove my stitches. These weren't normal stitches. They were large metal staples that ran in a line down the side of my spine. They were supposed to stay in place for two weeks, but my skin was starting to grow over them. The nurse had a device that looked like the sort of thing that gets staples out of paper. The ones at the top of my back were sore, but OK. The lower she went, the deeper they were embedded in my skin.

By the time she got to number ten, I screamed out in pain.

'Go on, swear at me,' she encouraged. 'There's nothing I've not heard.'

I was panting after number twelve and sobbing at thirteen.

'Ben, it might be better if we take you back to hospital and have these last ones taken out with an anaesthetic,' she said.

'Just take them out,' I insisted.

'Are you sure?'

The nurse looked at Mum and Andy.

'I don't want to go back to hospital,' I said. 'Just take them out.'

She had to dig into the skin to get the staples out and I screamed and cursed as loud as I ever have. But I knew that once they were out I could get on to my rehab, and that was more important. There are often points in my life when I'm in pain. I push past them. After pain comes sweet relief, and because I've always survived something worse before, I know I can survive anything. I wouldn't wish pain on anyone, but I truly believe what doesn't kill you makes you stronger, and that resilience is one of the benefits of adversity – so long as you choose to accept it.

Shep came up from Colville and Ian, my personal trainer, visited the next day. They devised a plan of exercises that I could do in bed to build up the strength in my back.

It was a really slow recovery. For the next two months I had to use the hoist to get in and out of bed, which I hate because I lose my independence. I wasn't allowed to walk. So it was exercises in bed and short periods in my wheelchair. And I was banned from doing big weights in the gym – for ever. That was a real blow. But if these rods fail there is nowhere else to go. I have to look after them. I focus on cardio workouts instead. I can now work much harder on the hand-bike and the grappler because I can sit straight.

And the positives were huge. Over time my strength came back. The muscles in my back recovered. The operation means I can sit more upright. I can walk and breathe more easily. Don't take these things for granted. For me, they are akin to miracles.

70

In March 2019, three weeks before I turned thirty-five – which was twelve and a half years after I was injured – a letter arrived from General Sir Mark Carleton-Smith, the Chief of the General Staff. He was the professional head of the army, a former commander of the SAS, and he had written to me to apologise.

'Dear Lance Bombardier Parkinson,' he wrote. 'I wanted to write to you personally ... to apologise on behalf of the army for the manner in which you have been treated as you pursued your service complaint. And for the frustration, stress and additional agony to which you and your family have been subjected.'

I have talked about the struggle I had at Selly Oak, and Putney and at Headley Court. But for most of that last decade, while I was focused solely on getting better, there was another battle in the background that Mum and Andy were fighting on my behalf.

They were fighting every single step of the way to make sure I received the care I deserved. If they hadn't fought that battle I don't think I would have survived.

Reading General Carleton-Smith's letter was a bittersweet moment. I was sad that the army – the army I love – had let me down so badly that a letter like this was necessary. At the same time I was happy because the letter was a victory. It marked the closing chapter in a decade-long struggle for the fair treatment that every wounded serviceman deserves. It wasn't just my victory, or Mum and Andy's win. I knew that other wounded veterans – the men with the most serious, complex and life-changing injuries, the people who need lifelong care – would all stand to benefit from the battle we had fought and won together.

All we had ever wanted was one thing: care. The appropriate care that would give me the best chance of recovery. Not just to be alive but to have a life, with the assurance that care would continue for as long as it was needed. In my case, because of my brain damage, I will need it for the rest of my life.

This should not have been a battle. A soldier hurt in the service of their country should get the care they need when they come home. It is such an obvious statement that most people assume it happens automatically, but it doesn't. Or at least it didn't when I was hurt. The system wasn't set up to cope with soldiers with my level of complex injuries. I would never have got the care I needed if it had not been for Mum and Andy fighting every inch of the way.

But there are parts of the story I haven't yet told you. Strap yourself in, because it gets very bumpy.

The first niggling sense that something had gone wrong came when Dad's wife, Sue, noticed I had been misidentified the first time they saw me in intensive care at Selly Oak. My hospital bracelet said I was a twenty-nine-year-old engineer, not a twenty-two-year-old airborne gunner. I had the wrong date of birth and the wrong service number, but no one paid much attention because they all thought I was going to die.

As the days went by and I survived, Mum began to ask more questions. They were simple questions at first, like What happened? What are my son's injuries? How are you going to treat them?

If the answers had been forthcoming, at least about what happened to me, that would have been the end of it. But the answers weren't forthcoming. In the end it took twelve years, two separate service complaints, an independent ombudsman's inquiry, which found the army guilty of maladministration, and a reluctant threat to sue the Ministry of Defence to get to this point.

The army spent those years redacting, obfuscating and delaying for no obvious reason. At best it was indifference. At worst it was the callous expectation that I would give up, go away or die. I was an anomaly and a nuisance. But they had underestimated us. They had underestimated Mum and Andy. The more the MoD tried to stop us, the more that made us think there was something they were trying to hide and that hardened our resolve to fight even harder.

To answer the first question – what happened? – the army convened a Board of Inquiry in February 2007. At that time, Mark Carleton-Smith was our new brigade commander at 16 Air Assault Brigade. He set the terms of reference and he signed off on the report in June, when it was completed. There was nothing unusual about that.

What was unusual was what happened next. For some reason, it took eight months for the army to let us see that report. Why did it take so long for it to be released? We heard all kinds of excuses.

'It is in the post,' they said.

'It missed the post,' they said.

'The names have got to be removed because of data protection.'

'We're sending it with a courier.'

'We can't send it with a courier because it's classified.'

'We can't give it to you if it's classified. We have to redact the classified parts.'

A man called Giles – our latest military liaison – told us that the main reason for the delay was that the surgeons' names had to be removed.

'Sheila will deliver it in person,' he said.

A lady called Sheila did turn up to a meeting, but she came without the report. She only brought more excuses.

Eventually, in February 2008 the army shared a document called 'Findings, Opinions and Recommendations of the Board of Inquiry'. Underneath the title it said, 'Redacted copy, for the family of 2511 9637 Lance Bombardier Ben Parkinson'. At least they had got my number right.

It was an eighty-page report that started with the terrorist attacks of 11 September 2001 and the reasons we were sent to Afghanistan and finished with a paragraph on the correct procedure for reclaiming travel expenses for relatives visiting Headley

Court. In between it explained the make-up of the MOG, the
type of armour on the WMIKs and the purpose of our mission in
the desert. It deliberated over whether the desert where I was hurt
was a 'minefield' or merely a 'mined area', and it asked whether the
wadi we crossed was really a wadi, or merely a 'shallow depression
in the plain'.

Parts of the report had been censored to remove information
that could benefit an enemy. All of the names had been redacted
for data protection reasons. Yet nowhere in amongst its 230
numbered paragraphs was there a mention of the surgeons who
amputated my legs.

It explained how my legs were thrown against the metal of
the gun turret as I was ejected. It talked about the medics, Matty
Oliver and Corporal Hamnett, saving my life with a surgical crike
and it rightly praised their actions as exemplary. It talked about
the ballistic characteristics of mines and of the incompleteness
of Soviet mine maps. It talked about the MERT spending twenty
minutes on the ground and it recommended the medevac choppers
carry blood products in future. But of the four long hours that
I spent in surgery at Camp Bastion there were only three terse
sentences:

> On arrival at the field hospital at Camp Bastion LBdr Parkinson
> was given a massive blood transfusion and underwent stabilisa-
> tion surgery. During this surgery both legs were amputated above
> the knee, a laparotomy was performed that led to the removal
> of the spleen, and the injuries to the chest and skull were exam-
> ined. The base of the skull fractures and the possibility of an
> intracerebral bleed were noted.

On the twenty-four hours I spent at Kandahar, waiting for a
non-existent brain surgeon, there were eighteen words:

> LBdr Parkinson was then moved to the Canadian hospital at
> Kandahar prior to being evacuated to the UK.

Why had it glossed over such an important part of my story? The board's terms of reference, spelled out by Carleton-Smith, had explicitly included medical care from the point of injury to repatriation to the UK. And why had it taken so long to release?

What were they trying to hide?

71

At Headley Court Mum started to notice that other amputees' stumps looked very different to mine. Theirs were messy, mangled stumps, criss-crossed with scars and pockmarked with puncture wounds from shrapnel and dirt. Mine were weirdly neat and clean.

Another thing she noticed was that other amputees had all met doctors who explained the reasons for their amputations. Mum had seen it when we were at Selly Oak. Someone would turn up and sit at the soldier's bedside and say, 'You were shot,' or 'You were blown up.' They would tell them what had happened, but because I was unconscious for so long, no one had done that for me.

All we really knew was what my mates had told us when they came to visit me in hospital. They said my feet looked like they had been dipped in a mincer, but my legs – which, the medics said, had felt like a sock full of snooker balls – were damaged but still intact when they carried me on to the Chinook. So why had they chopped them off? Maybe they needed to amputate my feet, but why both legs above the knee? Niggling doubts became gnawing fears.

Mum began to wonder if they had mixed me up with someone else. I had the wrong zap number on my hospital bracelet when I flew back from Afghanistan. We have all heard horror stories of surgeons making mistakes, taking out the wrong kidney or amputating the wrong limb. Maybe in the chaos of Camp Bastion the surgeons were confused. Maybe there was another patient who needed a double amputation and they chopped my legs off by mistake.

It might sound far-fetched, but in the absence of concrete facts it was the most coherent theory Mum could muster from the fragments of truth she had to work with.

In April 2008, she asked the army for a copy of my medical records and she requested, in writing, that a military medical expert explain the reasons for what had happened to me. At that time my mind was still too damaged to fully understand these concerns and Mum tried not to worry me while I focused on my rehab.

Her request was not unreasonable, but the army dragged their feet and the longer they took to respond the more Mum's mind began to burrow into a world of imagined catastrophes.

Four months after she asked for my notes, a retired colonel shared a sheaf of papers that he said was a complete set of my medical records. The papers were a slapdash bundle in no coherent order. Half the pages were duplicates. Some of them were blank. There were flight manifests but still no mention of the surgeons. There was absolutely nothing that explained the amputations. There were no results from the CT scans in Kandahar and there was nothing from the first twenty-three days that I spent at Selly Oak. The only thing we could ascertain from those papers was that my misidentification had started in Camp Bastion before I went into theatre.

My service number is 2511 9637, but on my medical notes from Afghanistan they had written two different numbers. They started 251, but after that they were totally different. The dates of birth are different as well. My date of birth is 31-03-84. The date of birth on my notes is 21-02-77. It wasn't like someone had misread a 1 for a 7, or a 3 for a 5, or transposed two numbers. The numbers were totally different.

Surely, Mum thought, if there was a simple, honest answer they would have told us by now. But we didn't get that answer for another seven years.

In 2008, the thing Mum wanted most were my X-rays.

'There are no X-rays,' the army said.

'There must be X-rays,' she insisted.

'What makes you think there are X-rays?' they challenged her.

'They amputated his legs, for goodness' sake!'

'It was a field hospital, in the heat of battle,' they said. 'There might not have been time.'

'Well how did they know that his arms and his ribs and his skull were all broken?'

'Mrs Dernie, let me assure you, you have a full and complete set of your son's medical notes. If there are no X-rays in those notes that means there are no X-rays for us to give you.'

In January 2009, Mum lodged a formal complaint with Lieutenant Colonel James Learmont, my commanding officer at 7 Para, about the standard of my care. Specifically, she asked why the surgeons had not fixed my broken back at Selly Oak. Why had they not relieved the pressure on my brain? Why had both my legs been amputated above the knee, and why were there no medical notes from Afghanistan explaining that decision? Finally, she asked whether an assumption that I was going die had led to the doctors' decisions.

As a result of that letter Lieutenant General Louis Lillywhite, the military surgeon-general, visited us in Doncaster in 2009. It was just before my back operation at Stanmore and I was home from Headley Court on leave. He looked at the notes that had been shared and told us that they made 'no sense'. As a result of that meeting, he commissioned a series of medical reports into my care. When those reports came back a few months later the most striking thing was that their authors had relied on records we had never seen. Again, we made the same simple request: please give us my medical notes.

Once again, in our minds, we had the same gnawing question. What are you trying to hide?

72

In 2011, two years after Mum's first complaint to Lieutenant Colonel Learmont, we were informed that we had been following the wrong complaints process. By that stage I had been transferred to the Personnel Recovery Unit (PRU), which was based at Catterick. My commanding officer was a lieutenant colonel, Mel Pears, who had joined as a boy soldier and worked his way through the ranks. He knew the army inside out. He told us we needed to submit a service complaint – it was a legally governed military process – which we did in September of that year. It was supposed to take twelve to twenty weeks to complete.

Two years later, in 2013, we were told to start the process again. My original service complaint had been ruled invalid because I hadn't signed the right piece of paper. Mum, who has lasting power of attorney, had signed it on my behalf but the army refused to recognise her authority. So we started all over again.

The two years in between were not completely wasted. We found out in the army's response to my complaint that initially my back was not operated on as there had been concerns about the risk of infection and that my abdomen might burst open if I lay on it. The army also explained that my treatment was not compromised by an expectation of poor survival and that we were instead given realistic assessments of the long-term outcome. Then, in 2012 we made a breakthrough on the X-rays. That summer Lieutenant Colonel Pears drove down from Catterick to see me at home and he brought with him a bundle of medical notes from Afghanistan. He still didn't have any X-rays but, buried in the bundle of duplicates and photocopies, we found proof that the X-rays had been requested. So it seemed very likely that they existed. One of the documents – which had the wrong service number and the wrong date of birth – was a Trauma Resuscitation Chart. It was a four-page form made up of tick-boxes and charts, a diagram of the human body and space for handwritten notes. On the second page was a box that said 'X-RAYS'. Next to the word 'CHEST' there was a tick. Next to the tick the medic had written '(L) FEMUR, (R) TIB FIB'. The same words appeared further down the page: 'X-RAY: (L) FEMUR, (R) TIB FIB'. It was proof we were right all along to try to get hold of them. If, as we could now show was likely, there were X-rays of both my legs, why would the army not share them?

Mum called Nick – her latest point of contact – and told him the good news and astonishingly, after years of querying whether these X-rays existed, he found them a few weeks later.

He couldn't release them to us. He said he needed permission.

'Whose permission?' Mum demanded. 'They are Ben's X-rays!'

'It has to go through legal,' he insisted.

Three months later, in late August 2012, a disc containing the images arrived through our front door. At last, we thought, we would see what the surgeons had seen in Camp Bastion.

We opened the files on our computer. The chest X-ray was clear, but the pictures of my legs had been redacted. All we could make out was the digital time and date stamp in the top right-hand corner. The main body of the plate was totally black. It looked like someone had placed a piece of paper or a piece of metal over the most important bit of the picture to obscure it. I would never have believed it if I hadn't seen the pictures myself, but it is true. The only sensible conclusion is that the X-rays had been deliberately covered up before they were photographed and sent to us.

The sense that this was a cover-up made Mum's fears ten times worse. On the same piece of paper which proved that the X-rays existed she found another detail, another fragment of evidence, which reinforced her darkest fears. The last thing the medic had written on the resus chart, before I was wheeled into theatre, was a note about the plans for surgery. 'PLAN. THEATRE – LAPAROTOMY, FIX.'

Only four words, but their implication was unavoidable. When they wheeled me into the operating tent they were planning to fix my legs, not cut them off. So why had they changed their minds?

We asked for clear copies of the X-rays. We asked them to send us the originals. We asked them to send the originals to our lawyers, but though it looked like the army were ready to release them, for some reason we didn't get them.

Eventually, in November 2012, which was six years after I was injured and four years after we had first asked for my medical notes, Mum and Andy were invited up to Catterick Garrison to meet a consultant radiographer, Colonel Gibb, who had the X-rays in his possession.

At first he talked them through my brain scans from Kandahar. Then he switched on a light box and laid out the translucent slides of my legs. Mum started sobbing. To her the breaks she could see looked like football injuries. There was one in each leg, simple breaks that could have been set. She asked Colonel Gibb for his opinion but he didn't comment. Andy snapped some pictures on his iPhone before they were ushered out.

In April 2015, almost nine years after I was injured, I heard from the surgeons who had operated on me at Camp Bastion, for the first time. Colonel Peter Hill and Lieutenant Colonel Grant Kane had been contacted in response to my service complaint and they took less than a fortnight to produce a detailed and joint report explaining the decisions they took in the operating theatre.

At last we had some answers.

The surgeons explained that they sawed through my legs to save my life because they had to get me as stable as possible as quickly as possible so that I would survive the flight to Kandahar. It was their opinion that I needed life-saving brain surgery, which they had thought would be available at Kandahar. They also said that it might have been possible to save more of my legs if they had done a longer operation that would have taken more blood. They also explained that there was a limited supply of blood in the hospital blood bank and conditions were rudimentary. They decided not to risk it.

'The dilemma we faced with LBdr Parkinson was that he had a severe brain injury requiring immediate treatment but also active bleeding. The priority was to stop the bleeding,' the surgeons wrote.

'To maximise his chance of survival we needed to evacuate him to a centre with a CT scanner and neurosurgery as soon as possible. This was in Kandahar. He also had to be evacuated in a state where he was not likely to deteriorate during the transfer from his other injuries.'

Initially they had planned to stabilise my legs with 'external fixators,' as indicated on the resus chart, but that plan changed when they unpacked the bandages and saw the severity of my flesh wounds.

'Both legs were amputated above the knee as the contamination had crossed the knee joint. This was a joint decision after discussion between the general surgeon, the orthopaedic surgeon and the anaesthetists and was not undertaken lightly. It was done to give LBdr Parkinson the best opportunity of surviving his brain injury, which was the next most likely to cause his death following control of the haemorrhage.'

For the first time since these men cut through my femurs we could start to understand why. It wasn't a mistake. It wasn't an accident. It was a brutal, life-saving decision that two experienced, trained men took in a tented field hospital without a CT scanner and with finite supplies of blood.

After nine years of cancerous doubt, which haunted Mum far more than it haunted me, we finally had an answer. These men had helped to save my life, so why had it taken so long to get that answer?

The surgeons sounded as surprised as we were. 'It was a pity,' they wrote, that they were never asked to meet us sooner to assuage some of our concerns. 'We would have been happy to,' they said, 'following our return from Herrick 4.'

Stray pages from my notes continued to turn up in dribs and drabs. Some time afterwards, we received a radiologist's report that had been written in Canada in 2006, based on brain scans sent from Kandahar the night I was injured. The most striking thing about the documents was not the diagnosis, which we knew all too well by then, but that someone stamped the scans 'non-urgent' by mistake, so by the time that they were looked at I was on a plane to Birmingham.

In the covering letter that came with the report, the army apologised for taking so long to share it. They said they had found it by chance, in a cupboard in a general's office which was being cleared out for redecoration.

73

Life would have been much simpler, for everyone involved, if I had done what everyone expected me to do in 2006, and died. Surviving was much more expensive.

To begin with, no one thinks about money. When your life depends on pipes and drugs and drains and round-the-clock hospital care, you are living minute by minute, hour by hour. It is only when your horizons expand and months stretch into years that worries about money loom increasingly large.

Life for a brain-damaged double amputee is surprisingly expensive. I save a lot of money on Big Macs, beer and dating but life is pricey in other ways. I need twenty-four-hour supervision and significant ongoing rehab, and while I have helped to raise money for charity I am yet to find a way that I can earn a living.

If I want a weekend away, for example, I can't just book the cheapest room. I have to get a disabled room. Most places only have one or two, so I have to book in advance. I can't get the last-minute discounts. Then I have to book a room for my carers. If it's a professional carer – by that I mean not Mum or Andy – and I am going for more than a night, I might have to take two carers so that they can work shifts, which means I have to book three rooms.

So long as I was in the army, the army paid for my rehab. My living costs came out of my wages and the NHS paid for my round-the-clock care, which Mum and Andy provided. But the time was fast approaching when I would have to leave the army. Their duty of care would end. I would no longer have a salary. They would no longer pay for my rehab and there was no way I could afford it on a lance bombardier's army pension.

Rehab is what I live for. It is what keeps me in the fight, but it comes at a hefty price. I have six hours a week with Shep, five hours' fitness with Ian, an hour with a specialist neuro-physio once every two weeks and an hour of speech therapy each month.

In January 2016 Mark Lancaster, the veterans' minister, invited us to Whitehall and told us that he understood my concerns. He said there was a plan to lift the most seriously injured soldiers into a 'higher welfare scheme'. It was exactly what I needed but it never materialised.

By November we still hadn't heard from Lancaster's team. The army published its response to my service complaint. It had taken five long years and it was a disappointment to all of us. They found no flaws with my care at any point; they said the five years it had taken them to get this far was not an unreasonable delay.

The only positive nugget, as far as I was concerned, was a recommendation that said it was 'vitally important' that I should be included in a scheme 'that provides appropriate care for so long as he needs it'. It was a reference to the higher welfare scheme that the veterans' minister had promised. The report was signed by General Nick Carter, who was then Chief of the General Staff, and General Sir James Everard, Commander Field Army. The fact that they had signed it gave me hope the scheme would happen.

At Christmas the MoD said the scheme would be running by Easter, but Easter came and went. Then in May 2017 they said the situation had changed. A man we had never met before turned up at our house and said there would be no higher welfare scheme after all; soldiers like me would have to rely on the best the NHS could offer. I knew from bitter experience that meant two hours a week on ill-fitting, blistering legs and zero speech therapy.

'It's not right, it's not fair!' Mum shouted at him. 'You, you . . . you have a legal duty of care.'

I love the army and I loved being a soldier but then, more than ever, I felt that I had been abandoned. Men's lives were reduced to budget lines. The grey men had betrayed me, and now they wanted me out of their hair.

It was with a heavy heart, and with no other choice, that we instructed our solicitors to sue the Ministry of Defence. We never wanted to sue them. It was no one's fault that I hit a mine. It was war. Bad things happen all the time and it was my job. I have never felt bitterness towards the army. I have never felt blame. But that was not a licence for the MoD to ignore me. Just because I am brain damaged, it doesn't mean I am stupid. Just because I'd been recognised in other ways – that I had carried the Olympic torch and collected an MBE – it didn't mean I would no longer need twenty-four-hour care and rehab every day for the rest of my life.

We had collected a range of expert medical opinions on the various aspects of my care. They confirmed, unanimously, that I owe my life to the men who treated me in the desert, while the dust of the blast hung heavy in the air. The experts also suggested that opportunities may have been missed, which could have made my lasting injuries much easier for me to bear. My brain injury might have been less severe, for example, if there had been blood products on the helicopter, a CT scanner at Camp Bastion or a neurosurgeon at Kandahar. If the hospital at Camp Bastion had even half the same resources as our military hospitals in Iraq in 2006, the surgeons would have had a better chance of salvaging one or both of my legs. If my back had been fixed when I first got to Selly Oak – though I now at least know why it was not – my rehab would probably have been fuller and faster. I might never have needed two subsequent operations.

Alice, our solicitor, warned us we would need a war chest of at least £50,000 to £100,000 to pay for barristers and court costs. There was only one place we could find that money.

In 2003, when I was in Iraq, Mum and Andy had bought a cottage on the shores of Loch Awe, in the Scottish Highlands. It had always been their dream to retire there. Mum was ready to give up work and Andy was planning to go part time. They were just months away from moving up to Scotland when I was hurt. All those plans went out of the window. Now they decided to sell their dream home to fund our legal fight.

The MoD jumped to attention. As soon as we issued a letter before action they invited us to a meeting. They assured us everything could be solved quickly and amicably. But that unleashed more meetings. Meetings about meetings with six-week gaps in between, where all they ever seemed to do was negotiate a date for another meeting. Each time the MoD sent a different representative, which meant they never had a clue what had gone on before.

It felt like they weren't really engaging with the process.

By the spring of 2018, more than two years had passed since Mark Lancaster promised to enrol me in a higher welfare scheme. But there was no sign of any progress on that front.

We decided our only option was to submit a second service complaint. Only this time I named General Nick Carter and General James Everard as the subjects of the complaint. The generals had said they believed it vitally important that there was 'appropriate care for so long as he needs it' in November 2016, in response to my first complaint. A year and a half later I still did not have it. It was twelve years since I had been injured. All I wanted was a way to live and fund my care when I finally left the army.

74

I never wanted to sue the Ministry of Defence. I never wanted to lodge a complaint against the army's top commanders. But it is fair to say things moved a lot more quickly once I did.

Within a few weeks of us firing both barrels, the defence minister, Earl Howe, took over the case. In September the MoD presented him with three options for my care. He scrapped the lot of them and appointed Helen Helliwell, the head of personnel support, to take charge.

Helen was a force of nature. For the first time in twelve years we felt like heads were getting knocked together. Things were starting to happen. Just before Christmas she came up to Doncaster and outlined a proposal.

The first thing she said was that the army would adjust my pension so that it was broadly in line with those of my peers. This was really important because I had fallen through the cracks. In the army, as with most employers, the longer you work and the more senior you are when you leave, the higher your pension will be.

That seemed really unfair to the privates who were blown up aged eighteen, so the MoD introduced a system to compensate. The younger someone was when they were medically discharged, the higher their pension payments would be, to take account of the promotions and career progression they had lost. So far so sensible.

Then, in 2007, General Richard Dannatt changed the rules about medical discharges so that people could stay serving. It was a brave and moral decision. It meant that people like me got the care we needed, even though there was no realistic prospect of us facing the enemy ever again.

I think that decision may have saved my life. It certainly helped me recover more fully, because it forced the army to pay for people like Shep, Judith and Ian when the NHS refused. But Dannatt's decision had an unexpected consequence.

It meant that I was leaving the army as a thirty-four-year-old lance bombardier, which is only one rank up from private. I hadn't been promoted since I was in my early twenties.

All of my mates who stayed in were sergeants or more senior. Phil Greenaway, who I got blown up with, has just made battery sergeant major. Martin Cartwright's on course to do the same. Even that joker Phil Armitage earned his third stripe – how, I'll never know.

My injuries meant that I couldn't get promoted.

Helen offered me a deal. She said they would adjust my pension as if I had been discharged in 2009, aged twenty-five not thirty-four. Then she offered me an annual allowance of £24,000, index linked, for life to cover the extra rehab costs and living costs that the NHS doesn't meet. Part of the deal was that if I accepted the settlement, I would park the service complaint.

It was a fair offer and I accepted. It means I will probably never know why or how I was misidentified, or if it made a difference to my treatment.

Ultimately, I don't mind. We can't change the past. I am focused on the future, and that is what this deal was about. It was a deal that offered me some form of stability to carry on my treatment indefinitely.

That is massive. It means I can carry on fighting to get better as long as I am able.

I have won many battles since the day that I was injured. I fought to stay alive, I fought to get the care I need and I fought have a life worth living, and I have won. But that struggle is not over yet. I want to keep on getting better. I want to walk more freely and I want to talk more freely. I work on that every day. I am lucky that I have people on my team who help me.

Perhaps if my experience proves one thing, it is that you don't have to be a soldier to win wars. My mum has never held a gun or run a log-race. She has never had to leopard crawl or face a minute's milling. She never fought a war. But she can battle like the best of them. She took on the faceless, heartless behemoth that is the MoD, and she won. She did it for me. And she did it for all the other soldiers like me whose lives have been changed irrevocably by service in the wars in Iraq and Afghanistan. There are countless soldiers whose compensation has been improved because of her struggle. If it wasn't for her our lives would be that much harder.

I believed in my fight, and Mum believed in hers. Whatever your battle, the most important thing is that you believe in it and you have someone to fight with you.

75

With the plan for my future care settled, the only thing left to do was say my farewells. Normally, when someone leaves a regiment, they have a 'dining out' in their honour. I ended up having about five, but the most memorable one was in London.

Mike Witt and Matt Hellyer arranged to host it in a private club where a few of the Pilgrims were members. They invited Pagey, Rudy, Phil Armitage, Martin Cartwright and all the folk from the Pilgrim Bandits. Ish was there. So was Andre, who had come with me on heaps of Pilgrim trips that I haven't had time to mention. So was madman Ricky Fergusson, Tyler Christopher and Jake Bartlett, my fellow amputees.

It was on 28 March 2019, my last day in the army. My friend Roberta drove me down from Doncaster. We checked in to the Union Jack Club next to Victoria station and she helped me to change into my Number Ones. It was a black-tie dinner and Mike had warned me there would be a surprise guest. I wondered if it might be my mum or someone from one of our expeditions. The last person I could have imagined I'd see at my dining out was General Lord Dannatt. The former head of the army, a four-star general and his wife, Lady Pippa, at the dine-out of a lance jack. I was totally blown away.

What happened that night is hazy, and perhaps this is a good time to blame my poor memory. I certainly can't remember the strip club that I definitely didn't go to with Roberta and Matt and the rest of the gang.

It is possible that Pagey, Phil and Martin might have got into some trouble for stealing someone's bowler hat. They may or may not have been told by some grizzly old throat-slitter that they would be wise to put the hat back. I do know it was after midnight when Rudy gave his speech, and that everyone was very drunk (apart from me – I don't drink any more). I know Lord Dannatt said a few kind words about my service in the army. Did I break into bawdy song while he was speaking? Was it a song about Matt Hellyer's sexual peccadillos that would make a sailor blush? I couldn't tell you. If I had done any of those things, then there would have been a very awkward silence. It's not really the done thing to interrupt a four-star general with a song about blowjobs.

Everyone looked at Lord Dannatt to know how to proceed. He was momentarily flabbergasted. His wife stepped in to save the day.

'Oh Ben,' she said. 'You are hilarious.'

I couldn't get into trouble by then. It was after midnight. I had formally left the army.

76

I have an amazing life. In the years since I was injured I have kayaked down the Yukon River and hand-biked the length of New Zealand. In the Pilgrim Bandits I have found a golden group of friends. I think I am a lucky man. That is how I choose to see myself. I focus not on my injuries, but on my survival, and that I'm alive to tell the tale. There are so many other ways I am lucky it would be hard to list them all here. I don't have any legs, which means I never have to cut my toenails. I can't remember the explosion, so I don't suffer from post-traumatic stress disorder. (I try always to see the upside.)

Most of all, I am lucky to have my mum and Andy. They put their lives on hold to help me. They fought my corner when I could not fight myself, and they still help me, every single day. If it was not for their unwavering love and loyalty, I would not have been able to tell you this story. This has been their story too.

I have no regrets and I harbour no blame. If you gave me my time again, I would do it all exactly the same.

You and I aren't that dissimilar. Everybody's life is made up of a series of battles: you can't always pick them and sometimes you'll lose. But you can also reframe them so you can win. This book has been split into the battles I think I've faced in my life.

I worked hard for what I wanted as a soldier because I refused to give up on my dream of being in the airborne.

All of us made the best of our time out on tour – we enjoyed the ride – rather than dwelling on the negatives.

When I was injured, nobody – not even my family – thought I would survive, but I held on rather than let go.

When I was in recovery, and doctors wanted to tell me what I could and couldn't achieve, I didn't let that dampen my spirits. I set my own limits. Everything is impossible until someone does it.

When I was forced to go to Putney, when my heart was set on Headley Court, I made the most of the opportunities in front of me. It was only by doing that wholeheartedly that I realised just how many opportunities I had there. I could have missed out on the chance by giving up, by feeling hard done by, but with the help of all the amazing people in that place I progressed even more.

When the army tried to tell me, the most injured soldier to survive the war in Afghanistan, that I didn't deserve the highest amount of compensation, we fought back, my mum at the helm. And we won. That improved the lives of countless others as well as mine.

There are things I can't do now that I used to do before I was injured, but I've found a new purpose, and have thrown myself into those initiatives. I will never feel sorry for myself. I have nothing to feel sorry about.

And every day I push myself that little bit further, try that little bit more, work that little bit harder. I don't know how far I'll go, but I'll carry on shooting for the stars.

Those have been my battles. I think I've won them all so far and mine have most likely been bigger than yours (this is my book, so I get to say that). I did defy the odds I was given, and even though I'm airborne to my core, I did it with a dollop of commando spirit: courage, determination, unselfishness on the part of my family and friends, and bucketloads of cheerfulness in the face of adversity. And if a thick-necked soldier from Donny like me can do it, then anyone else can too.

People ask me what I want for the future. I think I want the same as anyone. I want to drive a Maserati. I want to walk normally again. And then I would like to appear on *Strictly Come Dancing*.

Even with no legs, I can't be as bad as Ann Widdecombe.

Acknowledgements

After every battle there comes time for tea and medals.

I hope the pages of this book are proof of my never-ending thanks to the mates who risked their lives to save me, to the medical science that kept me alive and to the legions of friends and family who have showered me with love and support on the long and ongoing journey to recovery.

I wouldn't be here without you.

So many of you have gone above and beyond the call of duty:

Thank you to Brigadier James Learmont, who inherited me at 7 Para and fought for me tooth and nail. To your father General Sir John Learmont and you brother Mark, who picked up the reins and supported me in every way possible for the last twelve years.

General Lord Richard Dannatt, General Sir Freddie Viggers and General Sir Richard Shirreff, thank you for insisting things should start to be better for wounded soldiers.

And to your lady wives, Pippa, Jane and Sarah-Jane: you did more than anyone to make things happen in those darkest times.

Sisters Shirley and Angie at Selly Oak, you would make worthy army sergeants.

Leena, Gilsa, Christian and Marvin at Putney, you made the worst time bearable for me and Mum.

For Sonny and Tracey at Headley Court. Nurses and friends.

For those who worked so hard with me at home: Dawn, Nina, Aidan, Paul, Shep, Judith, Holly, Ian and James.

For Ros and Alan, who did so much for injured soldiers in Doncaster.

For Dr Fergus Jepson, Ned and Vicky, the amazing team at Preston Limb Centre, and Mr Alex Baker, who listened to me and pulled out all the stops.

For the PRU team from the army who 'handled' me and Mum for many years and ended up our friends – Warrant Officers Neil Davis, John Jarvis, Yvonne Youle and Lee Backhouse. Colonel Mal Pears, Colonel Steve Bostock and the gentleman who saved my mum's sanity, Colonel John Henry.

Everyone who makes Pilgrim Bandits what it is. Mike the Boss, Ang 'The War Department', Ish, Debs, Helen, Vinnie my marine wife, Jake, Tyler, James and Matt.

For Andre, who has looked after me all over the world in all sorts of ways that you don't want to know about.

For Rusty, who I am so proud to know.

For Roberta, my best friend.

For Pagey, with me at Harrogate when it started, who carried me from the helicopter in Bastion and ever present since.

For Crabbers. Gone but not forgotten, ever.

For Colonel Gary Wilkinson, always with me.

I have no medals to pin on your chests, but you all deserve a rack of them.

There is a custom in the army that if your name appears in print you have to buy a crate of beer for your mess. All of you above, consider yourselves crated.

For Emily Barrett at Little, Brown, thank you for having the vision and seeking me out at just the right time to make this book come true. Thank you, Jerome, for writing it all down, Kirsty and Maddie for keeping it legal, and my tireless editor Zoe Gullen for crafting it into the book you hold today.

Most importantly, I must thank my family.

Dad and Sue, my siblings Phil, Dan and Emma, your lives changed for ever when I was injured. You have never let me down.

Andy, I sometimes think your life has changed even more than mine. You have always been there for me and you have always been there for Mum. The level and length of your sacrifice is beyond words.

Mum. What can I say? You have fought with me in the trenches every step of the way. I said at the beginning of this book that I was born lucky. I am lucky to be your son. I love you. Thank you for being my mum.

Finally, for my lads. The fighting men of 7 Para RHA. You made me who I am. You made it impossible for me not to fight back. And thank you for not telling all you know.